LOVE IN
OLD AGE

HUNTER DAVIES is a prolific author, journalist and
broadcaster who has written for *Punch*, the *New
Statesman, Guardian* and *Sunday Times*. He is the author
of more than 100 books, including the only authorized
biography of The Beatles, biographies of Wordsworth,
Beatrix Potter and Alfred Wainwright, *Lakeland:
A Personal Journey* and *The Heath: My Year on
Hampstead Heath*. He divides his time between
North London and the Isle of Wight.

Also by Hunter Davies
and published by Head of Zeus

The Heath: My Year on Hampstead Heath
Lakeland: A Personal Journey

LOVE IN OLD AGE

My Year in the Wight House

HUNTER DAVIES

HEAD
ZEUS

An Apollo Book

First published in the UK in 2022 by Head of Zeus
This paperback edition first published in 2023 by Head of Zeus,
part of Bloomsbury Publishing Plc

9 7 5 3 1 2 4 6 8

A catalogue record for this book is available
from the British Library.

ISBN (PB): 9781801104098
ISBN (E): 9781801104104

Image Credits

1. Hunter Davies. 2. David Jones/Wikimedia. 3. CBW/Alamy. 4. Simev/Shutterstock.
5. Charles Chusseau-Flaviens/ullstein bild/Getty. 6. Jane Hilton. 7. Photochrom Print Collection/
Library of Congress. 8. Mypix/Wikimedia. 9. Spottedlaurel/Flickr. 10. duriantree/Shutterstock.
11. Print Collector/Getty. 12. Print Collector/Getty. 13. Duncan1890/Getty. 14. Keystone-France/
Gamma-Keystone/Getty. 15. CBW/Alamy. 16. Patrick Eden/Alamy. 17. SSPL/Getty. 18. Farmpix/
Alamy. 19. Chronicle/Alamy. 20. Bonhams Gallery/Wikimedia. 21. Keystone Press/Alamy. 22. Jason
Swain/Getty. 23. diana_jarvis/Alamy. 24. SSPL/Getty. 25. Antiques & Collectables/Alamy. 26. Peter
Noyce GBR/Alamy. 27. Keystone Press/Alamy. 28. Roland Godefroy/Wikimedia.

Typeset by Ben Cracknell Studios

Printed and bound in Great Britain by
CPI Group (UK) Ltd, Croydon CR0 4YY

Head of Zeus
5–8 Hardwick Street
London EC1R 4RG

WWW.HEADOFZEUS.COM

CONTENTS

CHAPTER 1

The madness of old age

On the Isle of Wight ferry, 1964

I don't know why we went to the Isle of Wight. It began out of the blue and the sequence of events has grown cloudy already, our motives and desires and fantasies still confused. It just seemed to happen, as if an unseen hand was leading us. We suddenly found ourselves besotted by the island and a particular house, and yet until that moment we had never ever thought about the Isle of Wight, far less about moving there.

Neither of us had any real connection with the place. Claire had been there once, aged five. She went with her mother and brother to a school camp for kids in Shanklin, she thinks, and absolutely adored it. But since then, she has never been back.

I went there last in 1966, my only visit. I was writing the Atticus column in the *Sunday Times* and interviewed the Governor of Parkhurst prison, the maximum-security gaol in the middle of the island. It was in the news at the time as some of the Great Train Robbers had been there.

A prison was not really the sort of topic which normally concerned the column. Atticus was a long-established diary feature, rather old-fashioned when I joined as the boy assistant in 1960. We usually covered eminent people, such as who will be the next archbishop of Canterbury or our ambassador to Washington, as if I cared. When I took over the column in 1964 I changed it, preferring to interview people I was personally interested in, such as gritty northern novelists, footballers like George Best and pop stars like The Beatles.

I was amazed when the Home Office agreed to my request to visit Parkhurst, or at least for the governor to appear in a diary column. I think I had seen a reference to the governor somewhere and he had sounded interesting.

I went across on the ferry with a *Sunday Times* photographer,

Kelvin Brodie, known as Steve for some reason. I have no memory of going on the ferry, or how we got to the prison, but months later, in the office, Steve gave me a photo he had taken onboard, unbeknown to me. I am sitting on the wooden deck lost in thought, looking very young – I had just turned thirty – and also nervous and a bit moany. In the background, out at sea, you can see one of the famous Palmerston Forts, which can immediately be identified by anyone who knows anything about the Isle of Wight.

The interview went OK, was quite jolly, or I made it jolly, but I have little memory of the governor himself, except that he was amusing. He told me a story about when he was governor of Dover prison. He was out on his scooter one day, about a mile from the prison, when he saw a man he recognised. 'What are you doing here?' he asked. 'Coming back with you, sir,' the man replied. He was, of course, an escaped prisoner. He hopped on the back of the governor's scooter and together they rode back to the prison.

I can't remember anything about the inside of Parkhurst. It was just another story, and the governor one of three or four people I interviewed each week, almost all of them long faded from my mind. In 1966 I had other things to get excited about, such as the World Cup and my first meeting with The Beatles.

It was when Claire happened to suggest going to the Isle of Wight for a couple of days that I remembered that ancient photo of me on the ferry looking dopey and I managed to dig it out. I could not recognise myself.

This was in July 2020, during the relaxation of restrictions that followed the first coronavirus pandemic lockdown, when we all thought things would now get back to normal. What foolish optimists we were.

Claire and I had been going out together for three years and had reached the stage of considering living together. Then we decided against it. I could not live in her house in Battersea, south London; it was too clean and white and immaculate for me. I would be scared to sit down. And she could not live in my battered Victorian house near Hampstead Heath, north London, too scruffy; it would upset her, she'd always be itching to change it all. So we continued to live alone, each in our house, though meeting all the time and going on lots of holidays together.

Then eighteen months ago I had this really daft idea. If I could not bear to move into her house, or she into mine, what if we started off afresh in a completely new house – buy something new to both of us? I would let Claire do all the refurbishing, decor and design. She would love that. Keep her happy and occupied.

We went to look at a rundown Georgian gem in East Heath Road, overlooking the greenery of the Heath itself, one of the best positions in all Hampstead.

The asking price was two million pounds. Don't gulp. This was Hampstead, best part. In good nick it would easily go for three million pounds. I would sell my house to pay for it. It cost only five thousand pounds when my wife and I bought it in 1962. Today, judging by other houses in the street, mine could go for three million pounds. The plan was that Claire would keep her house but rent it out to give herself an income. I bid £1.75 million. The estate agent said, Oh, no, he didn't think that figure would be accepted. So I then went up to £1.8m. Then £1.9m. By now the agent was suggesting we contact builders and architects, discuss it with them. I finally offered two million pounds – the asking price – as we had fallen in love with how it would look when it was all finished.

We went round it so many times, working out how the rooms would be arranged, what we would do, thinking how marvellous it would all be. For me it would feel like an emotional return.

When my wife and I first married we lived in a flat nearby in the Vale of Health, always promising ourselves if we ever made any money, we would return to Hampstead, our spiritual home, tra la. But, come the time when we might have afforded it, we felt so happy and settled where we were, in NW5, on the Dartmouth Park side of the Heath (which had been considered the wrong side of the Heath back in 1963), that we had no desire whatsoever to move.

Claire had lived around Hampstead as a single woman; then, when she married, she lived for many years in Muswell Hill, so she felt very at home in that part of north London.

Then one morning after I'd made that offer on the rundown place I woke up and thought – Bloody hell, Hunt, yer aff your heid. (I tend to speak in Scottish when speaking to myself.) It is the most stupid thing you have ever thought of doing. You can't possibly clear up and leave this house, your family home for almost sixty years. You love it so much. You have too many good memories. And far too many books and collections...

Anyway, at my age – which was then eighty-four – it would be sheer madness wilfully to take on a massive project, a wreck that might take two years to get right, which would involve fights with builders, architects, surveyors, planning authorities. Do be sensible for once, I said to myself. So I backed out. Withdrew my offer.

We were both relieved. We each had come to the same conclusion, that taking on a large house in Hampstead was far too big and complicated and worrying an endeavour at our stage of life.

When the chaos of Covid came, and the first lockdown was followed by a second and then a third... how we thanked our lucky stars that we were not involved in such a mammoth and really daft project.

But then, slowly, the same urges came back to us. Would it not be a wonderful way to seal our love and our commitment to each other to have a little holiday home? Somewhere we would find and create together and which had nothing to do with our families or past lives. A new project for our new lives together.

It would, of course, have to be a more modest plan this time, not a grandiose building venture like the Hampstead house, which would have taken all my capital and however many years I have left in my life.

How about a little holiday home in the Lake District, pet? Let's say a cottage in Glenridding, near Ullswater, close to where your mother used to live? Claire's mother was a teacher at Queen Elizabeth school, Penrith, and Claire has many happy memories of staying with her in her sweet little cottage. A one-bed Lakeland cottage would be sufficient, very simple, with no work. That would give us a project, something to create together, but a modest goal without aggravation.

For thirty years, my wife Margaret and I had a stunning country home in Loweswater to the northwest of the Lakes, but that was a proper home, with a study where each of us worked away on our books. When our three children eventually left home, we lived there for up to six months each year, from May to October, never returning to London during that period. Unless there were family dramas. We both loved Loweswater so much. It was like living twice, having an urban life in London and an isolated, rural life in Cumbria. Half of Margaret's ashes are buried in the churchyard at Loweswater. The other half is in my back garden in London, under a summer house.

I sold the Loweswater house when Margaret died in 2016. I gave all the money to our three children who then bought a seaside cottage just outside Broadstairs. Claire and I have been there many times but we always face competition from the three other families – my children all have children of their own now.

Claire always felt anyway that it was *their* house, decorated in *their* style, so she could not put her mark on it.

For a few months, we did look for a Lakeland cottage, concentrating on areas I did not know so well, such as Ulverston or Coniston. I even wrote about the idea of returning to the Lake District in the column I have been writing in *Cumbria Life* for twelve years. It was my son-in-law Richard who pointed out how hard it would be to drive up there for short stays. The time it took for Margaret and me to travel to Loweswater did not matter, as we went up there just once a year and stayed for six months. If we went to somewhere like Ulverston for a long weekend we would spend half the time driving.

Somewhere that was relatively easy and quick to get to from London, by train or road, would be more sensible – and perhaps also by the seaside. Being at Loweswater among the high fells was all very well when I was younger, but at my age – and with dodgy knees – something on the flat would be better.

Our minds were vaguely turning to places like Hastings or Rye when we got an invitation from a friend of Claire's called Donna. She lived in her street and, part-time, on the Isle of Wight with her partner Peter. She suggested that, now lockdown seemed to be over, we should come and visit them.

At the same time, I also kept on hearing from my lodger in the flat on my top floor, a young woman of twenty-seven, how wonderful the Isle of Wight was. She was working as a nanny for two of our neighbours in the next street, the actor Benedict Cumberbatch and his wife Sophie, a theatre director. I know Sophie and her mother, but I never knew they had a family home on the Isle of Wight. In fact, they got married there, and now seemed to be going back and forth between London and the island with their young children and nanny. If a family can manage it for a weekend, surely two mature, but awfully active, single people should not find it a strain?

We put it off for several months, waiting for what turned out to be only the first lockdown to be over, or eased, then we thought, in the summer of 2020, Yeah, let's go. It might be fun to have a couple of days in a pub somewhere we have never been before and see your friend Donna.

The Isle of Wight, being separated from the British mainland, seemed not to have suffered much from Covid. Hotels and restaurants were still open and we found somewhere to stay near where Donna and Peter lived, the Pilot Boat Inn, Bembridge, close to the easternmost point of the island. We booked a room overlooking the sea and were then told that lockdown restrictions had now been introduced. The inn was not serving meals and the bar was closed. We would have to pick up a key to our bedroom and let ourselves into a totally empty inn. Still, we were determined to enjoy our two nights on the island.

Before we went, Claire went on the Rightmove property website, just out of interest, to look at the local market, not realising that half the population of urban UK was doing the same thing. Lockdown had given everyone itchy feet – made them desperate to escape from their city prisons and head for the Cotswolds or Cornwall. Judging by the stories and pictures in the newspapers, the Isle of Wight did not seem quite so obvious or popular a destination as these perennial West Country favourites, and Claire quickly found a stunning-looking, sixteenth-century cottage for sale. It was just north of Bembridge – at Seaview, where our friends Donna and Peter live. How handy that would be.

But also, it looked like a totally unbelievable gem – Grade II, unspoiled, ancient cottage, full of original features, with gardens front and back, utterly charming and – My God! – what a bargain! It was on the market for only £385k! Hard to credit if you have lived your life in London and watched house prices rise obscenely these last fifty years. Bloody hell, for that price you would be lucky to get a garage in Battersea – let alone Hampstead.

There *must* be something wrong, I thought. Must be some drawbacks. Or is it just because all house prices on the Isle of Wight are sooooo cheap? Never having been interested in the place, we had zero knowledge of local house prices, or of the best places to live. We studied the photos of each room, went round the garden online, investigated its location, and blow me, it seemed to be all genuine – a total unspoiled gem. Wow. I couldn't wait to set my greedy eyes on it...

On 6 July 2020, I spent the night at Claire's house in Battersea; then next morning we set off for Portsmouth in her car. I don't have one. Gave it up after Margaret died and I sold Loweswater. We got lost trying to get on to the A3, which was not like Claire, who is normally an ace driver, but got to Portsmouth in just over an hour and a half. It was a bit complicated, driving through the city, trying to follow the mysterious blue arrows indicating the Isle of Wight ferry, but we arrived at the terminal in bags of time. In fact, two hours early, which I hate, as I have gone through life never waiting for anything.

I had originally wanted to go by train and hovercraft, which seemed much cheaper, but Claire insisted we had to have the car. Going to a new island and exploring, we would need a car; so, I had agreed. Even though I also hate being driven, almost as much as I used to hate driving. We had booked on the two o'clock ferry, the only one we could get. The various methods of reaching the island were so confusing, the booking systems labyrinthine, and the charge, ye Gods, it was still bugging me – £136 return! What a liberty. For just a forty-minute sail across the Solent, a distance of hardly more than five miles. We could have flown to Portugal and back for that price.

To fill the time, we wandered round the harbour and ferry terminal and discovered a rather well-stocked fresh fish shop in a warehouse, right by the docks. I said we must always come here – that is, if we ever come again, if we ever go on the ferry again, if we ever buy our own cottage, har har. Now I was getting rather carried away. I then realised we were near the cathedral. I didn't even know Portsmouth *had* a cathedral, though I did not know it hadn't got one either. It seemed rather modern for a cathedral. Being brought up in Carlisle, and then educated at Durham, I always assumed all cathedrals must be ancient – Norman, at least. Portsmouth's is on the site of a church dating back eight hundred years, which was being extended when war broke out in 1939. It was not completed and consecrated as a cathedral until 1991. Claire did not come in. She preferred to walk around. Would this be a handicap in the future, if I started rushing around the Isle of Wight looking at the buildings while she looked at the shops?

I love looking inside churches, museums and stately homes, though I usually only do a quick walk-through, taking in just enough to allow me to boast later that I have been there – 'Oh, yes, awfully interesting place' – giving a few details, generally with the help of a guide book. Same with new books. I read all the reviews, not the books, so I can sound knowledgeable.

Inside the cathedral was an old lady in a wheelchair, all her worldly possessions piled up around her. I counted twenty plastic bags. She seemed to be asleep. I spoke to an attendant and asked if the lady was a regular, perhaps even slept here at night. She said, 'No.' The woman leaves at lunch time. Because of lockdown, the cathedral was only open in the mornings.

Back at the ferry terminal, we were in time to see our ferry arriving from the Isle of Wight. I loved it. The sight of any ship arriving and docking, manoeuvring itself backward into a small space, is fascinating to watch. I felt like a child again with my grandmother, looking at the ships on the Clyde.

Our ferry turned out to be called *St Clare*. How apt. Once it was safely docked, the two drawbridges for the vehicles were let down and hundreds of cars and lorries began to stream off. It all seemed rather exciting and exotic, as if they had just crossed the Atlantic. It did now feel like an adventure, as if we were going abroad. Perhaps I would be able to forget about the awful cost of the journey.

Once it had tied up and was disgorging, the *St Clare* looked huge, towering above us. I could see five decks, plus what appeared to be open-air decks on top. Let's go up to the very top and sit outside, I said to Claire. We'll have a really good view as we leave Portsmouth's famous harbour, historic home of the Royal Navy and then again as we arrive at the fabled Isle of Wight on the other side of the Solent.

For our journey had become something of a fairy tale. In just two weeks, since we first thought of visiting the Isle of Wight, it had taken on a magical quality. So many people, neighbours and friends, once we mentioned we were going for a couple of days, said, 'Oh, lucky you, I used to go to the Isle of Wight as a child.' Then they started telling us about all the people they knew, or knew of, some of them rather well-known, who have a house there. Will I spot any celebs from the upper deck as we sail the ocean blue, I wondered?

No such luck. Because of lockdown, everyone had to stay in their cars. Oh, God, I was furious. For the whole of the damn voyage, we had to remain in the car, in the lower parking deck. If we had been in the upper parking deck, we might have glimpsed a bit of sea or sky. Instead, it was like being trapped in prison. We could see neither sea nor land. Just metal walls, stuck down below in the dark, satanic bowels of the ship.

Fortunately, Claire had brought a bottle of white wine and smoked salmon sandwiches on brown bread, her favourite loaf from Lidl. Yes, Lidl – their brown cob is excellent. And so cheap. We sat in the car and scoffed it all, trying to make the best of being incarcerated.

Then, of course, I needed a wee. Being a child. To use the

lavs, I had to call for a female attendant who came to the car. She helped me get out and squeeze between all the cars, parked bumper to bumper. Then she escorted me to a lift and we went up to the fourth deck to a lavatory. She waited for me outside the lav, then led me back down again to the car. It was like having my own prison warden. This must be what it's like when offenders are taken back and forward to Parkhurst.

Oh God, our first visit to the island, which I had looked forward to so much, and I was desperately worried that everything was going wrong already. Can I really put up with all this faff, the complications of booking, paying a fortune each time for forty minutes in an underground dungeon, to get across this short stretch of water to an island I know nothing about? We must be going potty in our old age.

I like to think I am a cheerful chappie, but I do moan on when given half an excuse. 'What have we done?' I said to Claire when I got back from the lavatory and sat in the car beside her, staring at the metal walls. We should have stuck to the mainland. We should have gone to look at something at Hastings, somewhere that is easy to reach from St Pancras. I was regretting this already.

We did not arrive in Ryde, as I had expected. Yes, bad research on my part. The car ferry lands several miles west of Ryde, along the coast at a place called Fishbourne. I had assumed Fishbourne must be in Ryde, but it was out in the sticks. And it appeared just to be a ferry terminal – there was no sign of any village or amenities.

We drove out of the ferry, along a ramp, and out on to a road, following directions to Ryde. The countryside was pleasant enough but looked very like, er, the English countryside, fields of green, ever so familiar, the cars and houses same as anywhere, not at all exotic and foreign. Being stuck in the hold of a ship I had felt a bit like a convict or a slave, as if I was being deported to Australia or the West Indies. After that journey, I had expected the landscape to be something a little bit different from boring old Blighty. We drove round the outskirts of Ryde, which looked like any old provincial town – perhaps Carlisle in the 1950s. The island seemed affluent and prosperous enough, but somehow rather old-fashioned.

Claire had put her TomTom on, her satnav system to which she is devoted, and a posh female voice was giving us instructions on how to reach Glynn Cottage, Seaview, the fab-looking cottage we had already fallen in love with. We planned to go straight there, before checking into our digs, as we were desperate to see it while the sun was still shining, which it had been doing for most of that summer, as if to mock the horrors of Covid.

Seaview is situated just south of Ryde, further down the east coast, but we seemed mainly to be driving inland, round lots of bends, and could see little of the sea or a beach.

As we drove, I studied again the details of Glynn Cottage from the estate agents Spence Willard, which I had printed out as I hate reading stuff online.

Attractive, charming sixteenth-century cottage boasting many period features with enclosed gardens and off-road parking... in a unique situation, tucked away on an elevated plot... fruit trees and slight sea glimpses. A short walk to Seaview with its prestigious yacht club, restaurants and shops and coastal walks to the sandy beaches of Ryde.

Just two bedrooms, quite sufficient for us, but a large sitting room and breakfast room. I still could not believe the £385k price – and, yes, it was freehold.

The TomTom led us a mile or two outside Seaview, up a hill, then along a little unmade track, which was pretty, suggesting it was all going to be hidden away, rural and undeveloped. We parked in the lane beside the cottage and a very pleasant woman from the estate agent came out to greet us and took us round the house.

The cottage looked just as it did in the picture – suitably twee and ancient, and detached; no cheating by the estate agent, no fiddling of the photos. It had probably been two or even three dwellings at one time, later turned into one spacious, bijou cottage.

We inspected the rooms, admiring the original features, the fireplaces, the old doors and cupboards. The cottage had not been overly modernised, but it did have central heating. There were still novels in an old bookcase, of the sort my mother used to read, by Somerset Maugham and A. J. Cronin, dating back to the 1930s.

According to the estate agent, the old lady who had lived here had recently died. Her daughter, who was selling the house, was outside in the garden, pottering away. Eventually she came in and said, 'Hello,' rather hesitantly, as if not wanting to be too sociable and meet yet more boring house-hunters, probably thinking us just here for an outing and to nose around.

Claire had begun sniffing the air and making faces. She whispered to me that she could smell damp. The owner heard and said, Yes, she and her mother had had some work done as there had been a patch of damp on one little cupboard near the front door. She took us to see it, which was honest of her. I can't say it bothered me much. Damp can always be treated.

I could tell Claire had clearly not fallen in love with the house now she was seeing it in person, though she rabbited on brightly enough to the owner and the estate agent, in her most charming PR manner.

My first impression had been how lovely and atmospheric it all was – and what an amazing bargain for a genuinely sixteenth-century house. It was only when we went outside, into the gardens at the front and back, that we realised that the cottage was in fact surrounded by houses on a newly built, small estate. You would never have much privacy in the garden. And from the garden itself, and through a lot of the windows inside the cottage, you would have to look out at boring, suburban semis.

I asked how far it was to the beach, and how far to the town. The daughter, who had now become more interested, said she was about to walk into Seaview village and would show us a back way on a path through some fields. She had lived here for some time with her mother.

It was a very nice walk, very rural, though we did pass a few other modern suburban houses. We left her in Seaview, near the yacht club, which looked so attractive that I longed to go inside, sit in the sun and have a drink watching the boats, were it not closed because of lockdown. I assumed you would have to be a member anyway. Perhaps Donna and Peter were members and would take us there some time.

Claire and I sat on a wall overlooking the sea, outside the Old Fort pub, and had a glass of wine. I looked at her. She made a face. I could tell it was thumbs down.

Claire was against the cottage because it was so dark and damp inside. I said I had not really noticed that and it did not worry me too much. We agreed the worst thing was the existence of the surrounding modern houses. The photos had shown no hint of them. The cottage was detached with its own garden; in close-up shots you could not see other buildings.

In our simple, romantic minds, we had been looking for a love nest in a pretty spot by the seaside or a rural retreat in unspoiled countryside, not an old house next to a Wates estate. I know, it sounds snobbish, but we had persuaded ourselves that Glynn Cottage was the hidden gem of our dreams. My other worry was the walk down to the harbour and coast. It would take a lot longer than I had imagined from the map and it was much steeper. I had a new knee ten years ago and I can walk fine on the flat, but I do try to avoid any hills or steps. The Broadstairs cottage owned by my children is stunning, but you have to go down some incredibly steep steps to get to the beach at Stone Bay. It always knackers me.

At the age of eighty-four, an exhausting walk to the beach is the last thing I need. I want the beach and sea on my doorstep – not necessarily in direct view, but close by and on the flat. Presumably my legs will get worse in the years ahead, so why lumber myself with a tiring walk?

So, that was that. Our romantic dream of a cottage on the Isle of Wight was over. We had come all this way just to be disappointed.

I sent an email to the estate agent, thanking her, and asking her to thank the owner for her time, but making it clear we would not be making a bid.

On reflection, I decided, it was probably just as well the cottage had turned out to be such a disappointment. Could I really stand being driven all that way to Portsmouth and travel forty minutes on the ferry every time we came to the island? No doubt we would also have to suffer delays and cancellations in bad weather, particularly in the winter, when the seas were rough. In our minds, the cottage was going to be our main home all year round, though we would pop back regularly to see our grandchildren.

So much for our love nest in which to live and bond together. So much for getting away from it all, having a place of our own by the sea. So much for the fantasy of having a perfect project to amuse us both in our twilight years.

Yes, I realised now it was all madness. The madness of old age...

CHAPTER 2

Is this our fantasy cottage?

A view of Ryde from the sea

That evening, we had supper with Donna, Claire's friend from her street in London, and her partner Peter. Donna kept her London house and moved in some years ago with Peter to his house in Seaview, which he had owned for some time. They both regularly popped back to the Main Island, as locals refer to the rest of England, to see their children and grandchildren.

I moaned about the cost of the ferry but they pointed out that once you are an Isle of Wight resident – if we ever were, which now looked unlikely – you get a discount on all the ferries. All the same, Peter reckoned that the previous year he had spent as much five hundred pounds on ferry crossings. I had not reckoned on that expense when I had been lying awake at night these last two weeks, fantasising about that sixteenth-century cottage, doing sums in my head.

Peter's house turned out to be modern, in a quiet and a pleasant cul-de-sac, but it did have a long garden which Donna lovingly tended, with lots of trees and fruit bushes and vegetables. At the bottom of the garden, it also had a rather dinky old railway carriage, very dilapidated, now used as Donna's tool shed.

I suppose I had expected them to live in a Grade II gem, being people of taste and discernment, but then I am a snob about old houses. I always think any period house, of whatever period, is always preferable to anything modern, however glam, however convenient.

My London house is not quite a listed gem, just Victorian, circa 1860, but I expect one day it might be. Claire's house in Battersea is also Victorian, but a bit later, 1880. It has three storeys like mine and, also like me, she has a lodger on the top floor.

Donna and Peter filled us in on the social pecking order in

the Isle of Wight. Seaview and Bembridge are probably the most desirable and expensive places to live. The old part of Cowes, on the west bank of the River Medina in the far north of the island, is also much sought after, but you really have to be a yachtie to appreciate its location and amenities. Newport, the capital, is more or less in the middle of the island, with council offices and lots of supermarkets, but they did not know anyone who lived there. Outsiders who come to the island, to retire or have a holiday home, much prefer to be near the coast. Yarmouth, on the Cowes side was also desirable and expensive.

All these places were still just names to us, as was Ryde, the biggest town, where the hovercraft and fast catamaran services come in. Ryde, apparently, has some handsome houses but is considered by the folks in Seaview and Cowes to be rather run-down and neglected. They made it sound a bit like Margate, Broadstairs's scruffy and less respectable – but much cheaper – neighbour. In the last few years, however, Margate has had something of an upturn, attracting hippies and arty types. Perhaps Ryde would come up in the world as well.

We sat outside in Donna and Peter's garden and quizzed them about life on the island. Peter was thinking of buying a boat. He already had the pink corduroy trousers. This is partly an island joke. All the yachtie types wear brightly coloured cords, even if all they do is sit in the yacht club and drink gin. The favourite shade is 'Cowes pink'. Shade of the corduroys, that is. Though it's probably the preferred colour of the gin as well. Peter was looking for a little motorboat, in fact, rather than a yacht, perhaps with a cabin to sleep two, which he thought he might get for under twenty thousand pounds. Donna was against it, considering it a waste of money.

Claire and I were the opposite, in that she likes sailing and I don't. I did have a boat in the Lakes at one time, which I kept on Derwentwater, though I never actually learned to sail properly. I never could understand the winds. I bought it for the image, to parade on a trailer behind my Volvo, not for the water sports. I believe the best thing about yachts is looking at them out at sea. Actually being on one is thoroughly boring. But I agree yachts make a good photograph. I said to Claire that if we ever lived on the Isle of Wight – fat chance, of course – I was sure she would find someone rich with a large yacht who would take her for a sail. She did once have a rich boyfriend who had a large sailing boat, thirty-eight feet long, but every time she reminisces about him I change the subject. 'Keep it to yourself, my darling. I am sure it was fun and he was handsome with floppy hair and went to a frightfully good school.' 'How did you know?' she replies.

Back at the Pilot Inn, it felt strange letting ourselves into the empty pub, creeping down corridors and being startled by remote security lights suddenly coming on. But the room was quite comfortable, if a little basic, with a good sea view.

Before bed, Claire went onto her laptop and looked again at Rightmove. I think women all over the UK do this every night before bed. It really is a form of pre-bed property porn.

And amazingly, as before, she immediately found what looked like another stunning cottage – and this one was £100,000 cheaper than the one in Seaview. She certainly has the touch, does our Claire.

But it was in Ryde, the supposedly run-down town. And we had not thought of ending up in a town. From the beginning our fantasy love nest was going to be tucked away in a yummy little village or by a little hidden beach. We were still going to keep our urban homes, but with a lodger in each, just in case wherever we bought did not work out – or we fell out, and none of it worked out. Why would we want another urban house in an urban street and another urban life when we had that already?

All the same, it did look pretty – a pink-washed, Grade II cottage. And even more of a snip than the other one – asking price just £285k. Of course, despite the pretty prose and equally pretty pictures, there might well be unseen and unknowable problems lurking behind that pink façade…

I rang the estate agent before we went to sleep and left a message on their answerphone as it was so late. I begged for a chance to see it the next day, just for a few minutes. We were only here for one more day, so it had to be tomorrow. Please, please do your best, Mr or Ms Estate Agent, do fit us in, just for a quick look. And we are cash buyers, oh yes.

Next morning, we went for breakfast in the nice little beach café across the road, since there were no facilities at our inn. We liked the woman in charge, Michelle, and her assistant, a young man who tuned out to be still in the sixth form at the local Ryde school. We liked it so much we booked a table for supper that night and rang Peter and Donna to invite them to join us.

We drove to Ryde, parked the car and wandered around the town. It seemed much more attractive and interesting than the image we had picked up. There were plenty of solid, handsome Regency and early Victorian houses – some of them, on the front, were exceedingly grand. Some, admittedly, were a bit in need of a spot of tender loving care, but none of those we saw were derelict or had been turned into squats.

I kept ringing the estate agent, on the hour, begging for a viewing. Eventually, one of their staff agreed to come and show us round, but it had to be very briefly. We rushed at once to the address – we'd just been killing time, poking around town. We went up and down the street, gawping through all the windows. The estate agent was a young woman in stilettos and a tight skirt who seemed very pleased with herself. In all her years as an estate agent, so she immediately told us – as if it was all her doing – she had never known business to be so good. Her firm was bombarded by people who were desperate to flee the mainland, escape the stresses and strains of urban life – especially in London – and move to the Isle of Wight. So many people were stuck at home during the pandemic lockdown, working at the kitchen table and homeschooling their children – which they might have to go on doing for years to come – that there was a sudden longing to get up and away, to move somewhere with more space, to have a garden, to be near greenery and – most of all – be near the seaside.

I thought she was making it all up to keep us keen and put up the price. But the estate agent turned out to be right. As we were about to find out, that very day, 8 July, the chancellor Rishi Sunak announced a stamp duty 'holiday', which meant people would pay less tax if they bought a house before the end of March 2021.

The papers would soon start reporting what the estate agent had been boasting about – a mass exodus to the country. People would fight like cats for a house in or near a honeypot location or with a sea view; some people apparently, offering cash without even viewing the place.

We had timed it badly. Our house-hunting had nothing to do with lockdown or the economy. We were not following the middle-class herd in a Gadarene rush to the country, to acquire a house with an extra bedroom and a garden where the children would grow up in touch with nature, tra la. No. Our motivation was romance. We had fallen in love with each other and wanted to find a quiet place where the two of us could be together. And also to have a project, to fall in love with a new house, a new place. But, oh God, we seemed to have chosen the worst time in living memory to buy a place by the seaside. The Isle of Wight had been unknown, as it is to most British people, and at first it had seemed to be cheap. But now it looked as though we could get caught up in a bidding war, before we had even been inside the house.

Our awfully helpful, eager-beaver estate agent was talking on her mobile phone as she arrived. Before opening the front door, she told us that this house had already had three offers – and it had only just gone on the market.

Bullshit, I thought, estate agent cobblers. But, there again, it could be true. If the house seemed half-way desirable, we had better get our skates on.

We were being allowed just a very quick viewing and the estate agent spent most of her time on her phone. I suspected she had not been in the house before, but she did condescend to give us a bit of background. She explained that the house was a very successful holiday let, occupied most of the year round. In fact, a new holidaymaker was coming the next day, so the owner did not want any more prospective buyers trailing round it. Anyway, she had got enough offers.

The house, Victoria Lodge, had four bedrooms, as the online details had listed, but one bedroom was very small. There was no garden as such, just a largish courtyard at the rear. That did not bother either of us much, as having to look after a proper garden might be a bit of a drag. The courtyard was south facing and the sun was already streaming in. So that was a plus.

It felt much bigger inside than it looked from outside. There was an interesting extension at the back, which you entered down a little corridor, leading to a large bedroom, with an adjoining bathroom and toilet. It was nicely hidden, like a West Wing, perfect for guests to have their own space and privacy.

There were three WCs, two upstairs, one down at the back of the house in a utility room. I noticed they each had a notice, 'septic drainage' – warning users to treat them carefully and put nothing down them. We had had septic drainage at our Loweswater house, as the house was so remote there was no mains drainage or water or gas. Our septic tank was in the garden and was always going wrong. But why did they have a septic tank here, in a built-up area? That suggested some sort of problem.

I asked the estate agent, when she was off her mobile for one brief instant. She waved vaguely through a window towards the courtyard, indicating the septic tank must be out there. She clearly had no idea about the drains. But she had to rush, the world was desperate, making endless offers on all her other houses. Without further ado she ushered us out, leaving us on the pavement as she continued her busy, busy, estate agent's day.

We stood and looked at the house from the outside, then looked up and down the street. There was a palm tree in the little front garden and there were lots of other tropical-type trees growing in front of other houses along the street. Next door they had a much bigger garden at the back than ours, which seemed to contain a complete tropical rain forest.

The path to the front door was laid with pretty Victorian tiles; there was stained glass in the door and 'Victoria Lodge' was spelt out in pretty letters on a pane of glass above it.

The estate agent had led us to believe that it could sleep eight people, which was hard to believe, but I could understand why it had been very popular. The owner was a local businesswoman, she said.

We then walked to the beach, to Ryde Sands. I made Claire count the minutes, to see how long it took to get to the actual beach from our street, no cheating – and, oh my God, it was three minutes max. And all on the flat. Our street was just one street away from the Esplanade, the handsome street overlooking the beach. And it was a nice little stroll in itself, across one street, through a little garden and you were there.

To the left was Ryde Pier, over half a mile long, stretching out to sea. To the right there seemed to be some three miles of perfect open wide sands, with scatterings of families still playing. It was late evening by now, but still light and warm, so we set off to walk along the front. I do like a seaside walk at the end of the day, when people are putting away their belongings, packing away their memories.

At this end, the Ryde Pier end, there were quite a lot of traditional seaside amusements: a mini-golf course, a pirate's castle for the kiddies, a small and rather restrained amusement arcade and ice cream stalls and caffs, all of them open and working. None were noisy or tacky. With age, one does like a bit of peace and quiet – certainly no rowdy teenagers. The visitors seemed to be made up of families with pretty young children, couples holding hands, people with dogs. It was the seaside I remembered from my youth, but a gentler, less threatening version.

After about a hundred yards' walking along the front, the funfair and children's amusements were left behind. There was a nice-looking café with a funny name, The Big Kahuna, which was also the lifeguard station, with a couple of lifeguards on the roof, watching the beach.

On the right, inland, was a large lake with swans and ducks. There also appeared to be a swimming pool at this end of the lake, with a glass roof. Oh, bliss, right on our doorstep. I wondered whether the roof opened… And I saw what looked like a posh restaurant, the Duck. Again, right on our doorstep. I was getting carried away, as if we had bought the cottage already.

The walk was slowly but surely becoming more upmarket: the beach huts were well-tended, and we saw more middle-class families on the beach. We appeared to have now reached Appley Beach. We passed a rather smart café, with a restaurant above it, the Three Buoys, and then a strange stone tower that looked as though it had once been part of some grand Scottish castle, right on the edge of the beach; it was clearly some sort of folly. At the far end of the bay, after walking for possibly three miles, just as we came in sight of Seaview, we encountered an even nicer, posher café, the Dell.

We were both entranced. All these lovely amenities and attractions, so much to see and do, right on our doorstep, just a pleasant stroll away along the beach front. Meanwhile, out at sea, there were so many different vessels to gaze and wonder at: yachts and smaller sailing boats, ferries and cruise liners and massive container ships heading for Southampton or Portsmouth. I do like an ocean view which offers a bit of visual action.

And all of it was on the flat. I would never have to worry about my dodgy knees. And if I ever needed a rest, there were loads of seats, pretty, wrought-iron seaside shelters and a choice of eats and drinks, from chips to chablis. It was all utterly wonderful – just what we wanted. And yet until that moment, until that day, we had not known it *was* what we had wanted. Much better to be in a street with a lovely cottage on the edge of an interesting seaside town with direct access to a fab beach than stuck out in the countryside, however pretty. And so real, my dears. Ryde seemed to be a town full of real, ordinary people – not second-homers in pink corduroys.

We retraced our steps to take another look at our street. We walked to the end and discovered that, minutes away, round the corner, was a little row of shops – an Indian grocery, an Indian newsagent, a chip shop, a launderette, a greasy spoon caff, a dog parlour, a hand car wash. All the things real ordinary people need these days, right on our doorstep. And two pubs – one in our street and one round the corner.

Right on the corner of our street, just before the shops, was an antique shop and café which seemed slightly out of place, as if it should be on Portobello Road. The name of the shop appeared to be 'Madeira'. In the window were a few Portuguese prints and views. I wondered how someone from Madeira had ended up living in Ryde. Would he know Cristiano Ronaldo? I must go in some time when it is open and speak fluent Portuguese. That will be a surprise for them.

It was closed but I pressed my nose against the window and admired the vintage treasures, the old fireguards, tables, pokers, plates, paintings. I love that sort of stuff but, alas, Claire does not. She hates clutter and ornaments or anything that might harbour dust.

I hoped we would never come to blows, if we ever came to furnish and decorate Victoria Lodge. That is, if we ever got to buy it.

CHAPTER 3

We make an offer

Ryde Pier in the early twentieth century

We drove back to Bembridge and let ourselves into our room at Pilot Inn. Claire went online again and tracked down more details of Victoria Lodge. We knew it had been run as a holiday let and she managed to find a promotional video. It was very swish and professional, with music and graphics. It gave you a tour of the house and then the beach, complete with aerial views, presumably done by a drone. Estate agents are so smart these days. The video included lots of close-ups of a beach hut at Appley Beach, which appeared to be part of the let for holidaymakers, presumably for an extra fee.

Claire even managed to find the name of the owner, Catherine, and an email address. Did we dare contact her direct? That would really piss off the estate agent. And might annoy the owner.

That evening, the last of our two days on the island in that trip – perhaps our last-ever if we didn't get the cottage – we took Donna and Peter to the Harbour View Café, opposite the Pilot Boat Inn. Right on the beach, very natural and untrendy. It did not even have a lav – you had to cross the road to reach one on the road. But such wonderful seafood – fresh crab and lobster. The other three had half a lobster each, what guzzlers.

The café was empty except for a grandmother with two grandchildren and we were able to chat to Michelle, the manager. I told her what we had done that day, how we had just seen a lovely house in Ryde and were probably going to make a bid. I gave the address and she exclaimed that she had been there. Her sister had looked at it once, when it was for sale, and she had gone with her to inspect it. And loved it. But it all fell through. She couldn't remember why. Perhaps it was taken off the market. Anyway, she clearly remembered it well and how she loved it. She wished us luck with our offer.

Before bed, I left a voicemail for the estate agent. I offered £280k, cash. This was just below the asking price of £285k, which I though was a fairly generous opening offer.

I also sent an email to Cathy, the owner, whose surname I did not know. I said we had made an offer of £280k for her house, which we thought was so lovely and which we were really, really keen to buy. I hoped that would be a hint that we could offer a little bit more.

I know it is not done for prospective purchasers to contact an owner direct. That is the unwritten rule. You must always go through the estate agent. But what the hell. We had nothing to lose.

Then we went to sleep, dreaming about Victoria Lodge. Wondering perhaps if it was real or a fantasy from a children's story.

Next morning dawned fine and sunny, we were even more convinced this was it; this would be our love nest. I rang the estate agency to check they had received our offer. I pleaded with him to let us see the house again this morning. But he said, 'No.' A holiday let was moving in. And there was something else. The owner had given first refusal on buying the place to one of her regular holiday guests. That person was now trying to get the money together. So, for the moment, the owner did not want the agent to show new people round. And anyway, they already had two other offers: both in cash and both higher than mine.

So the boastful young woman we met at the house the day before had been right. The world was indeed rushing to escape to the country – and too many of them now fancied the Isle of Wight. It was time to leave the island.

On the way to the ferry, we made a detour to look at the street and the house once again. There appeared to be someone in. I tried to peer through the front window, which was hard, as the little front garden was dominated by a large cactus as well as the palm tree. I knocked at the front door and a young woman eventually opened it, having been interrupted in the middle of cleaning and dusting, ready for the imminent arrival of the next holiday guests. I asked if she was Cathy, which I doubted she was. She said she was Cathy's daughter. I explained that we had made an official – if brief – visit, and that I had made an offer. We now just wanted another quick look at the house before we went back to London. I said we had left a message for her mother. I wondered if she had got it?

'Oh, she is very busy at the moment, with all her businesses.'

I said, Please, please, could we just have a quick look round? She looked hesitant but eventually agreed to ring her mother on her mobile. By the sound of it, her mother had neither received my offer, nor knew anything about me and Claire being interested. But she agreed we could come in for ten minutes for a quick look – provided we took our shoes off.

So we did. Another quick ogle. Which only confirmed how much we loved it.

We raced to the ferry, worried we might miss the boat – but also worrying about the house. I wondered whether I should make another offer? And should I do it now or later? And what would be my maximum?

Claire said, 'Don't make another offer now. You haven't heard about your first one yet. Just wait. You are always in such a hurry. Anyway, it looks as if this other person has got first refusal, so we will just have to wait to see if that falls through.'

'If this other person exists,' I said. When bidding for any house, you don't always know the motives of the vendor or if they or the estate agent are telling you a load of bollocks. Capitalist pigs, able and willing to buy a second home, do not of course deserve any sympathy.

As we drove to Fishbourne and got on the ferry, we felt rather churned up. Three days earlier, when we came over on the ferry, I was fantasising about what my life might be in a stunning sixteenth-century cottage at Seaview. I could just see myself there, popping down to the yacht club for drinks with the chaps in corduroy. Now I was in love with a totally different house in a different part of the island with a different set of attractions.

On the boat, we had wine and smoked salmon again, our new ritual, but this time we were allowed out of the car and could go up to the top deck. During the ferry crossing, we could talk about nothing except Victoria Lodge. But would we get it? Perhaps Cathy was not even selling, just testing the market. Was it all a game?

I said, 'Let's both write down on a piece of paper, without conferring, why we want to buy it. Try to list up to five things that make us really love it and want it. And also five reasons *not* to buy it. Just off the top of your head. The order is not vital.

'If we are both in accord that we still want it, then the minute we get back to London, I will put in another offer. Whatever happens, I will file both lists away when we get home. In a few years' time, I will chance upon them again, read them out, and will have no idea what we were on about. Where the hell was Victoria Lodge? What were we thinking of? Were we potty or what?'

On the other hand, in twelve months' time we might have been happily living there for a whole year and still considering it to be the best thing we have done since meeting each other. I will have framed the lists and hung them on the wall in the kitchen, as a daily reminder of past and present bliss.

Claire's reasons to buy the cottage

1) It will be a true commitment to one another
2) Our first home together
3) I love the beach, new places, new adventures and excitements
4) I will never be bored there – so much to do

Claire's reasons against

1) I don't think I would like to be there on my own
2) I fear if we get it, we might argue over the furnishings

Hunter's reasons to buy the cottage

1) I love the house soooo much
2) I love the location, the beaches, local amenities
3) I love it as a project, for us to do together
4) It will cement our relationship

Hunter's reasons against

1) I am eighty-four
2) The ferry – might be a right drag getting there
3) We already have access to the family's seaside cottage in Broadstairs – it is pure greed to have another
4) Unseen problems in the house – things are bound to go wrong and drive me mad
5) What if we fall out...

The reasons against were pretty minor, piddling and hypothetical. It was clear we both loved it dearly and for the same sorts of reasons.

I gave Claire a kiss and said, 'That's it, we have decided. I will put in a higher offer...'

CHAPTER 4

Gorrit!

The *Island Flyer* plies the Southsea-to-Ryde
route across the Solent

We returned to our respective houses in London; all shook up. I'm in love, I'm all shook up, hmm, yeh, hey, all shook up.

Not just in love with Claire, of course, but in love with Victoria Lodge. In love with the street, the beach, the walks, the lovely town of Ryde, the whole damn thing. What a project; yet an easy project – in that, by the look of it, there would be so little to be done on the house. What excitement, for my old age.

We were together for half of each week, at Claire's house or mine, not breaking any lockdown rules, oh, no, because we were in our bubble. We talked about VL all the time, what to do next and how to move things along, but in practical terms we were stuck until we had heard whether Cathy, the owner, had agreed a deal with the holiday let or had put the house back on the market again.

To hurry things along, or at least keep our interest alive and active, I emailed another offer to the estate agent – £300k. This time I indicated it would be my last bid. I was beginning to feel a bit sorry for the estate agent. If it was true that Cathy planned to sell the house to one of her holiday tenants – and who knows what is truth and what is fiction in the strange world of house-selling? – then presumably the estate agent would not get their percentage. Should I put in a higher offer? Try to contact Cathy direct? Chat her up and at least find out the real state of play?

One night, I lay awake thinking of all the cottages I have bought in my long-legged life. Seemed a lot, when I counted them all up.

The first we had, when our three children were small, back in the 1970s, was a cottage called Keechbrook in the village of Wardington, near Banbury. We went there every weekend, bustling them out of school, then into the Volvo estate and whoosh, up the M1. Just like so many other middle-class families in our area. I had by then begun to admit to myself that Margaret and I had become middle class, despite our modest Cumbrian backgrounds – both of us having been brought up on a Carlisle council estate.

I suppose it was a university education, which at the time was only enjoyed by 4 per cent of the population, which allowed Margaret and I to rise up the socio-economic ladder. That and writing books and films, which was lucky for me, as I always believed Margaret was the creative one. It meant that for many years we had two good incomes.

I can't remember what we paid for Keechbrook. Possibly twenty thousand pounds. Nor what we got when we sold it – which we did in a hurry after only four years. Margaret had to have a double mastectomy and we thought for many months she was a gonner. So much for thinking we were so lucky, with our yummy Oxfordshire cottage. You never know, do you?

Amazingly, Margaret recovered, returned to full health, far healthier than me, which was quite easy really. I have always had to have something to moan about, from my asthma to my arthritis. So, about ten years later, we bought another country cottage, this time up in Cumbria, in a hamlet called Parkend, just outside Caldbeck, at the edge of the Northern Fells. We wanted somewhere for the school holidays, not weekends this time, as it was too far away for that. And we wanted to be near Carlisle as both sets of parents were growing frailer and we wanted to visit them frequently. With the money we got from the sale of some film rights, we bought them a bungalow each in Carlisle, next door to each other, thinking they would keep an eye on each other.

I bought the Caldbeck cottage at auction, I think for thirty thousand pounds. Must have the details somewhere as I have always been obsessed by money. (I'm always asking people how much they earn or how much their house cost them.) It was a seventeenth-century cottage, sturdy and basic as opposed to pretty and twee. Inside, it was rather dark and damp. But it felt very genuine, a real Cumbrian farm worker's cottage, rather remote, out among the open, barren fells. While we still owned it, it became Grade II listed, partly I think because of some historic connections. It was called John Peel Farm, after the famous Cumbrian huntsman.

We eventually sold it when our children were going off to college and our parents had died. We decided we could now indulge ourselves, this time have a real Lakeland house, in one of the pretty parts, near a lake, with enough space for each of us to have a study to work in. It would not be a holiday home, where we went for quick visits, but a proper house, where we would make our lives for six months every year.

In the spring of 1986 I went up for the day on the train for the auction in Cockermouth. The guide price was eighty thousand pounds. I promised Margaret I would not go above that figure. What a fib. I had to pay £92k to get it, but I was thrilled. It gave us such joy and pleasure for the next thirty years. Margaret loved it, which is why her grave is in Loweswater churchyard. It was Margaret's death, in February 2016, which made me sell up.

In a way, buying another cottage, to share with Claire, felt like a rebirth, a new beginning, a second chance at being in a couple, being happy together with someone you love.

They are so unalike, Claire and Margaret. I think that rather alarmed my family and friends. Margaret was not a social animal, did not like parties or events, which I do – though with age my boredom threshold has got lower, but I still do like going out. I always say, 'Yes,' to almost any invite. Claire is much the same.

Claire is glamorous, wears makeup – which Margaret never did – she's a fashion plate, still the same weight and has the same figure she had when she was a girl. She likes classical music, which Margaret and I never did. She does read – her favourite author is Jeffrey Archer, and I can hear Margaret tut-tutting at this. Margaret was incredibly clever, the brainbox in her school, gifted at so many things. And also very outspoken, whether she was asked her opinion or not. People did say they were a bit scared of her, being so direct and clearly clever. Which was daft. She was not at all scary or a bluestocking. And she loved *EastEnders* and *Casualty*.

Claire is always charming and friendly and outgoing; she talks to everyone, and is very popular. Unlike me and Margaret, she has rather a posh southern accent – though over the years Margaret's accent definitely softened. I remember listening to an old *Desert Island Discs* recording of Margaret, after she died, and was surprised to find she did not sound like a lass from a Carlisle council estate, as I had always imagined in my head. I suppose her three years at Oxford had taken the edge off her native accent. I went to Durham, which today is quite posh, but in my day, 1954–8, most students were from northern grammar schools, like me.

I then made another offer for VT – £305k. I said it definitely was my last offer. I did not want to get into a bidding war with people unknown who might have loads of money, intending to install their mistress in the house or use it as a lucrative source of holiday-let income (apparently, Cathy was getting £1,500 a week in rent at the height of the summer season).

The estate agent rang back to say hard cheese. The other two buyers had put in higher offers – and in cash. One was offering £321k, to include buying the holiday let business and all contents.

Oh, bugger. That's it, then. Little use going any higher. The top offer was sixteen thousand pounds above mine. As a gesture, I put my offer up by five thousand pounds, to cover all the contents and the holiday business, which I did not want, but seemed to be part of the deal. I was definitely going no higher. Where do people get the money, in these hard times? So that was it. End of story.

We might now start looking in Hampshire, perhaps, or Dorset, somewhere on the south coast anyway. More sensible, really, than a place that forces you to make a ferry crossing to reach it.

The next day, which was 21 July 2020 – a date that I will mark forever red in my diary – the estate agent rang to say the owner was accepting our offer. You what? But it is £310k compared with the other bid of £321k! It was up to the owner to tell me why she preferred my bid.

I had never heard of a seller going for a lower bid when both were cash. How strange, how mysterious – but how wonderful. We had done it!

Except, of course, there then began the long and protracted and agonising struggle to complete. I rang the solicitor in Scarborough I had used for a few years, purely because one of the partners there had been at school with Caitlin, my older daughter. I had known the partner since she was a little girl, so I always felt I could boss her around, though of course I did not say that. Her firm had handled the sale of the Loweswater house and the purchase of the Broadstairs cottage for the family, and probate for my wife. That last got complicated, but they did it all calmly with no fuss, and for a very reasonable price. Alas, it turned out that their conveyancing solicitor had been furloughed and was not working.

What was to be done? I wanted to get started as soon as possible, so we could move in while it was still summer. I knew from experience that you don't really need a solicitor with local knowledge these days. They all use the same sort of search companies, so they could be based anywhere. I was on better terms with my estate agent, now that my offer had been accepted and her firm would get their whack. I felt able to ask if she could recommend someone on the Isle of Wight. She mentioned a firm and I asked for a rough quote. We wanted to complete as soon as possible and all the money was in my bank.

I was fortunate that my money was coming from one simple source – my National Savings Certificates, the ones that me and my wife had invested in throughout our married lives, since we first had any savings. They can be cashed in twenty-four hours – no tax or paperwork needed. I got the details online and then printed them out – taking care to delete my actual National Savings and Investments number (not totally daft).

The recommended solicitor seemed willing and efficient but alarmed me by saying it would take at least three months, but could be longer because of Covid. Every office, every business in the world was using Covid as an excuse for delays. He said it was not their fault. He blamed local government offices – 'they are miles behind' – and not just because of Covid but owing to the huge stampede to buy country cottages before the stamp duty holiday expires.

Oh, God. My fantasy of swimming and sunbathing on Ryde Sands all summer was slowly disappearing.

I probably drove that legal firm mad, constantly bombarding them with questions, asking if there been any progress, when we might reach the next stage. I suspected my solicitor was working at home, probably had kids crawling all over him, but hard cheese. He always seemed to blame other people for the endless delays, either the local council offices or the vendor's solicitor.

After a month, we decided to go on a quick trip to the island, just to ogle the house again and see if it was still as marvellous as we thought when we first saw it. Perhaps on a second, cold, clear look we might see loads of faults. This was during a pause in the lockdown drama, and we were able to book a room very near the house, at the Royal Esplanade hotel on the front near the pier. I refused to go on the car ferry again, in case we had to endure the same hellish incarceration as last time. I persuaded Claire to go by train and hovercraft instead.

We met at Waterloo and travelled down to Portsmouth together. I was confused by what station in Portsmouth we were supposed to get off at, as there seemed to be two, but we found the right one and found our way to the hovercraft departure station – only to find it had been cancelled. Oh, bloody hell. Stormy seas.

We went to the catamaran office – they were running a service, but all their boats were full. This is becoming a nightmare. We had made a date to meet Cathy the owner, who was going to take us personally round. Now we were unlikely to get there on time – and she was a busy businesswoman.

The only alternative was the dreaded car ferry and the terminal was quite a way away. Claire had packed a huge case for our two-night stay, as of course she always travels with enough clothes for a world cruise. I just had a little rucksack, as I don't need many clothes. We couldn't see a taxi and it was very windy. We set off walking and got lost in the back streets of Portsmouth. Claire does not wear high heels, being naturally quite tall, and was in sensible plimsoles, but she still struggled to push her large case against the wind over uneven cobbles.

We made it. This time we didn't have a pre-booked ticket, as we were foot passengers. But at least we weren't imprisoned in the car in the bowels of the boat and were able to sit upstairs on the deck. Claire emailed Donna, telling her what had happened, how we were not arriving at Ryde Pier after all but miles away at Fishbourne. We now feared we would be late. Donna immediately offered to get Peter to come to Fishbourne and pick us up – which was so kind. And he drove us to Victoria Lodge.

Cathy, the owner, was already there. She turned out to be a very attractive, slender, blonde, athletic-looking woman of about fifty, with a northern accent. Her husband Andy was from the Isle of Wight. They had lived in the house at one time, about twenty years ago, then bought another house to live in, on the outskirts of Ryde. They had been letting out Victoria Lodge for about ten years, very successfully. In fact, they had bookings all the way to Christmas, but cancelled them when they decided to sell.

Why sell, I asked? The main reason appeared to be that they had another much bigger business, go-karting, which had not been earning money during the pandemic. Letting the cottage had been successful enough, but it was stressful, getting people in and out, cleaning it, repairing it. We complimented her on how beautifully maintained the house was and how tasteful. Holiday lets usually look like holiday lets, with tired furniture, lumpy beds, dodgy-looking carpets, nothing matching, cheap curtains.

She took us round the house and answered all the queries which the estate agent could not. The septic tank notices were a ruse. There was no septic tank. With up to eight people in the house at any one time, there was always a chance of someone putting something down the lavs. So, this way, guests had been warned to be careful. And it had worked, she said.

I asked about various points the solicitor was now raising, such as an alteration that appeared to have been made to some of the glass in the bedroom window. This was, in theory, against the law as the house was Grade II listed. The window in question is very handsome and rounded, Regency-style, one of the distinctive features of the house, which I had noticed on other local houses when walking round the town. I couldn't actually see what the problem was. Cathy said it had been like that when they bought the house. She went on to explain the things they had done in the house, and why, and what to look out for. There really was nothing to worry about, that I could see. We loved the house, even more than the first time.

Claire had been adamant that we had to have a survey. That was what she had always done, in the three houses she had bought over the years. I agreed in the end, although I said surveyors just frighten you, they have to cover everything, warn about the most piddling thing, so they are covered if sued. When we bought our Loweswater house at auction I never had a survey done, which everyone thought was stupid. I imagined I could see the roof was OK, could smell no damp, and that we would be doing a lot of work anyway, as there was no central heating for a start. If you are getting a mortgage, you have no choice, of course. You have to get a survey done, otherwise they don't lend you the money.

I had already contacted a local surveyor in Ryde, Tim Smart, whom Cathy had suggested. He turned out to be very quick and efficient and had just delivered his survey, a copy of which Claire had printed, reading it as we walked round the cottage. Tim's survey report seemed fine to me. Even Claire agreed. He had spotted some damp in an exterior wall in the dining room, but I couldn't smell it or see it, so chose to ignore it.

Back at the Esplanade we had a lovely evening. It is an old-fashioned grand seaside hotel, overlooking the harbour and Ryde Pier, with some very nice staff. We had booked a room on the third floor, right at the front, overlooking the sea.

The only problem was not evident till around six o'clock in the morning when we were awakened by the most thunderous noise. It was as if war had broken out and there were planes overhead, with explosions going off, and bangs and blasts rending the air. Claire, being much younger than me, has no memories of the war, which I, born in 1936, still have. I can still clearly see and hear being in Glasgow at my grandmother's house, going into the Anderson air-raid shelter in the garden when the sirens sounded, watching the barrage balloons, the 'Nazzie' planes – which was how we pronounced it – being shot at, the air battles, the ack-ack artillery, God, it was brilliant, I loved it.

The deafening noise I was hearing now was in fact the first hovercraft of the day, a giant creature bursting into life. We had yet to experience hovercraft travel, of course, as the one we had booked had been cancelled. I jumped out of bed and rushed to the window, which was all of six inches away, as it was a pretty small bedroom. It was as if a massive spaceship had landed outside our window, just fifty yards away, and didn't think much of what it had seen, so it was now hellbent on leaving. It thundered, chundered and juddered its way across the sands – gosh, it was exciting! But I think, really, on reflection, hearing it once a day would be enough. Imagine being in this bedroom all day long. Unless of course you are a member of the Hovercraft Fan Club. I have made that up, but I am sure such an organisation exists.

We felt so happy we still loved the house, and thought that the solicitor's faffing on about the window was complete nonsense – and then he informed us that, because of flood danger, we should on no account buy the house. Apparently, there had been a history of local flooding. An underground stream, which flows from the recreation ground behind our street and then into the sea, had burst its banks two years ago and flooded our street.

I had eventually had a coffee with my new friend at the corner from Madeira, the one with the antique shop, and he had told me his cellar was flooded. But he assured me the council had spent millions on flood prevention locally. My solicitor seemed to be unaware of all this work or maybe the firm that did the searches on his behalf did not know about it. Oh, God. More problems. He said we would not get a mortgage – which of course we did not need – or any flood insurance.

I rang Cathy, my new best northern friend, and she said she had never had flood insurance. You just had to live with the danger. Andy, her husband, who was a surveyor, had checked the new flood defences installed by the council, which had cost twenty-five million pounds, and he assured me there was little danger.

There was silence on the legal front for a week and I thought, Hurrah, we are sorted at last. Or will he find something else to worry about?

Thinking back over the houses I have bought, I realise I had never known a conveyancing lawyer bring up so many objections – and to advise me *not* to buy. I might have forgotten, of course, which you do in life with most things which at the time are really annoying.

The whole process so far had been an obstacle race – with all the obstacles being thrown in our way by the lawyers. Their advice always seemed to be pessimistic or negative. You long for any experts you have hired, medical or architectural or whatever, to be on your side, to be positive, to think of ways round any problems, to get you over all the hurdles. Fortunately, my attitude has always been that problems are there to be overcome. Rejections and refusals are a challenge.

I told the solicitor, bugger the floods – I was willing to live without flood insurance.

Immediately, they discovered another obstacle. Local searches, they said, had revealed there was a sewer right under the house, possibly dating back to the 1850s. This was now illegal and highly dangerous. If it all exploded, the house would fall down. Their advice was – you've guessed it – 'Don't buy it.' They sent me copies of these ancient drainage plans, no doubt dug up by some third party they had hired, based in another part of the country.

I rang Cathy and discussed them with her. She said this was always happening in Ryde – and that drainage plans from that early period are often inaccurate. Claire, however, being a sensible gel, was worried; she was inclined to accept the legal advice and call it a day.

I rang around and contacted a drainage firm, saying it was an emergency. I spoke to its boss, who sounded helpful – he knew our street as he used to live there – but alas, he was off to Cornwall tomorrow on his annual holidays. Oh, God, more complications... but not to worry, he said; he would send his chaps round tomorrow morning and they would forward the results to him to analyse and he would do an immediate brief report.

I got Cathy to arrange for them to get a key and they arrived first thing. They put CCTV cameras down all the drains in the house, front and back, checked every one – and there was no sewerage pipe under the house. It was in the yard, where it could always be easily reached if things went wrong. The old drainage map was clearly rubbish.

I was furious. I had been thinking that if the legal advice about the drains had proved correct, I was not going to back out of the sale, but I might use it to get the price down. This is what you often do with a poor survey. It's hard luck on the vendor, who is probably completely unaware of the problems that need extensive work. But in this case, I had got a good price – especially so in that there had been a much higher bidder. And we both liked Cathy and trusted her.

So why had she chosen us? Cathy later revealed what had happened.

A rival offer had come in, from a woman who lived in Birmingham, whose funds had been verified, but then she started laying down conditions. She offered ten thousand pounds up front, before contracts or completion, on condition the house was taken off the market at once. Cathy's husband Andy, the surveyor, had an idea of what the woman was up to. Once they had agreed to sell to her, and taken her ten thousand pounds, she would make more demands and try to get the price down. She was probably doing the same with several other houses, then going for the one where she got the best price. It all sounded jolly complicated to me, but Andy had had dealings with such people and smelled problems ahead.

So, after weighing things up, he and Cathy had chosen us. They decided that we, rather than the woman who lived in Birmingham and had lots of properties, would complete quickly and would not mess them around. They could see that we loved the house, the neighbourhood, the Isle of Wight. We wanted to contribute to the community – and in fact I had already agreed to appear at that year's Isle of Wight Literary Festival.

Also I was from the north, like Cathy, which I dragged in to our chats. Leeds is not the north compared with Carlisle.

We felt that we had made new friends in Cathy and Andy; that they were people who could help us to fully understand the house and integrate into local life.

The full drainage report, when it came in after the boss's holiday, indicated exactly where the main sewer was, and all was well, though he said that a little rainwater drain in the yard needed a new flap, so no rats could get out. The quote was four hundred pounds. But it was not urgent and we could do it sometime after we moved in. Cathy agreed to pay half, which was very nice of her.

The solicitors were still faffing on, still saying their advice was not to go ahead, unless we got indemnity from the vendor about future expenses, on the bedroom window for example, which was mad. No vendor is going to agree to that.

So, we said sod it; as far as we were concerned, everything was in order. We were going ahead, regardless.

Completion finally took place on 18 September 2020, three months after we had first seen it. It seemed much longer, with all the aggravations and delays and of course we had now missed the summer. Ah well, there would be many more summers to come, we hoped.

But we had done it. We had secured our love nest.

CHAPTER 5

Paradise postponed

Messing about in boats, Ryde, 1906

Our first day in paradise was on 20 September 2020. OK, it might not turn out to be paradise. There might be disasters ahead. Or Claire and I might fall out, have a row and one of us would then storm off. But where do you storm off to, on the Isle of Wight? Unless you own a helicopter or a power boat, how do you suddenly leave an island? We were told that was one of the reasons the crime rate was relatively low. Burglars find it difficult to leg it in a hurry with their loot.

I suppose if we fell out while walking along Ryde Sands, one of us could storm off into the sea and swim all the way to Portsmouth. I think Claire could do that. She is a jolly good swimmer. I swim all the time, three times a week, and could not wait to try out the local pool, but I can only manage ten lengths these days. I would probably get no further than the end of Ryde Pier before I sank.

We decided to take the car ferry. For weeks Claire had been buying and collecting stuff for the house, so her car was crammed to the roof. We were expecting thirty packages from IKEA to be waiting at the new house. God knows what. I let Claire do it. I agreed from the beginning she could be in charge of all household purchases. I would probably regret it, when the bills started coming in. I find I can spend money on big things, like a house, but with piddling, day-to-day expenditure I am so mean, always looking for bargains. It drove my wife mad.

We did the drive to Portsmouth in an hour and a half. It was so easy. I almost – but not quite – said, 'Oh, I am enjoying this ride,' but I held back. The A3 is such a nice road, dual carriageway all the way from London, few of the thundering lorries or boy racers you usually get on motorways. I used to dread going up to Loweswater each year on the M1 and the

M6, sheer hell; I couldn't wait till we could turn left at Penrith.

The ferry was a delight. No, I really mean it. I took back what I had said about never going on it again. We sat on the top deck in the sun, had our wine and smoked salmon, our treat for ourselves. One of many. Now we are old – well, I am old compared with Claire – I promised it would be constant treats from now on

We were beginning to tell ourselves we were regulars, we knew where to find the best seats on the Wrightlink ferry – a comfy, nicely upholstered sofa and two easy chairs with a little table, right beside the window, so we could look out and see everything, on land and sea. The thing about the Solent is that there is always so much happening, all sorts of boats and yachts, chugging away.

I had announced to my family and friends that the ferry was in fact part of the adventure of going to the Isle of Wight. It was a delight in itself, not a drag which had to be endured. That first awful trip in the car deck was probably helpful in the end – made us appreciate, when we could travel on top deck, how wonderful it all was, spotting all the landmarks, ticking off the stages, recognising the little island forts, looking out for the church spires, spotting Ryde in the distance.

We arrived to find we couldn't get in the front door.

So that rather ruined my good mood and led to effing and blinding from me. Cathy had told us the code number to put into a little black box where a key had been kept for new holiday lets. A good system, which we intended to continue, in case one of us ever lost our key. Such as me.

I had not actually asked Cathy how the little safe thing worked, though I had written down the four-number code. It didn't work. I must have written it down wrongly or could not read my own writing. I tried another number and eventually I heard the mechanism click into place. But I still could not work out how to swing it open. With age, my fingers have grown very stiff and I have little strength in my hands, not that I ever had much. Any strength I had was in my thighs, through playing so much football until I was fifty. But elsewhere I remained a weed and weakling.

I was about to ring Cathy and cry for help, which would have been pathetic. But then – Hurrah! – the key box suddenly swung open and there was the front door key, like a magic jewel on a little pad, waiting to be enjoyed.

We stepped into the hallway into bright sunlight which was streaming down from the glass door at the end that led into the back courtyard. We stood together for some time, holding each other and hugging. Then we congratulated ourselves on being so clever as to find such a treasure of a place and also on our perseverance in making it all happen in the face of the problems thrown at us. We also thanked our lucky stars, as it had been luck really, that Cathy suddenly had decided she wanted us to have it.

It was also such stunning weather – another lovely bonus for our first stay. It felt as though summer was still with us, even towards the end of September.

We opened all the doors and windows, and the big sliding doors in the kitchen which led out into the courtyard. Cathy had left outside a metal table and four chairs, which was handy, so we were able to sit outside in the sun. We looked up, trying to work out when the sun would go down over the back wall of our garden. We also wondered what was behind the back wall. It was clearly another building. Luckily, there were no windows in it, so no one could see us. We could easily bathe naked.

'Let's crack open a bottle of fizz,' I said. 'You have brought some, haven't you?'

I don't actually like champagne, so I don't know why I said it. Just tastes fizzy, no taste or body, might as well drink Coca-Cola. Claire had gone off it as well, saying it affected her stomach, but she had brought some Prosecco. I took one sip and decided I didn't like that either. Fortunately, Claire had also brought some excellent Marlborough Sauvignon Blanc, my current favourite white wine.

After lunch outside – salad with avocado and tuna – I went upstairs to our bedroom for my afternoon rest. I wasn't going to break a habit of a lifetime. Well, since 1986, when this habit began. My wife and I went to Barbados on Concorde for my fiftieth birthday. It was so hot at midday and I drank so much at lunchtime, that we both got into the habit of having a siesta every afternoon. I have kept it up ever since, over thirty-five years now, regardless of where I am. Claire was a bit surprised, never having known any of her previous boyfriends take to their bed every afternoon – on their own.

I take off my trousers and socks, pull the curtains, get under the duvet, and am usually asleep in minutes. Having two glasses of wine every lunch is a help of course. When I tell people I drink every lunchtime, as well as in the evening, they say, 'Goodness, I couldn't drink at lunch. I would fall asleep.' I say, 'Precisely. That's the point.'

Most times I sleep soundly for forty minutes. If for some reason I can't sleep, I just lie there for thirty minutes, then get up. I have at least rested. I am ready to do some more words, shift some more sentences. Claire never has an afternoon kip, well – she is so young – but she is always frightfully busy all day long, doing household jobs – washing, ironing, cleaning, hoovering; she is always gainfully employed.

I didn't sleep, of course, that afternoon in Ryde I was too excited. So, after thirty minutes, I got up and wandered round the bedroom, wondering where I was. This happens to me all the time. Even in my own bedroom. I think I should leave chalk marks on the floor, so I can find the lavatory in the night.

Claire was busy chucking out the curtains, sheets and towels which Cathy had kindly left, saying, 'Ugh, horrible!' as she did so. I couldn't see what was horrible about them. But I didn't want to have an argument on our first day. Decor and furnishings are subjects we always differ on. She thinks my taste is appalling, that I am colour-blind.

I explored the whole house again, all ten rooms – four bedrooms, front sitting-room, dining room, kitchen, utility room, two bathrooms, plus three WCs. Even though it is on just two floors, it felt very spacious. We had decided the smaller bedroom, downstairs at the back, which had a single bed, would be turned into my study, in due course. We would still have enough bedrooms when our families came to stay. They would go in the south wing, as we called it, the extension leading off the staircase on the first floor, down a little corridor, with its own bathroom and loo. Handily hidden away for visitors to feel independent.

We then went off to explore the beach. We turned right, heading along the promenade, and soon left the amusements behind. Not that I minded them. They were all traditional seaside attractions, like the pier itself, part of English social history and architecture for 150 years. Even this late in the season, there were still plenty of families about, enjoying themselves on the sand. And there were no rowdies, no horrible music, nothing to disrupt the peaceful scene.

I decided to have a swim. I had put on my cossie just in case I should be tempted. Claire refused, however. Her ear had been perforated while she had been having her ears syringed back in London, so she was keeping out of the water until it healed.

I had noticed some families paddling at the edge of the water or building sandcastles, but I couldn't see anyone actually swimming at this end of the beach. The swimmers mostly seemed to be further down, towards Appley Beach. But I couldn't wait. I wanted to go in, now. The sand was deliciously warm to walk on and the water was so inviting.

The tide looked a long way out, though it was probably only half out. At Ryde, the tides are enormous. At the lowest tide, the sea is at least half a mile away. I don't think I have ever seen a beach where the tide goes out so far, leaving a wonderful empty expanse of perfectly clean and smooth, yellow sand with no rocks, no seaweed, nor flotsam or rubbish. When the tide is right out, you must be exhausted by the time you reach the sea itself, and then you have to wade on until the water is deep enough for you to swim.

I put my shorts and T-shirt and sandals down on the sand on the beach and gave Claire my mobile. I switched it to camera mode and said, 'Hold this, pet, I want you to do some shots of me swimming.'

'Do I have to?'

'This is historic stuff, pet. My first swim ever on Ryde Sands. The first day of our new life. I want to send shots to all my family and friends. They will be well jeal—'

But Claire carried on walking.

'Oh, don't be rotten. Just a few shots. Perhaps a video as well. And make sure you get me properly swimming, OK?'

I started swimming as soon as I was in the water, even though it was still quite shallow. The worldwide audience would never know the actual depth from the video. I turned and waved frantically at Claire. Look at me, oh, look at me, oh, I'm dancing, I mean swimming... I could see her filming, and she waved back. Then I swam out a bit more, till I really was in deeper water. I did my flash backstroke, a few yards of my stylish crawl, then my sedate breaststroke, wondering how many other people on the beach were admiring my amazing bathing feats and thinking to themselves, Goodness, he is a jolly good swimmer for his age.

I did a really fast racing crawl, with my head down, well, at least six strokes, then started waving at Claire again. But I couldn't see her. That's funny. But then I didn't have my specs on, that must be the reason. I wear specs for long distance sight, not for reading (unlike Claire).

Where the hell is she? The rotten thing. Oh, God, she has walked off down the beach, not waiting for me. I want her to take more lovely pix of me. She must be jealous.

As I scanned the beach, the families I had noticed earlier had also seemed to have walked on. Which was strange. Perhaps Claire had spotted someone with a dog, and gone off to talk to them. She is a sucker for any dog, always bending down and patting them, slobbering over then, then starting some boring, doggie dialogue with the owners. Where the hell has she gone, and all the others? Where have they moved to?

Then I realised it was not Claire or the other people on the beach who had moved – it was me. I thought I had been doing so well, but in fact I had been swept along by the incoming tide. I was now being carried by a swirling current and was heading straight for Ryde Pier. If I had not realised in time that I was being swept along by a fierce current, I might well have been dashed against its pillars. Oh, God, how stupid of me. I managed to summon up all my feeble strength and struck out for shore. No wonder no one was swimming at this end. Unlike silly old me, the locals knew all about the strength of the tides.

I eventually managed to drag my poor old body back onto the sand and lay there like a beached whale. Then I hauled myself to my feet and staggered about two hundred yards back along the beach – where I saw that Claire was standing at exactly the same spot I had left her. And she was indeed talking to some woman with a dog and had not seen that I had been swept away.

Typical of me in a way. Even at my great age, I am far too impulsive for my own good, always wanting things done now, at once. But I learned one thing on our first day in paradise. Don't swim at the Ryde Pier end of the beach. Head towards Appley Bay, where the quality swim and play. And the sensible.

That evening we had supper outside in our courtyard. Claire lit candles, put cushions on the chairs and set the table beautifully. It was awfully romantic and lovely. We drank a lot and once again congratulated ourselves on being so clever and fortunate as to have found not just a lovely house, but one with so many attractions and wonders, right on our doorstep.

We went to bed quite early, as it had been a pretty exhausting, if enjoyable, day. I think sea breezes do make you extra tired, but nicely so. We were just settling down when the most awful noise started – a screeching, wailing sound, coming on for a minute, then going off for a minute before starting up again. Oh God, what the hell can that be? What have we left on? Is it the oven or stove? The air extractor? We had not yet investigated all the kitchen and utility room items we had inherited. Or perhaps it was a burglar alarm? Though I had not noticed one yet.

Was it coming from outside? Was it the hovercraft or the catamaran revving up to take off?

We decided the noise was coming from inside, somewhere downstairs. I made my way gingerly down and finally located the source of the trouble – a smoke alarm on the high ceiling of the hallway. For such a small disc, the noise was horrendously loud. It must be waking up the whole of our street.

Claire came down to join me, wondering why I was taking so long to switch it off. I just couldn't reach it. She found a wooden pole used to close the curtains and I tried to stretch up as far as I could, poking at all the switches on the smoke alarm, in the hope that one of them would turn it off.

I am not all that tall, 5 feet 8 inches in my socks, and Claire is the same, though she looks taller, being so slim and slender, with very long legs. I looked under the stairs where we had noticed a few tools, hoping there might be a stepladder, but alas there was no sign of one.

I balanced a pouf from the front parlour on a dining-room

chair, which immediately fell over. I tried again, this time with Claire holding it, shouting at me not to be so stupid. I had drunk quite a bit at supper, so was even clumsier than usual.

I eventually got my hands on the smoke alarm. I pressed various buttons, but this only made the noise worse – louder and, this time, constant, accompanied by flashing lights.

Finally, using both hands, I managed to unscrew the damn thing, took it off the ceiling, brought it down and threw it on the welsh dresser – where it started going off again. Oh, God. This is a nightmare. How can a small thing make such a big noise? I opened it, found a battery, took it out, opened the back door and threw the alarm on the courtyard floor. Where it persisted in making a noise for several minutes, like a worm continuing to move after it has been sliced in half.

We returned to bed and were just settling down again when another version of the same, ghastly noise started up again. This time the source was in our bedroom, just above the door. Fortunately, the bedroom ceiling is not as high as the hallway, so I just needed one chair to reach the alarm and unscrew it. But by now I could hear another one going off downstairs. What on earth was happening?

I went round all the rooms and discovered there were smoke alarms in every room, which we had not noticed. Clearly, Cathy had had to install smoke alarms for up to eight holidaymakers to comply with health and safety regulations. They must have been there for a few years, but for some reason – whether as a reaction to our (very classy) cooking, perhaps, or simply owing to a malfunction? – they had all decided to go off at the same time.

So much for our first night in paradise.

CHAPTER 6

All about Claire

Hunter and Claire at Victoria Lodge

'Who is Claire? What is she,
That all our swains commend her?'

My mother used to sing that song about Silvia – 'Who is she?' –
as did most mothers brought up in the 1930s. The vital line that
Shakespeare never managed to include in his original verse is –
how did you meet her? That is what most friends and relations
ask when someone new comes into your life. Well, that is what
friends have been continually asking me, these last three years.
Especially about this someone not just new in my life but a
rather stunning, exciting, wonderful addition to my life.

Claire was born well after the war – a year during which
interesting things happened on the national stage. I was born in
1936, another year in which interesting things happened on the
national stage. We had three kings that year. George V died on
20 January 1936, two weeks after I was born, and was succeeded
by his son Edward VIII, who abdicated in December and was
followed by his brother George VI, who had a good run till his
death in 1952, when Queen Elizabeth II took over. So, during
my lifetime there have been four different monarchs. I used to
boast about this to my three children and now grandchildren
who, of course, have known only one monarch. I think they
think the Queen has always been Queen and always will be.

Claire was brought up in a big house in Blackheath. And it
was big – I have seen the photographs. Her dad worked for
United Glass. Her mother taught at various well-regarded girls'
grammar schools, including the one Claire herself attended –
Mary Datchelor school, in Camberwell, south London.

Mary Datchelor has long gone but I have seen the programmes
for their annual speech day and spotted Claire Thornton's

name, listed as a prize winner. The ethos of the school – with a house system, uniforms and 'streaming' (i.e. classes arranged – and named – according to pupils' perceived ability) – was very similar to the Carlisle and County High school which my wife attended. I went to Carlisle Grammar school, which had similar traditions.

Claire did A-levels but did not go to university, as few did at the time. She went to a smart secretarial college and her first job was as a secretary at the Royal Opera House. She then worked for the Royal Ballet, where she was responsible for looking after star performers such as Margot Fonteyn and Rudolf Nureyev, when they were performing abroad.

She then moved on to do PR for the London Philharmonia Orchestra – and got married to a viola player, one of the rising young musicians in the orchestra. They had a baby, a son, but alas the marriage collapsed. You never hear of that happening, do you...?

Claire then brought up her son all on her own, all the time still working in PR. By now her parents' marriage had also broken down and her mother had moved to the Lake District and become head of English at Queen Elizabeth Grammar school, Penrith. But she was able to help Claire out during the holidays.

Claire managed somehow, out of her salary, to send her son to a Highgate prep school and then a north London public school, Mill Hill. She never remarried, but over the decades she has had several suitors and serious swains, as she quite frequently tells me. But she never went in for casual or short affairs. I should think not.

She had three relationships which lasted a long time, around ten years each, though she never properly lived with these boyfriends; she always kept her own house. By the sound of it, her men were all wealthy and handsome and took her to the racing at Ascot and on exotic trips around the world. Another was in property. The one she talks about most was a film producer, who was a bit older. She helped care for him when he fell ill, nursing him until his death.

For a spell she went off to Australia, where she worked for the Sydney Opera House. She returned to London and resumed work in PR, this time in the theatre and film world. She worked for the actor and director Bernard Miles, who opened the Mermaid Theatre, and Ray Cooney, at the Theatre of Comedy Company.

Then she worked for a well-known PR agency which specialised in films. One of her jobs was to promote Hollywood films when they opened in London and across the country, organising media interviews with the stars. And this was how our paths crossed. In the 1980s and 1990s I was doing a lot of interviewing with so-called famous people – for the *Sunday Times*, then the *Independent* and also the *Mail on Sunday* magazine. When you do this sort of job, you work hand in glove with publicists – they help you when you are stuck for someone to interview and you help them when they are being pushed by the production company to get publicity for their film.

I became friendly with three or four of the leading publicists in publishing, music and films. I would have lunch with them every three months or so – at their expense, of course – to hear what they were working on. I can't now remember all the Hollywood films that Claire worked on. But I recall that one of them starred Jack Nicolson and I was delighted when he agreed to give me his only London interview.

It got off to a bad start. I turned up at the wrong hotel – the Connaught not Claridge's – which caused the assistant publicist who was minding him to have hysterics. Nicolson was a right pain at first, as he insisted on wearing sunglasses, which meant I couldn't really see his eyes. I said I would leave now and forget the interview, if he didn't take them off. Cue more hysterics from the minder. But he eventually did as I asked and it turned out to be a good piece that pleased the PR company and the film company. Then I gave up doing interviews – fixing them up every week was too much like hard work. For the last twenty years I have concentrated on writing books or columns in various places. It's much easier work as it all comes straight out of my head. I don't have to go anywhere.

When my wife died in 2016, her obituary was in most of the papers. Lots of friends I had not seen for some time sent their condolences, asking how I was getting on, and would I like to have lunch or a drink some time. One of them, to my surprise, was Claire. She said she remembered me, had followed my progress and had read and enjoyed some of Margaret's books.

I remembered her name and what jolly, lavish lunches we had had, but I could not remember what she looked like. Which rather ruins my description of her as being stunning. I also could not remember whether she was married, if she had any family, or where she lived. These lunches with publicists in the nineties were very much business lunches, oh, yes. And anyway, I was a happily married man.

When Claire wrote, I was still trying to sort out probate, my wife's estate and the copyright of her books, and also trying to decide what to do with the house in Loweswater. I wrote to Claire and said, How lovely, I do remember you, yes. When things have settled down a bit, yes, let's have a drink.

I wrote back to her about three months later. By this time I was thinking I would like a chum, a female chum, to do things with, go places with, have holidays with. I did not want to get married again or live with someone; that was not in my mind. I certainly did not want to do online dating, as I did not want to meet a stranger. I reckoned there must be a lot of women at my stage of life, single and available, whom I had met over the last fifty years, while working in newspapers, magazines, radio and with publishers.

I wrote a piece in the *Sunday Times*, describing the fantasy creature I had in mind. Aged sixty-five to seventy-five, single, either divorced or widowed, with her own family, her own interests, her own house and her own teeth. This last was partly a joke. In my mind, it meant being fit and well.

I auditioned quite a few likely women. They obviously did not know they were being auditioned. That was just in my head. I am not that brazen. I just invited likely ladies of a certain age whom I had known for some time, or were friends of friends, to have a drink or a meal. There are a lot of single women around. More than single men of my age. Lucky men.

I chatted them up about their lives, and what they were looking for. Quite a few made it clear they were not looking for an intimate relationship. They were quite happy going on holidays with their girlfriends, rather than men, and living on their own at home with their dog, not a bloke. Jilly Cooper and Joan Bakewell, both of whom I have known for decades, and were now single, made it clear that, much as they really liked me, romance was out of the question, thanks for asking.

I invited Claire for lunch at my local bistro – Bistro Laz on Highgate West Hill. I did not reveal I lived round the corner, and I did not invite her to my home. We chatted non-stop over lunch and I asked her about her life. I discovered she was living in Battersea, had her own house, was a stalwart of the Battersea Society, acting as their membership administrator. She had loads of friends, women and men, and seemed to be on the go most of the time.

She had lived in Muswell Hill, in quite a big house while bringing up her son, but had sold that after he had left home and got married, thus releasing some capital to help him buy a house. He now lives with his wife and three children in Bushey, near Watford. Claire is devoted to them, visiting all the time, despite it being a long journey across London. She does their ironing and collects her younger grandchild from school, as the mother and father both work.

When Claire first downsized she moved from Muswell Hill to a house by the sea at Christchurch, Dorset, which sounded very posh and had its own swimming pool. I have never quite understood this move or what prompted it. I suspect it must have been a bloke, but she says no. She just wanted to get out of London, live by the sea and be near her close cousin.

After two years, she realised what a mistake she had made. She had no real friends down there, or interesting work. She managed to sell up quickly and not lose any money, and came back to London, buying an old wreck in a quiet, up-and-coming street in Battersea. At the time, one of her well-off boyfriends was living in this street, hence the connection. But all that finished about ten years ago now.

After our first meeting at Bistro Laz, I walked her to the Overground at Gospel Oak and put her on the train back to Clapham Common. I remember thinking how tall and fit she was, a faster walker than me and so glamorous and well-dressed. I remember also that, at one point as we were walking, she took my arm. I wondered what it meant. Was it because I was an old bloke who might stagger? (I do have an awful, shuffling walk.) Or was she just being friendly and affectionate? (As the best PR professionals always should be.) Or was it because she comes from down south? (Where they are forever kissing or hugging people they have only just met; not like us gritty, reserved northerners.) Claire herself has no memory of holding my arm on that first walk, after our first meal. She thinks I must have imagined it. Ah, well.

A few weeks later, she invited me for lunch at her house. Then I invited her to an event at the Royal Albert Hall, in a box. I have had no interest in classical music since I was a teenager, when I used to go to the Edinburgh Festival or hitchhike down to London for the Proms. I can hardly believe it now. I gave up all that classical stuff when rock'n'roll and then The Beatles arrived on the scene.

But it so happened that the Royal Liverpool Philharmonic Orchestra were playing. I had done a performance with them, or at least with their string quartet. They did a couple of concerts of Beatles tunes and I gave a short talk between each one about the origins of the lyrics. I had got free tickets from a chum in the orchestra for their Albert Hall concert.

Then I invited Claire to a *New Statesman* party, which was a very impressive and jolly affair. I have been doing a column for the *NS* – on football – for over twenty years. We were getting on so well that I invited her for the weekend to the family's Broadstairs cottage, which she loved. We had long walks, long talks, lots of meals and lots of wine. I suppose that is where it properly began. And we became a couple.

I wondered at first what to call her when I introduced her to friends. My companion? My chum? My partner? The latter sounds so formal, as if it is a business arrangement. As a joke, sending myself up, I called her my girlfriend. Which I still do. Unless we are staying at a hotel. In which case I say 'partner'. Sounds more formal and serious. Which is what it is now.

One of the many joys of finding love in old age is that you find yourself not just with a new partner but the new partner's family, friends, history, house, interests, pets, pals, pleasures and pains. I have got to know all her family as she has got to know mine.

And also, in a way it's like going backward, regressing to one's youth. I found myself reacting just like a dopey teenager. Why has she not called? Why did she say that? Has she gone off me? Why is she sulking? What have I done wrong? What have I said now? You don't actually slam doors, like a teenager, and you don't run off down the street shouting that you never want to see her again – how could you with your dodgy knee? But you can still manage a glacial look which you hope will pass for withering, if she has her best specs on.

It also meant I had a companion for going to events such as book festivals. I had been about to give them up; it is boring, going off somewhere on your own and staying in a strange hotel. The same went for supper parties: it's not much fun giving a supper party when you are on your own. But perhaps most wonderful of all was having someone to share my holidays with. In that first year, we went to the West Indies, on a Mediterranean cruise, to Portugal, to the Lake District and various other places.

After two years, we had a slight hiccup. We fell out on the Caribbean island of Grenada when I got it into my head she did not love me any more. So, in a fit of pique, I said that's it, we might as well part, no use continuing together. At Gatwick railway station, when we got back to England, I said goodbye, thanks for everything, have a good life. Bye-bye. I cried on the train, going home to my empty house. We had done so much together, been to so many places. Then suddenly it had all blown up.

It was Christmas two weeks later. I was still in mourning, so I said bugger Christmas, I'm not sending any cards. First time in sixty years. And I love doing Christmas cards, homemade ones, of course, full of really good jokes. Nor would I go to any Christmas parties. On Christmas morning, two of my granddaughters rang and said, 'Humper, please, please, you've got to come, it's not a family Christmas dinner if you are not there.' So I gave in. And, of course, I enjoyed it.

I began to miss Claire so much, thinking of her all the time. I sent her emails and she replied, 'Leave me alone.' But then, out of the blue, in January, she left me a late birthday present behind my dustbin. She happened to be spotted by my next-door-neighbour, Prue, who asked how she was. Prue then told me that Claire looked awful and was very depressed. Oh, God, I thought, what have I done? What a fool I had been.

Then Covid arrived, and the first lockdown, and I was stuck at home on my own. The loss of Claire was even harder to bear. We had been so happy together, so good for each other. Why had I been so stupid? When lockdown restrictions began to ease, in the late spring of 2020, I suggested meeting for coffee on neutral ground, just to talk it all through. She eventually agreed.

We sat on a park bench, holding hands in the dark. She told me that in Grenada she had been in great pain, with the most awful toothache. I was too stupid to have noticed it. She had to have an emergency operation the day she got back. I apologised for being so hasty and melodramatic, for having announced in Grenada that that was it and immediately cancelling all the lovely plans we had made for the next year.

She eventually agreed to come to my house, on condition that I wrote to all the women I had been seeing via a dating website and never saw any of them ever again.

I had told my family and friends about the split. I always find it hard to conceal anything, whether I am asked about it or not. They all rolled their eyes. 'You two are worse than teenagers…' What's wrong with that? Love in old age is like love at any age. Will it last? That's what we all want, however old we are.

Moving to the Isle of Wight was a sign of commitment, on both our parts. That we wanted to be together, stay together, make our home together.

At the time I am writing these words, the hiccup had taken place more than a year ago – and we have promised each other not to go over it again. It just leads to, 'You said…', 'No, you said…', 'No I didn't, it was your fault…', 'No, it wasn't…', 'Oh, gawd, this is giving me a headache, let's open another bottle…' Yes, just like teenagers, only in this case we now open better bottles.

I never did any cooking when my wife was alive, during

fifty-five years of marriage. Once I was living on my own, I had to make an attempt. Today, I can cook for myself, after a fashion. I try to insist when Claire comes to my house that I do the cooking. It is my kitchen.

But at Victoria Lodge we had already fallen into the pattern I had with Margaret. Claire does all the cooking and cleaning. Plus, painting, decorating, shopping, cutting the hedge. She even fills up my glass, before I have finished the first one, something my wife refused to do.

My wife did bring me tea in bed in the morning, which Claire now does. Margaret would even turn on the radio for me, as my arms are so awfully tired in the morning. Claire does not yet do that, lazy thing. But like my wife, she runs my bath for me. Oh, it is so lovely not having to sit and wait while the water is running. I hate any sort of waiting.

Claire always puts a dash of Johnson's Baby Oil into the bath, while my wife used Radox bath foam. I eventually decided the foam was giving me a rash, so when Margaret died I stopped using it. When Claire arrived in my life, she introduced me to the baby oil. It is brilliant. My skin is so soft and tender these days. Just like a baby's.

Claire, over these last four years, has seen me through various health scares. I first had heart trouble when we were together in Portugal. I collapsed on a walk, suddenly could not breathe, had to sit down. There were no pains, so I thought it would pass, which it did, and I managed to walk back to the house where we were staying. I had a cup of tea, lay down and rested for a while. Then I felt so much better that I decided to go for a swim. Claire thought I was being stupid, as the waves were so huge. But I was fine.

I remained fine for several weeks, then I had another sort of mini-attack, feeling dizzy and out of breath. It happened this time while I was cutting the grass at home, nothing really too energetic. After a third incident, I went to the Royal Free Hospital A&E in Hampstead and ended up in St Barts hospital, Smithfield, having a triple heart bypass. Three arteries were blocked, one of them by 90 per cent. Claire was with me all the time. She drove me to Barts and then visited me. My children all visited as well, but it was Claire who drove me home.

I had to stay in bed for three weeks, till the stitches started to heal. I was not supposed to be living on my own, so my son Jake stayed for a couple of nights and then Claire came to live on my top floor for a week. I rang a bell when I needed her to come down and be Florence Nightingale.

Later, I had another operation – for a hernia – which took place at a hospital in Barnet. Again, it was Claire who drove me there and back.

Love in old age, eh? It is bound to be fraught with health scares and the weaknesses and problems which the years bring, but I tend not to think or worry about them, once I have recovered. I am convinced it won't happen again and that, really, I am still thirty-nine. Same with Claire. Except she looks it.

I know and appreciate that Claire has been a brick, an angel, a godsend. She has looked after me so well in my times of need. Am I not a lucky feller to have fallen on my feet?

At first, I think my children were a bit suspicious of Claire – a younger, glamorous woman suddenly coming into my life. I don't think they worried that she would be off with their inheritance – just that I might end up unhappy. When they first heard she was staying the night, re-arranging the furniture, doing the cooking, taking over the kitchen, they did not wish to know any more, did not want to know the details of our relationship.

But were they not happy that I was happy? I asked them and, of course, they said, 'Yes.' But don't worry, we were not going to get married, just be together, go places together. She had her own life, her own house, her own family.

When I took Claire down to the family's seaside house in Broadstairs, in the early months of our relationship, one of my granddaughters, aged eight, over the evening meal, suddenly asked, 'Is Claire your girlfriend?'

'Yes,' I said.

'Have you kissed her yet?'

I said no, but I was hoping to very soon. The adults sniggered and then quickly changed the conversation.

When we had our little hiccup, after Grenada, I naturally gave my children a suitably sanitised but one-sided version of what had happened and Claire did the same. Which resulted in our respective families taking sides, Claire's lot thinking I was a bastard to make their dear beloved mother and grandmother so unhappy. While mine were equally upset but tried to cheer me up by suggesting I had had a narrow escape.

It is always a mistake to pass any comment on the love lives of your nearest and dearest, whatever the generation. I remember when one of my daughters broke up with a boyfriend and was distraught, my wife said, 'There, there, don't worry, you are well out of it, we didn't like him.' Naturally she was back with him within the month – and my wife cursed herself ever afterwards for having expressed an opinion.

During our hiccup, I always felt we would get back together; in fact I wrote it down in my new year predictions for 2021. Now I think both our families are very happy that we are happy. And they can't wait to come to the Isle of Wight, knowing that Claire will have made the house so lovely and knowing how generous she is at entertaining. And pouring out the drinks. We have put off having any of them to stay until the house is completely sorted, until Claire feels everything is in order and she has it as she wants it to be.

I have to wait till she is happy with the house and happy with me. And we are happy with each other.

You never know. I might fall ill again. We might fall out again. You have to say these things. You can't take anything for granted at our age or at any age really, least of all when it comes to the good things in life. That's life...

CHAPTER 7

We can rent a cottage in the Isle of Wight

Appley Tower, early twentieth century

'd forgotten with a new house all the things you have to do – most of them boring and time-consuming. You then begin to think, Why didn't we stick to staying in hotels or holiday lets? No wonder Victoria Lodge had proved so popular for so long with holidaymakers. Cathy had been so organised.

We had to transfer all the utilities into our names, all the usual stuff. But because of Covid, all the council people seemed to be working at home and not answering the phone. We accumulated so much rubbish and could not work out the system for the dump, which meant registering and booking a slot. We also needed to be registered for council tax to get parking permits, either vouchers for visitors or residential permits. Oh, God.

On the third day, still dazed and confused with all the bureaucracy, Claire got done for illegal parking. In our local streets there are lots of signs saying two hours free, but it is hard to work out which side of the street and which hours. Claire had only parked outside for ten minutes. She got fined eighty pounds – sixty pounds if we paid quickly.

Cathy had paid council tax as a business because the house was a holiday let. She went through all her documents and found her number and a note that she had paid up to the end of the month. In theory, that was proof the house was registered. A kind neighbour gave us one of his visitor permits, so we were safe for the rest of the day.

I discovered that daily visitor permits were issued at the local library in the centre of Ryde. Using Cathy's registration number for the house, I managed to get two months of tickets – only twenty pounds. Even better news, I was told that next week, the price was going up four times. So, I got the cheap ones just in time. Wow, what a bit of luck. Clever old me.

We had agreed Claire could use the third bedroom as her own private dressing room. It had two single beds, which would probably be rarely used until our grandchildren came to stay. Claire had decided that one entire wall would be given over to a mirrored, walk-in wardrobe. It looked from the pictures of the new storage space as if she would have enough space to hang all the costumes for the Royal Opera House, where she used to work. I did not say so, of course; I didn't want to get into an argument in our first week.

But the problem was – how do we get all this stuff assembled and put in place? In all, there were thirty-two different IKEA packages. Oh God, darling, what have you done?

There was an old-fashioned, dark mahogany wardrobe in the main bedroom, which seemed perfectly OK to me, suitable for a seaside holiday home. But Claire had taken violently against it the moment we moved in. She could not bear having it in the house a moment longer. We had to pay to have it taken away and dumped.

There was an even bigger, darker, more old-fashioned wardrobe in our bedroom. Claire would not be able to stand waking up and seeing it. We had some fairly amicable discussions – no plates flew, there was no bad language – and we agreed to keep it for my clothes – but that Claire would paint it white. Otherwise, she would have nightmares.

The monster new IKEA wardrobe, to go into her dressing-room, with the mirror fronts, is like the one she has in her own bedroom in Battersea. Personally, I have always found it unsettling. You see yourself at every angle in the bedroom. Then you walk into your reflected self or can't find the door.

The stuff from IKEA eventually came, including white shelving for the front room, which I had decided I was going to call our 'parlour'. The delivery cost a fortune as there is no IKEA on the island. Alas. The boxes filled the entire hall. Claire had boasted she was ace at putting IKEA stuff together. But when she looked at the dozens of packs, and the pages of instructions, she had second thoughts. She made a start on unpacking them before finally realising she herself could never fit them all together, clever though she is. She would have to go online and find a local handyman. But we were strangers, in a foreign land, so how do you find them? At our age, you do have to rely on the kindness of strangers, or at least family and neighbours, to do any heavy lifting, but we knew nobody.

I can hardly open an envelope these days, so I knew I would be no good with the Allen keys and fitting parts together. Another reason why starting such a big, new project at our advanced age in life was really rather potty.

Several know-alls had already told us that handymen on the Isle of Wight are hellish to find – and that even when you do, they don't always turn up. I hoped this was not true. Know-alls had also told us Ryde was run-down, but I could already see this was a fib. Surrounded by piles of half-opened cardboard boxes and weirdly shaped bits of wood, we ended up having words. I said how stupid it was to have ordered such a complicated and massive wardrobe. And the cost, goodness, the cost. The wardrobe was seven hundred pounds! Dear God, I could have bought a car for that.

It was silly, of course, to waste energy on such a pointless row. But it is sometimes hard to resist the temptation to score points and tell your partner: 'I told you so.' So I did tell her so, feeling rather virtuous, probably several times, until she shouted at me that if I couldn't help, I should get out.

I left in a huff, slamming the front door. Much better to let her sort it out. It was all her doing anyway. I walked along the beach and stopped for a coffee at The Big Kahuna café on the front. On my regular beach walks, I had already been there a few times and talked to Wayne, the owner, who was very friendly, and seemed to spend most of his time talking to customers, old or new, giving them advice. Just my sort of person.

Wayne was not there but I met his wife for the first time, an attractive-looking woman aged about fifty with well-cut, very fashionable, short, blonde hair. I complimented her on it and asked where she had had it done. I explained we had just arrived locally, told her the house and street and said my partner was searching for a decent hairdresser, as she needed her hair regularly coloured. She gave me a name and a number, down in Shanklin, which seemed a bit far, but I said I would pass it on.

Her name was Iso, at least I think that is how it is spelled, and she said she originally came from Namibia. How amazing, ending up here on the seafront at Ryde, working with Wayne in his beach caff. I wondered how that had happened. I said how much I loved Namibia. My wife and I had a couple of great holidays there when our older daughter Caitlin lived in Botswana for twelve years.

I told Iso I had left Claire struggling with thirty-two boxes containing an IKEA wardrobe and bookshelves. Did she by any chance know of a handyman? Oh yes, she said, she knew a very good one – their maintenance man for this caff and the two others they ran along the front. She rang him and, amazingly, he said he could come tomorrow.

I finished my coffee and ran home, jubilant. I had sorted Claire's problems, the ones she had created. Clever old me. I let myself into the house and ran down the hall shouting, 'Hi, darling, I'm home,' as in the best sitcoms. 'Your problems are all over.' There was no reply. I looked in the kitchen, I shouted upstairs. Still no reply. I went into the spare bedroom, where the wardrobe was going to go, and there was a strange man, lying on the bedroom floor. Beside Claire.

Bloody hell, I leave her alone for half an hour and she has invited a bloke into her bedroom.

'Sorry to interrupt, pet,' I said. 'But I have solved your IKEA problem. I have arranged for a highly recommended handyman to come tomorrow…'

'I already have one,' she replied. 'Adrian is doing it for me – aren't you, Adrian?'

The man lying on the floor, unpacking boxes and studying diagrams, grunted some reply.

'Get out of here,' hissed Claire. 'You are getting in Adrian's way.'

It was only at lunch that I found out what had happened. After I left the house to go for my walk, Claire had gone out into the street, hoping to ask some kind neighbour if they could suggest a handyman. There she encountered a middle-aged couple with a dog, who had just walked from the beach. Claire patted and fussed over the dog, as she always does, ever so charming and gushy, in her best PR mode. She explained we had just moved in, we were totally new to Ryde, and desperately in need of a handyman to assemble some shelves and a wardrobe.

Did they by any chance know anyone local?

'Him,' said the woman, pointing at her husband.

He looked a bit taken back, clearly not having thought of volunteering.

'Adrian will do it for you. He is good at putting things together.'

Claire immediately smiled and beamed and ushered him into the house before he had properly digested what was going on and what was required. Meanwhile, his wife walked on with the dog. They lived not far away, up Monkton Street. Perhaps she was pleased to get rid of him for a few hours.

Adrian stayed for three hours that first time, fitting all the new white shelves in the front room. Next day he was with us for nine hours. Working on his own, he managed to install Claire's magnificent, dazzling, shimmering, glass-fronted wardrobe, which now occupied one entire wall. Oh, and of course we paid him handsomely for his handiwork. What sort of people do you think we are?

Naturally, I had to be suitably grateful to Claire, for her having solved her own problem, and to express unqualified delight in the end result. But then I went and ruined it by pointing out a very small, hairline crack in the top corner of the glass. I was duly ushered out of the room.

I rang Iso's handyman, explained what had happened, and apologised for having to cancel him. We were sorted for the moment, but I was sure in the months ahead there would be countless jobs we would need help with. We would definitely call him.

'Just one week, eh, pet,' I said to Claire, 'and we have secured two handymen.' How smart is that? Who says you can't find handymen on the island?

I then decided I would contribute to our new project by organising something really important and vital which needed to be done, at once, as everyone who has ever moved into their dream house will understand and appreciate – house cards!

By that I mean prettily printed and designed little cards showing our lovely new house, in colour, of course, with our names and address, letting all our relations and friends know where Claire and Hunter are now living – lucky them, in such a gem – and encouraging them to visit. It's all just showing off, of course.

I found a nice photo of the house that Claire had taken when we were first looking at it, in the sun, all lovely and pink, with its sweet little tiled path leading to the front door. I also remembered some very special words written about the Isle of Wight, by none other than Paul McCartney. You must know them – they come from his song 'When I'm Sixty-Four'. Paul first wrote that song before The Beatles became famous, when he was still very young. Eventually, it was knocked into shape and appeared on the *Sgt. Pepper's* album.

A lot of people on the Isle of Wight, and elsewhere, think The Beatles' song 'Ticket to Ride' was really about Ryde. You see and hear the phrase used in local headlines and stories, but it does not refer to our Ryde. The authentic reference to our island comes in two less well-known lines at the end of 'When I'm Sixty-Four' about renting a cottage in the Isle of Wight, 'if it's not too dear'.

I happen to have a copy of the original lyrics, in Paul's handwriting, which I reproduced in a book about The Beatles' lyrics. I am sure most people on the Isle of Wight have never seen it. I decided it would make an amusing house card, which we could use when inviting people to supper or thanking new chums for their hospitality – if we made any friends here, that is...

To use the lyrics in my book, my publisher had to pay a fortune to Sony, who maintained they owned the copyright of all The Beatles' lyrics, even original versions with words and lines not used in the recorded version.

I photocopied the two lines which mentioned the Isle of Wight and stuck them at the bottom of the card. I wasn't remotely worried about copyright on this occasion: this was not a commercial card – I was not selling it or publishing it. It was just a private, homemade amateur card to give to friends. I got a hundred copies printed at a local print shop on good quality card. They weren't cheap, but come on, this was a very important announcement, after all. We were telling our close friends this is what we have done, this is where we now live. Look at us. Lucky us.

Apart from the cards, my main contribution so far to our new house had been to stand around criticising, moaning about the expense and generally getting in the way. Claire had made all the decisions, bought all the stuff, done the painting and decorating, washed everything and hung new curtains. I did not let her forget I had done one thing: I had secured parking vouchers for her car. That wasn't easy, pet.

Having got the new shelves and new wardrobe installed, the old brown furniture painted, and lovely house cards created, it was time to start our social life. Claire and I are social animals, always up for some social intercourse, even if after half an hour we are thinking, Oh, no, what have we done? I would rather be at home watching footer.

Because of the pandemic lockdown, we could not have a proper housewarming party. That would have to happen some time in the future. God knows when that would be. People on the Isle of Wight seemed very obedient and law-abiding, wearing masks in shops, always booking when they went out for a meal, then social distancing when they sat down. Unlike in London at that time, all the pubs and restaurants were open, as were the shops. It all felt pretty normal. But goodness knows when it would be all over and we could all have a proper social life.

The rule of six was in operation – i.e. you were allowed to entertain up to a maximum of six people – so we decided that for our first supper party we would just invite the two couples we were most indebted to: Claire's friend Donna and her partner Peter, who had been our reason for visiting the Isle of Wight in the first place; and long-time residents Cathy and Andy, from whom we had bought the house.

I gathered that Donna used to be a teacher, at a top prep school in London, while Peter had worked in PR, specialising in computing and technology. I knew that Cathy was originally from Leeds and Andy was born and brought up on the Isle of Wight. I didn't know how they had met, but I knew they had at least one child, the daughter who had been cleaning the house when we doorstepped her. We were surprised the two couples did not know each other, despite both living on the island. But, of course, that was a sign of our being newcomers, who didn't understand the island. We were beginning to realise that people in Ryde think Cowes is a far distant country.

Our guests all brought bottles and flowers and plants, being well-brought-up, middle-class people, just like us, and we had drinks and nibbles and laughs, sitting in our smart new front parlour, now equipped with all-white shelving units and a new rug.

I took Cathy round the house to show her the changes we had made. She admired the repainted bookshelves, wardrobe and chest of drawers, now gleaming white, thanks to Claire's efforts. I don't think Cathy was all that thrilled that Claire had chucked out her curtains in the front room, together with the carpet, and – Oh! – where is the large wooden games table? Visitors loved that. It had gone to the dump and been replaced by a glass table from Habitat… Cathy smiled politely and said, 'Lovely, what a good idea.' She seemed a bit disappointed, too, that the chandelier in our bedroom had been altered – the hanging bits had been taken off. She could not quite understand that. Easy, I said. Claire just woke up one morning and said, 'I hate those bits, they will have to go.'

She was astounded by the new mirrored wardrobe in the second bedroom, Claire's dressing room, the size of Wembley stadium. I think she would quite have liked that in her own house.

In a Grade II house you can't make any structural changes, and we didn't want to, as the arrangement suited us perfectly, but you can change the use of the rooms. The only thing I wanted done in the house had not yet happened – turning the little fourth bedroom into my office. Funny, that. It had taken hardly any time for Claire to bring about the changes she demanded. I was still looking for an old-fashioned desk in dark wood with a leather top. I didn't want any of that all-white IKEA nonsense which Claire loves, not in my room. Really, she would have everything in the whole house white, given half a chance. That is how she has her own house. I always complain it is like living in an institution. I let her have her way two years ago when I gave up having a car and converted the garage at my London house. I turned it into a garden room and let Claire do all the furnishings and décor. It is cool and elegant and has been much admired. And feels a bit like a reception room in a posh Caribbean hotel.

But in my London house I have always preferred colour and clutter. One of the main attractions for Claire in buying Victoria Lodge was that I agreed she would have her way. Well, mostly. And I have to admit she had done a brilliant job in a short time.

Peter and Donna and Cathy and Andy all said they loved my house cards. They particularly loved seeing Paul McCartney's handwritten 'When I'm Sixty-Four' lyrics. They were aware of the reference to the Isle of Wight, but had not seen the original. Andy started singing the song and we all joined in. Well, we had had quite a few bottles by then. Andy turned out to be a really good singer, a strong, rich baritone. He had been head chorister as a boy at St James's church, Ryde. He still sings today in various groups and also plays the guitar – the singing surveyor.

I rushed to get my mobile phone, which I can never find when I want to, especially after a few drinks. I wanted to capture this touching moment on video: our first party in the house – historic stuff!

Andy then moved on to other Beatles songs, and other tunes, with everyone joining in lustily. Goodness, it was such fun. I hoped the neighbours on both sides – one of whom, a youngish couple, we had still not met – were not getting pissed off by all the drunken singing and laughter.

Alas, next morning, when I opened my mobile and tried to play the video, I discovered none of it had taken as I had clearly not selected the video function. Stupid me.

So, it was gone for ever, the evidence of our first supper party in our new fantasy home. At least the evening and the music will remain in our minds for ever...

CHAPTER 8

The Isle of Wight Literary Festival

Northwood House, venue of the Isle of
Wight Literary Festival

Our first outing, our first adventure, our first expedition away from our little love nest and our lovely Ryde Sands, which had now become so familiar and friendly, was to go across the island to the Isle of Wight Literary Festival.

Alas, it was not happening, in the normal sense. No flesh-and-blood audience, no massive queues and crowded tents, no over-excited, middle-class folks in their best frocks and straw hats having drinks and nibbles after another awfully stimulating talk, then queuing up to buy a signed copy of the book by the famous author they had just been listening to.

These days the queues are anyway not always for authors in the old-fashioned sense, those who spend their life hidden away writing words, but more often for people whom the audiences have seen on TV, a news presenter perhaps or even a weather forecaster or possibly, oh joy, a well-known and much-loved cook or gardener. How can humble writers, who live totally by their writing, compete with such modern celebs? But never mind. The celeb has written a book, or been helped to write a book, or put his or her name to a book and so is an author, hurrah; time to make his or her publisher really happy by turning up in the flesh, spouting some well-rehearsed chat and oft-repeated, amusing stories and then signing loads and loads of books.

When I first became an author in the 1960s we got invited, if we were lucky, not to a literary festival but to a literary lunch, to somewhere like Leeds for the *Yorkshire Post* literary lunch. It was a proper lunch, sit down, usually starting with melon and ham, followed by chicken, then ice cream for pudding. There would be about a hundred local worthies, mostly women, who had paid twenty pounds to have lunch and then listen to three authors.

During the meal, the author would usually find himself next to a local councillor, the mayor and his wife, or someone on the organising committee, and have to make idle chat all the way through, trying not to use up their few amusing anecdotes over the chicken.

At the end of the lunch, often while coffee was still being served, and cigarettes smoked, each author would be given ten minutes to stand up and delight the audience and, of course, plug their book. No questions were asked of them. Their main job was not to overrun.

Afterwards, the three authors would be ushered to a large table piled with their individual books while the audience rose from their meal and queued up to buy a copy from the two or three shop assistants drafted in from the local W. H. Smith who had had to sit, bored rigid, listening to yet more authors chuntering on, showing off, about their dreary books, mostly destined for the remainder shelves.

It was all pretty competitive. The authors who were famous off the telly or the West End stage, and who were well-versed in delighting an audience, and could speak in public beautifully, usually got all the laughs and the applause – and a long queue at once. The poor author who never went out in public, never met anybody from month to month, found it hard to compete. He would try to engage the two or three innocent folks who, perhaps by mistake, had joined the wrong queue, spin out his inane chat for as long as possible, then afterwards lie about just how many books he had signed.

I remember going to one literary lunch and was pleased to see quite a few women of a certain age were in my queue.

'Is your wife with you?' asked the first one. 'It's your wife I really wanted to meet.'

When I said, 'No, sorry, she does not do literary lunches,' all the women turned and left my queue.

If the lunch was running late, because one of the show-off authors with a booming voice had got carried away, there was then a mad rush by all the authors to get to the station and catch the train back to London. The ticket would have been bought and paid for by your publisher. You did not want to have to catch a late train and fork out your own money. You did not stay overnight; it was purely a one-day gig. And you did not get paid for doing it. Just a free melon and chicken lunch.

Today, those literary lunches hardly exist. In their place we have book festivals, many of which are enormous, lasting five days, with scores of events, hundreds of authors appearing, all day and evening long. The organisers are full-time professionals, working all the year round. The authors stay in a smart or bijou hotel, all expenses paid, with their spouse or partner. During the day there is a green room just for authors, where they can drink and stuff their faces and gossip. Best of all, they get a fee for appearing, usually £150, even for a humble first novelist. The TV stars or famous ex-politicians can of course negotiate their own, much more handsome, fee, as nationwide promotion for the festival usually features their mugshot.

There are now at least five hundred book festivals in the UK each year, even in out-of-the-way market towns miles from a mainline station, such as Hay-on-Wye. It has become a mark of local pride to have your own little book festival, enhancing the status of the town and bringing in visitors. The big festivals get national sponsors, usually a leading newspaper, while the local ones get local council support or a grant, as it is culture, innit.

The Edinburgh Book Festival or the Cheltenham Festival, both long established, have up to one thousand authors appearing each year. They can charge ten pounds for a talk, fill a hall or tent with five hundred people, and therefore bring in five thousand pounds, enough to cover most expenses, and bring a warm glow to the town, to the authors and the audiences.

One of the attractions for the modern audience is the getting to see and meet and listen to someone they have heard of – in the flesh. So much entertainment these days is remote, electronic and packaged, with people living their lives on their laptops, tablets and mobiles, staring into a screen all day long, for work and for pleasure. To actually get out for a change and listen to a human being perform is a different experience, a little event in itself.

The authors love it. They get a chance to go to places they would not otherwise visit. They get a free night in a hotel. They get a small fee. And a chance to sell some books.

Publishers like it and encourage their authors to take part but, in reality, the publishing economics of it is a nonsense. Let's say an author sells twenty of his or her lovely books at twenty pounds each. The author's share will be about two pounds a book – if they are lucky. So, they will have earned just forty pounds in royalties for giving up a day and a night of their lives.

The publisher has also lost, because they have to pay the hotel and the train fare for the author, which can come to up to five hundred pounds. Their share of the proceeds from the author's twenty sold books is probably much the same as the author's. But – ah, ha – they see it as general publicity and promotion for their author and their book, giving them a public presence. The local papers and radio usually cover the events. The local bookshops put you in the window.

Yet until I met Claire, I had given up going to book festivals. It was such a fag, trailing off for two days on my own to Hay-on-Wye or Wigton, staying in some boring hotel. Over the decades, I have been to most of the main festivals anyway. Why do it again? I've had that experience. Meeting other authors can be fun, especially for those of them who otherwise sit at home all day, but I meet enough interesting people in my normal life anyway.

For about ten years I was on the board of directors of the Edinburgh Book Festival, so I saw the organising which went on behind the scenes, as well as turning up each year to take part. Even Margaret used to agree to appear and, for about ten years, back in the eighties, we went every year, staying in the same digs. But when Margaret fell ill and stopped travelling, it was not such fun.

Since meeting Claire, I have been to a few festivals with her, such as Cheltenham, and one which was in Chiddingstone Castle, knowing the location would amuse and entertain her, which it did. Her working world had been in the theatre, music and films, not books.

When the Isle of Wight Literary Festival approached me, I did not even know the island had such a thing, yet it has been going for ten years. I said, 'Yes,' at once, thinking it would be a festival I could attend on our doorstep and I would meet some interesting locals – without really registering that, because of Covid, it was going to be online, without a live audience. Oh, God, how dreary, how pointless, can I really be bothered?

Then it was explained they were holding it in their usual venue, a stately home somewhere near Cowes. I could come over at my convenience, they would film my talk, then put it online, with other authors and the whole lot could be accessed by the public for free on a certain date. The volunteers running the event were committed to keeping the festival going, for people on the island and elsewhere to still be aware of the festival and able to enjoy it. Fortunately, they had some money in the bank from generous local benefactors and sponsors. The clincher was that someone would come over to Ryde, drive us there, and give us lunch afterwards. Wow. As newcomers to the island, we jumped at the offer to ingratiate ourselves.

It was arranged that one of their little helpers, Josy Roberts-Pay, would pick us up. Yes, I should not use such a derogatory term as 'little helper', but all festivals have such lovely, willing, friendly, cultured people who help. Local volunteers, usually awfully well-bred, mostly retired, who work over the whole of each festival, picking authors up at the station in their own car, taking them to their hotel or the venue.

When Claire and I went to the festival in Kent, the one held in Chiddingstone Castle, we were put up for the night in the grand home of one of the volunteers and also attended a cocktail party in another stately home. Claire loved it. Being islanders, we did not need accommodation on this occasion.

Josy arrived at our front door in a large and very expensive-looking Range Rover. She got out to let us in. But she could not open the rear doors. It was such a state-of-the-art locking system that she had not mastered it yet – the car was not, in fact, hers. She had borrowed it to drive us in style. Shame we couldn't get in – although Claire gamely offered to climb over the seats into the back. How we teased her.

When we finally did make it inside the car, we drove across the middle of the island towards Newport. Claire had been this way a few times in her own car. All the big superstores seem to be around Newport and Claire loves shopping. I hate it.

The traffic around Newport was so busy, not helped by works on the ring road. I had got it into my head that the middle of the island would be all countryside. That Ryde, being the biggest town, would be the only place affected by traffic jams. In fact, Newport, the capital of the island, was far worse. With the River Medina piercing its centre, Newport sits as a spider at the centre of a network of small roads reaching out to the far-flung edges of the island.

We got through eventually and headed for Cowes. The island is only 22.5 miles across, but it was quite an expedition, going from the east coast of the island to the north – almost like crossing a continent.

We were heading for a stately home called Northwood House, which has been the venue for the Isle of Wight Literary Festival since it began. It is a large Georgian mansion, with extensive grounds, dating back to 1799. The estate was acquired and developed by a London merchant, George Ward, and it was where he gave lots of parties and concerts. Queen Victoria's children often popped over from nearby Osborne House to take part.

Today it is owned by a charitable trust who somehow manage to keep it going and in good order by hiring out the richly decorated rooms for weddings, conferences, parties and other events. Perched on a hill overlooking Cowes and the Solent, the grounds are free for island residents and visitors to enjoy.

There seemed to be some sort of fair and exhibition going on in the grounds as we walked through, but when we entered, the house itself was empty. I met first Janet Allan from the organising committee, who had invited me, Maggie Ankers – the chair of the Isle of Wight Literary Festival – and lastly Steve Ancell, the producer who was doing the filming. I was taken to a nice reception room where Steve had rigged up some lights and a camera, turning it into a little film studio.

I sat down at a desk, as instructed, facing Steve, who was behind his camera. The lights were a bit bright and hurt my eyes. Claire was seated in a corner of the room, along with Josy, our chauffeur and helper, but I could not see them. I asked Steve to turn the lights down. Steve was on his own, without an assistant, doing all the technical stuff, which was very impressive. He began with a voiceover, introducing me, then left me to it, to chunter on for forty minutes, talking into the camera. It was like talking to a blank wall in an empty room. So disconcerting not having any human reaction. Steve was concentrating on his camera and mic. Claire and Josy were sitting silently, somewhere in the dark.

I had not written anything down or prepared what I was going to say. When Janet had invited me, she said I could talk about any of my books, or anything really, so I had said I will talk about The Beatles, how I came to do their biography, and will explain the song 'Ticket to Ride' and 'When I'm Sixty-Four'. I had brought a photocopy of the lyrics in Paul's hand, which I gave to Steve to drop in when he edited my chat. That was one of the few advantages of doing it on film, rather than live, in the flesh. It can be edited or added to. I did suggest he dropped in some Beatles songs as a background, such as 'When I'm Sixty-Four', but he was hesitant, saying there might be copyright problems. I said the video was non-profit-making, no fee was being charged, surely he could take a chance? But, he said no, they couldn't risk a claim.

I did forty minutes – and Steve said my time was up. I missed the lack of questions afterwards, the live audience, which I always enjoy answering.

I never saw any of my fellow authors who were appearing at the 2020 Isle of Wight Literary Festival. We all did our bit on different days and different places, but they included Alan Titchmarsh, Joanna Trollope, Jeremy Irons, Anna Pasternak and Robin Hanbury-Tenison. The whole festival went out digitally on 9 October 2020 for three days. Hurry, hurry – you can find it on catchup, if you twiddle the right knobs.

I did watch myself – well, for a bit, just to see how boring I was and if Steve had dropped in any music (which he had not) – but you were able to read the manuscript lyrics online. My talk, apparently, got nine 'likes' online the next day while Alan Titchmarsh only got seven.

Afterwards, Josy took us on a walk round Cowes, as we had never been before. We walked up and down the High Street, which was very pretty, lots of nice caffs and gift shops. It seemed much more touristy than Ryde, which does always strike me as a real town, with real local people going about their real business. Cowes reminded me of places like Grasmere and Stratford-upon-Avon, visitors cluttering up the pavements, taking selfies, hoping to see the famous sights. Must be hell in Cowes Week, but I assume in the winter it goes very quiet, if not dead.

We then walked along the Esplanade to our lunch venue – the Royal Ocean Racing Club, where we were joined by Maggie, Janet and Steve. It was a sunny day so we had drinks on the lawn first of all, looking out over the Solent.

I had assumed, for no reason, apart from ignorance, that there would be only one yacht club in Cowes, the world-famous royal one, called, er, whatever its full title is. Turns out there are five yacht clubs in Cowes, several with royal connections, each with their own handsome premises and slightly different history, rules and regulations.

Over lunch, I gathered there is and always has been a clear social pecking order among the clubs, which might not be obvious or apparent to total newcomers, like me and Claire. At the top, so everyone I talked to agreed, is the Royal Yacht Squadron, the RYS. You have to be invited to become a member – you can't just ask, much less pop in for a drink. And new members have to be agreed by existing members, who can blackball hopefuls. None of the people at our lunch table were members, but I made a note to myself to write to the commodore or the secretary to see if we could pay a visit some time. After all, yachting is what the Isle of Wight is probably most famous for.

I picked up lots of rumours and gossip about goings-on at the Royal Yacht Squadron in the past, which I was told was situated right next door, over a wall. When the aristocrats and members of the royal family came to Cowes for the season, a lot of them brought their mistresses and girlfriends. As women were not allowed in the RYS, they would sit in the garden next door, ordering endless bottles of champagne. When they had finished, they would throw the empty bottles over the wall into the grounds of the Royal Yacht Squadron, just to show what they thought of their silly rules...

Next in the social pecking order, or so my fellow guests told me, is the Royal London Yacht Club, founded on the Thames in 1838, which moved to Cowes in 1882. It is quite a formal club, with many barrister members, evening dress rules, and much polished brass and silver. Third in status is probably the Royal Ocean Racing Club, the one where I was lunching. RORC was founded in London in 1925 to support offshore racing. It still has a base in St James's, but they have a club house in Cowes with twelve rooms for members.

Then there is the Island Sailing Club, which attracts a rather older clientele, who do a lot of lunching and drinking. It describes itself as the most popular sailing club on the island – perhaps because of all the drinking.

The fifth yacht club is the Cowes Corinthian Yacht Club. Compared with the other four, it attracts more local sailors (and drinkers) who are less well-heeled. Naturally, it does not bill itself as such, but that is its image in Cowes. The RORC and the Royal London attract more wealthy local members and the 'down from towners', well-heeled yachties who come for the sailing season, or have holiday homes on the island.

I have probably got the differences and social order wrong, and will get duffed up next time I walk through Cowes, but that was what my lunchtime colleagues led me to believe, all of whom were locals. But then it was a rather jolly lunch.

All of the yacht clubs on the island have bars, restaurants and often accommodation. Most have reciprocal arrangements with yacht clubs elsewhere, so get very busy in the yachting season – apart from in the Covid pandemic.

I walked along the Cowes harbour front, studying the fronts and entrances to the five yacht clubs, trying to get my snotty nose up against the windows; goodness, they are impressive. Funny how they have all congregated together, like doctors in Harley Street or as our newspapers all used to huddle together in Fleet Street.

Josy then drove us back to Ryde. She is a marketing consultant – a busy, energetic, cheerful and capable woman. She has lived on the island for six years. On the way home, near Newport, she happened to mention that she and her husband Owen live in a house which was formerly a railway station and station master's house in Queen Victoria's time, originally designed for sole use by the monarch herself.

'How amazing,' I said. 'I would love to see it some time. Oh, I do love old railways and old stations.'

Many years ago, I wrote a biography of George Stephenson, father of the railways, and visited all the places associated with him. Later, I did a book walking disused railways lines all over the UK. I wish I had known about this one on the Isle of Wight, I said. It would have been great to walk it.

'You still can,' said Josy. 'The public footpath runs beside our garden.'

'How wonderful. Any chance of a quick look now?'

I can be very pushy sometimes. Well, all of the time.

We turned off the Newport Road and went up a long lane, passing a crematorium, then on to a dirt track – and there, at the end, I could clearly see what had once been a Victorian railway station, hardly changed or modernised.

I walked round the outside, in the garden, and could see where the tracks had been. Josy opened her front door and took us inside, apologising if it was a bit of mess. Owen, her husband, was rather taken aback by the sudden arrival into his house of two total strangers. He was in his old clothes, covered in paint stains, up a ladder. But he came down and was charming and said, yes, of course, we could have a quick tour of the house.

The station was officially Whippingham railway station and was just a mile away from Osborne House. Queen Victoria and her family and guests would be driven there by coach, then on to the train to join the paddle steamer at Ryde or to visit the south side of the island, using the extensive rail network that sadly no longer exists.

It is uncertain how many times Queen Victoria did actually use the station. One of the few recorded occasions was in 1885, when she travelled to Ventnor to open the National Consumption hospital. Lord Mountbatten, as a young man, was known to have used the station while he was staying at Osborne House. The line from Ryde to Sandown is still running today, with old London tube carriages bumping along all eight miles of it. Well, it is supposed to be running. So far, every time we have gone to the station hoping to go from Ryde down to Shanklin or Ventnor, it has been closed. Work on the line. Waiting for new rolling stock. Or other excuses.

The little branch line and the railway station at Whippingham was closed to all traffic in 1953 and lay derelict for some time. In 2015, when Josy and Owen bought it, the old station was being advertised for sale as a unique, five-bedroom country house by Fine & Country, the upmarket estate agents. The asking price was £625,000. Seems a lot, compared with Ryde, but then it is a rather grand house with gardens – and it does have all those royal connections.

Josy drove us home. We thanked her profusely for a lovely day – visiting Northwood House, lunch at a Cowes yacht club and, for afters, a surprise and delightful tour of Queen Victoria's old railway station. Who knew there was so much to see on the island? But you have to know people in order to know what is going on and where to look.

Over supper, I told Claire what I had decided I wanted for my next birthday in January – pink corduroy trousers.

Stepping out of Victoria Lodge and going for my morning walk on Ryde beach in the years to come, I will always wear my Cowes pink cords, if just to amuse the local dog-walkers. Some will probably scoff and titter. In Ryde they tend to be more down-to-earth than the carefully cultivated, hearty yachties over in Cowes. But I don't care. In the summer, I will add a straw hat. Look out for me...

CHAPTER 9

Man about the house

Union Street, Ryde, 1970s

So far Claire and I had been pretty much in agreement on what we wanted to do in the house. I allowed all the white stuff to be installed, despite considering white to make everything institutional – give me colour every time– but I did admit it made the rooms look cleaner, fresher, brighter and, yes, more modern – except… who wants modern? I can never imagine how a room will look when it is redone, so that was one reason I was often unenthusiastic about changes.

My wife and I, during our fifty years in our London house, never fell out about furniture and fitting – mainly because I had no views, no tastes; I just let her get on with it. I always agreed with what she did. Saved me thinking about it. She liked lots of colours, mainly yellows and browns and oranges, which I always think look good and bright and friendly. While allowing her to decide on curtains, carpets, wallpaper and all such boring, fiddling, tedious stuff, I did insist on commandeering the best room in the house as my office. It was originally our posh sitting room, on the first floor, with double windows, a nice marble fireplace and an attractive balcony. But I did let her take over the much smaller room I then vacated, which we had built as a back addition. So kind of me.

Our big difference of opinion, house-wise, was that I like clutter, wanting all my various collections and objects to be on view all over the house. My wife was against this, maintaining they just collected dust. She had no interest anyway in any of my collections, though she knew they kept me happy. She always used to say, 'If you go first, it's straight to the skip.' Not meaning my body, I hope, but all my so-called 'treasures'. She would bin them right away. Don't you know how much I paid for them? Don't you know how much some of them are worth? Right, that's it, I'm never dying...

I was allowed to have all my clutter in my big office, which she agreed never to touch, and my Beatles collection hung on the wall of the stairs on the top floor, but that was it.

Claire is much more fierce in her tastes and opinions and would not let me have anything cluttering up the house or the walls anywhere, except in the very little room at the back, downstairs, which she agreed was going to be my office. It was the so-called 'fourth bedroom' when we bought the house, but so small I can't believe anyone slept there. It is only about six feet across, leading out of the kitchen and into the utility room and the downstairs lavatory. It was as much a corridor or a passageway, as a room. But I knew that having a lavatory adjoining would be a blessing for a bloke of a certain age. Not for women. Margaret never seemed to go to the lavatory in our fifty-five years of marriage. Very strange. Claire does, though not as often as me.

Men have it fairly easy, if they are caught short outside, but it is harder for women. Nevertheless, Claire has no compunction about stopping and going under a tree and pulling down her breeks. That's a Scottish word, which my mother used. Once on the way back from Broadstairs, we got stuck for ages in a massive traffic jam just outside the Blackwall Tunnel. Claire suddenly got desperate. We pulled into a side turning and Claire got out, carefully leaving the side door of the car open when she bent down in order to conceal herself – or so she thought. She had not spotted the major road thundering above, just yards away. God, the peeping and hooting from all the lorry drivers, shouting and yelling and pointing, practically driving into each other.

In my new little office itself, I was determined to have a proper, old-fashioned, chunky, dark wooden desk in my room, not one of these slim white flimsy nonsenses from IKEA. I wanted one with a green leather top and lots of drawers with brass handles. I looked for a long time in Union Street, going up and down, convinced there would be some antique shops. This is Ryde's high street, which I found a bit confusing at first, as there is a street actually called the High Street, but that is a continuation of Union Street, going further up the hill.

Union Street itself is a handsome, broad street leading down to the sea. From almost all points, you can see the pier and right across the Solent to Portsmouth and the Spinnaker Tower, if the sky is clear. This is a clever architectural joke, building the tall tower like the sail of a ship, dominating Portsmouth harbour.

Union Street itself has some magnificent Victorian buildings and shop fronts, some of them adorned with pillars and statues high up, so you don't see them at first. This tarting up started when Queen Victoria moved to the Isle of Wight. They wanted to make themselves seem grander and more regal.

There are some excellent, long-established independent shops in Union Street, such as Hurst the ironmongers, which we haunted in the first few weeks, buying tools and stuff for the house. No chain stores, no McDonald's, and only one supermarket, a fairly small, discreet Sainsbury's, though there is a fairly big Co-op, not far away, hidden up a lane.

I frequented a shop called Frame when we first arrived, as I liked the look of the local artwork and their old photographs, prints and documents to do with Ryde. I bought quite a lot. I fell in love with a limited edition print of Union Street, in full colour, looking down Union Street, which I was told had lots of real local people on the pavements, plus a camera crew on the roof of a house, which was funny. Claire was not so enamoured. After some relatively amicable discussions, she agreed it could hang in the entrance hall, replacing a rather tatty, cheap tourist map of the island, presumably placed to help holidaymakers.

I also bought a black-and-white poster dating back to 1888 at Frames, published by a local estate agent, which listed all the houses for sale – in our street. I was thrilled by the coincidence. The artwork was typographical. When I started in journalism on the *Sunday Times*, back in 1960, it was still hot metal, with linotype machines and letters laid out in blocks, so I was fascinated to count up all the different type sizes and fonts employed in this one, simple poster. I got to twenty, thinking of all the old printers who laid them out then turned the handle of the printing machine. I raved about it so much, pointing out to Claire how it had been done, and she kindly allowed me to hang it in the hall as well.

The place I like best in Union Street is the Royal Victoria Arcade, entered through most handsome, wrought-iron gates into a genuine Victorian building filled with about a dozen shops, mostly selling collector's items, the stuff I love, plus a computer repair shop and a little café which is done up like a 1950s' mid-west diner. There are stairs and a poster enticing you to what is billed as the world's only Donald McGill museum, about which you will read more in Chapter 26.

I eventually found two antique shops in Union Street and in one of them, Deja Vu, I did spot a Regency desk, so it said, in good nick, nicely polished and the leather covering in good condition, price £220. I got it for two hundred pounds and the woman agreed to deliver it, no extra charge. She brought it the next Sunday morning – by taxi. That must have eaten into her profit, if she had to pay for the taxi. I assumed the taxi driver was a friend.

I then insisted on a Turkish carpet on the floor – which Claire eventually agreed to. In fact, she bought it for me – a modern version of a Turkish carpet, from IKEA, I think. Then I covered my new office walls with photos and other images of the area I had bought – cartoons, posters, leaflets and old newspapers. It's my room. I can do what I like with it.

The big problem was what to do about a computer. I had brought my laptop with me but I find that so hard to use as the keyboard is small. Should I get another, proper computer? I would then, of course, need a local techie to help me set it up, as I am an idiot. Also, the wifi connection in the office, at the back of the house, turned out to be very poor. I bought a booster, which made only a marginal difference. Oh, God, all these boring things you have to do, setting yourself up in a new house.

Having done the front room, our so-called parlour, which looked good with its new white carpet, white shelves and new curtains, madam then turned her laser beam eyes on to the dining room.

Along one wall, on the left as you go in, was the enormous Welsh dresser we inherited, over six feet high and six feet broad. We both found it most attractive. It had been painted a light green – or at least I think so, but then I am colour-blind. Claire maintains it is turquoise. Anyway, a very acceptable and fashionable shade. And it was very useful. It had lots of drawers, a good flat top and lots of shelves above, on which we had arranged framed photos. Claire installed little battery lights on the shelves which we put on in the evening, now that it was autumn, when we were having supper.

One morning Claire got up, jumped out of bed and announced she had decided the Welsh dresser was in the wrong place. And I thought she had been sleeping soundly. It should be on the other side of the room, she declared. The dining table should be in the space instead, near to the window. It would give us a view into the courtyard and more light while eating.

I said, Yes, dear. Good idea, dear. Thinking it will never happen. It will need at least two strong men to move it. And, anyway, I said, it is probably securely bolted to the wall. And the weight must be enormous. Now that lockdown is back as the pandemic surges, we won't be having any strong men coming into the house. And I am certainly not up to it. I can't open an envelope, far less take out all those drawers in the Welsh dresser. If I so much as tried to pull one out, my hernia would go again. We don't want that, do we, me falling ill? In a new house, with a new life, where we don't even know where the local hospital is.

Then I forgot about it. It was just her daft and unnecessary idea. How potty, wanting to move a massive piece of furniture from one side of the room to the other. I'm all for projects to improve our life, but not something as pointless as this.

A couple of days later, I went to bed after lunch as usual for my rest. I slept for exactly forty minutes and felt really refreshed. Claire had said she was going to do some painting while I rested. We were lighting a fire in the evening, now the cooler nights were coming, and she had decided she hated the colour of the fireplace. We had admired the fireplace when first going round the house, although it did not appear to ever have been used, though there was a nice fireguard and an old-fashioned black kettle in front of it. The fire turned out to burn excellently – a really good draw, with no smoke fumes in the room, and loads of heat. Then she said the fireplace surround needed touching up; I said, fine, if you insist. I can see a few scratches. But while I am asleep, no singing, dancing or shouting please. And if you have BBC Radio 3 or Classic FM on, do try to keep it low.

I came down after my rest and looked in the parlour to see if she had finished painting the fireplace. Which she had. But she wasn't there. Hmm, perhaps gone for a walk.

I went into the dining room – and, blow me, I didn't recognise it. It was a different room. Everything had been changed round. The giant Welsh dresser was no longer against the right-hand wall. Had we had burglars while I was asleep? It would need pretty strong burglars to have stolen that monster. Then I realised the dresser was still in that room – but had been moved across, a whole twenty feet, to the far wall.

I found Claire in the utility room, doing yet another load of washing, looking very pleased with herself.

In the forty minutes I had been in bed, she had finished painting the fireplace, then attacked the dresser. Firstly, she took out all the drawers, emptied the cupboard below, cleared the shelves, unscrewed the bracket which had fixed it against the wall, then moved it right across the floor. By hand. All on her own. I could not believe she was so strong or agile and adept. Are you Pansy Potter, the strongman's daughter, I asked her? But she didn't get the reference, being too young to remember the comic-strip character from the *Beano*, which I had read avidly as a little boy back in the 1940s and 1950s.

I had to admit the room was better. It was a nicer, lighter room. She had done good, without involving me or getting in any strangers from the street. So I gave her a kiss, and a round of applause. Well done, pet.

But later that week, late on the Sunday evening, we had our first, well, our first words…

Just before we were going to bed, after I had been doing some writing in my office, I had gone into the utility room to check I had put the light off. The light switch also turns on the air freshener, which can then run all night and overheat.

I noticed that the little sink in the room was full of water – rather mucky, dirty water. I didn't remember using that sink all day, apart from washing my hands that morning on return from the beach. Where had the water come from?

I went upstairs to ask Claire, who was now in bed. She had no idea what I was on about, so came down to look

We agreed that the sink must be blocked for some reason. I looked underneath, with a struggle as these days I try not to bend down too far. I could see the pipes and how the water ran away. I examined the bend and wondered if some gunge had got lodged, though God knows how I could get access to it. We had as yet few tools in the house. Anyway, these days, aged eighty-four-and-three-quarters, I am not strong enough to use them.

Claire is very handy, as she has had to be, living on her own for over thirty years, bringing up her son, running her own house, able to fix or, at least, understand most of her own problems and she knows roughly what to do in most domestic emergencies. My wife was not handy in that way, and never attempted to be. All our married life, either in our house in London or the Lake District, I sorted all the simple household problems – putting new washers on taps, unblocking lavatories, climbing on the roof and fixing the slates, doing basic electric repairs. Mostly they were botched jobs, done badly, but usually sufficient to keep us going till we got in a proper plumber or electrician.

When I first became a householder, back in 1963, I tried to understand roughly how lavatories and electric switches and fuse boxes worked, as we could not afford to call in experts all the time.

In my London house, on my own, I still attempted to mend most simple things, but God, they have got so complicated. Fuse boxes have changed. Lavs flush a different way. Worst of all, with age, I can't do any screwing, no silly jokes please, or climb up on roofs.

When staying with Claire in her own house, over the last three years, I never presumed to offer to mend anything. Claire clearly knew how her own house worked and could sort most things. I kept out of it.

Now, for the first time, we were living together, joint householders, jointly responsible, neither of us really in charge. And, of course, with a new house, neither of us really knew what was wrong. The guts and entrails of the property were all foreign to us.

We leaned over the blocked sink, studying the horrible, nasty water, with bits floating in it, neither of us knowing what the problem was – but that did not stop us telling the other, 'What you need to do is...'

This soon led to us shouting at each other, even a bit of pushing and shoving. Then we started blaming each for being stupid, knowing nothing.

Claire stormed off upstairs, to the bathroom and lavatory in the room above, to investigate. She discovered that the water in the lavatory pan had not properly run away, even when the chain was pulled. It appeared somehow to have backfired.

We had three lavatories and sinks and two bathrooms, which we were very pleased by, but we did not know how they were all connected, or where everything flows.

We had been in a right panic when buying the house and the solicitor had announced there were sewage pipes running under the house, but eventually the experts had put cameras down and proved this was not true.

Yet, clearly, we had got some sort of blockage – but where and how and why?

It was late at night on a Saturday. I had taken out house insurance cover, I think, must have put the forms somewhere, but what were the chances of dragging out an emergency plumber at this time of night, during lockdown, in a town in which we knew nobody?

'Don't worry,' I said, trying to appear a capable householder. 'I have coped with this sort of problem before.'

'No, I'll sort it,' said Claire. 'I know what it needs.'

She grabbed her coat and ran out of the front door. She returned five minutes later with a monster plastic bottle of unblocker, bought round the corner at the Indian supermarket, which fortunately never appears to close.

Meanwhile, I followed her out of the house, but only to go next door. I had spoken now and again to our next-door-neighbours, a youngish couple, but did not really know them well. They had not yet been in our house for a drink and we had not been in theirs, because of Covid. But as we are attached to their house; or rather, semi-detached, I hoped they might know about our pipes and whether they had had similar problems.

They came to the door and I explained our problem. How were their drains? All fine. I then asked if I could possibly borrow their plunger.

I have always had at least a couple of plungers in my house in London, and in the Lake District, handy for emergencies when you have loads of grandchildren and friends visiting. I love using a plunger. It is rather dramatic when, after a few violent plunges, the nasty, horrid blockage suddenly clears. Well, mostly.

Claire and I arrived back at the house at the same time – me with the plunger and she with her bottle of chemicals. We rushed to the blocked sink and started pushing each other, determined that our way would sort it.

'Don't be daft.' I said. 'Don't put that poison down now, it will take twenty-four hours to work. Let me try the plunger first; come on, don't be stupid, move out of the way.'

I accused her of always being far too ready to rely on nasty, dangerous, environmentally damaging chemicals and patent potions. She buys loads of them, for cleaning every possible surface – different bottles for different types of dirt, all expensive – which I maintain are a con. Elbow grease, that's the best way, pet.

I then complained how she has our washing machine on every day, and the dishwasher, just for two people. Madness. You are so wasteful, ruining the planet.

As for all the paper towels you get through, ye gods, using sheets of it to mop up the smallest drip. And the lavatory paper, dear God, you are almost as bad as my granddaughters. They use miles of it, just to annoy me. I hear the toilet-roll holder rattling and rush to bang on the lavatory door, telling them to stop it, at once.

And the bleach. You are always buying bottles of bleach. What do you do with it all? Drink it? No wonder the beaches of the world are so polluted. I am going to report you to the *Daily Mail*...

All of this was, of course, nothing to do with the problem in hand, the blocked sink. You do that sort of thing – drag in other annoyances – when you are both fraught, upset and bad-tempered.

After we had shouted at each other for about half an hour, pushing and shoving, calling each other names, we collapsed, exhausted. Ranting is very tiring.

OK, I said, you go first, do it your way. Let's see what happens.

She poured about half a gallon of her chemicals into the sink and the upstairs lavatory, while I had to look away, upset by the waste and the expense. We waited a few minutes, then it was my turn to have a go at my solution. I used the plunger in both places, but I hardly had the strength or the dexterity to make any effect. But I did not want Claire to use the plunger. This was *my* miracle cure.

Nothing at all happened; the sink and lavatory were still obviously bunged up, so we said, 'Let's have a drink.' We went into the front parlour and opened a bottle of Beaujolais.

Eventually, about an hour later, when we had calmed down, and were on the second bottle, we decided it was so late we should go to bed. But first we had another quick look at the sink in the utility room, not expecting anything to have happened.

Miracle of miracles, the sink had cleared. Claire then rushed upstairs to look at the upstairs lavatory – and it was now flushing properly.

Who had cured it? Whose method had worked?

I maintained it was my plunger what had done it. Her stupid

chemicals could not have worked in just an hour. She said it was her method which had worked, obviously. Mr Muscle always works miracles. Mr Expensive, if you ask me – and Mr Polluting The Planet.

We managed not to start arguing and fell into bed, totally knackered. But at least we had sorted our first domestic drama. And had our first words.

Fortunately, it was all caused by a pretty minor domestic problem. It had become heated, but about nothing really serious or personal. Though as we all know, trivial arguments about trivial things can all too easily become a proper, personalised, awful slanging match if you are not careful. Damage can be done and you can later regret what you said.

I went to sleep, hoping that would never happen.

CHAPTER 10

Needles and needling

The Needles, three stacks of chalk extending
into the English Channel

One afternoon, when we had finished lunch and were wondering which way down the beach to walk, on a whim we decided instead to go off in the car. We would have an outing to some of the places we had still not visited. There were loads of them, but we felt we just had to go and see one in particular which is, probably, perhaps, may be, the most photographed bit of landscape on the island – the Needles. It has been famous in stories and legends about the Isle of Wight and in paintings and drawings since the eighteenth century. As an image of the Isle of Wight, it is probably the only one which the rest of the nation is likely to recognise.

How do you find the Needles? Look in a haystack. Har-har. Very old joke. In fact, the Isle of Wight has loads of such topographical jokes, enjoyed by primary school children of all ages, such as *moi*. There is one well-known postcard, decades old now, but still in print, which shows photographs of the main places of the island with ever so witty captions underneath. Such as 'Cowes – where there aren't any', 'Ryde – where you can't' and 'Newport – which is very old'.

In fact, we did have some trouble finding the Needles – mainly because we did not know what we were looking for. Was it a lighthouse on a rock, miles out at sea? Was it off the shore? Or was it just a stretch of coastline? Or perhaps it is no longer a lighthouse but some sort of park?

It turned out that, from Ryde, the Needles are across the other side of the island, down on the far tip, where the island comes to a point – so perhaps that was why they are called the Needles?

We took several wrong turnings before, at last, coming to a

sign saying 'Needles car park' – but with no sign of the Needles. Just a sort of empty stretch of undulating coastline, overlooking the sea. The charge for parking was six pounds, whether you stayed ten minutes or all day: what a cheek.

There appeared to be a fairly good path along the cliff top, but no access for cars. The weather had turned cold and windy and we began to wonder if we should save the Needles, whatever they were, for another day and instead go and poke around Freshwater or Yarmouth. But it seemed daft having come all this way not to spend at least ten minutes having a quick look. So I paid six pounds, still moaning, and set off to walk along the grassy cliff path, to see what we could see.

Down below, to our right, there was the interesting-looking Alum Bay, with different coloured cliffs, different sorts and layers and hues of stone. I tried to take a picture, but it was too far away and too misty for my phone camera to do it justice. There seemed to be a little pier at the bottom of the bay and what appeared to be a chair lift to reach it. That might be fun to do one day, in the summer when our grandchildren come to stay.

The cliff path went on and on, leading us nowhere, with occasional little tracks leading off uphill, which I wasn't going to take, not with my poorly knee. Eventually, we came to some signs pointing to a 'Battery'. What did that mean? Yes, bad research. I normally try not to go anywhere new without mugging up about it first. This was a sudden decision.

We kept to the coastline, thinking, We are bound see the Needles some time. We eventually came to a sort of encampment, old concrete buildings which looked like they were left over from the Second World War. And nearby was an open-top tourist bus parked outside, which I did think I had seen from the car park. So I had not imagined it. We should have taken that instead of walking, if we had known where it came from

Looking down at the old buildings, which I presumed must

be the military battery, there appeared to be an entrance where presumably you had to pay. I felt I had already lashed out quite enough in parking.

'You go, pet,' I said to Claire. 'You tell me what is there. Daddy is too tired. I'll wait here.'

That's what I used to say to my children, when I was being lazy and would send them off to inspect shops or caffs. Oh, and here's a shilling, get me an ice cream as well.

Claire disappeared over the hillside. I decided to explore a little bit, hoping to get a view. And I did. I eventually managed to catch a glimpse in the distance of those famous, world renowned, total icons – the Needles.

They are – calm down – three smallish-looking stacks of chalk sticking up in the sea, just a few hundred yards off the tip of the coast.

Beside the third and last stack is a lighthouse, admittedly a rather pretty, red-and-white lighthouse, not very big or tall, but artfully and rather precariously situated.

This is the little lighthouse you see in all the millions of pictures and paintings of the Needles, but I assume most of them are either taken from the sea or from the air, to get a clear and unobstructed view. On the land, looking down, as I was, it was hard to get a proper perspective. In fact, they looked a little bit – dare I say this without the Isle of Wight tourist people chucking me off the island? – rather titchy. It's the dramatic photos taken close-up, in a wild sea, which make them look so huge and magnificent.

Claire came back and said, 'Yes, it is a National Trust building and you have to pay to go in.' 'Oh, no. Let's leave it for another day,' I said, 'with better weather and this time I will research it properly.' Which I have now done.

The lighthouse dates back to 1859 and became automated in 1994. There were, in fact, four stacks of rock making up the Needles at one time. One of them was rather pointy and was called Lot's Wife – a biblical reference, from the Book of Genesis. Lot's wife looked back on the city of Sodom, when she was told not to do so, and was turned into a pillar of salt. The Needle known as Lot's Wife was destroyed in 1764 in a storm, so it's now hard to tell how pointy it was, although drawings and paintings exist. It was because of its pointed, sharp-looking head that the Needles first got their name.

There are two batteries, meaning military artillery establishments. One is Victorian and the other, which Claire went to look at that day, is indeed left over from the last war. It was also the site of a firing station which in the 1960s employed about 240 people, working on rocket launchers. But I never saw any signs of that.

That afternoon, in the rain and mist, I did not see much to write home about or take photographs of and send to my dear children. In fact, I did not see a Lot. Well, she did fall over all those years ago...

On the way home, we decided to pop into a pub for the first time. It had always appeared so nice through the window – log fire, pretty garden, handsome building, possibly Regency, like our house.

It was almost empty, which was good. Claire and I, at our age, with our hearing not what it used to be, do prefer quiet places. There were just two other customers. One was a fairly old man, sat in a far corner near the garden quietly reading the paper. A younger man, about forty, was at a table in the middle. He smiled when we came in.

Claire and I sat down in the other corner and discussed what we wanted. Claire likes beer, which I have not drunk since I was a student. Could not believe it, when I first met her. But it is her fave tipple when we are out and have walked somewhere and also at home, in the house, when she has been working and has got up a sweat – sorry, ladies don't sweat. Me, I drink dry white wine, with lots of ice cubes. What a jessie.

There was a telly blaring away, showing some sort of news.

'What channel is that?' I asked Claire.

'Southern,' said the younger man in the middle of the room, unasked, clearly dying to chat with us. I squeezed Claire's arm, indicating don't reply, don't get involved, or we'll never get away.

We started a pretend conversation with each other, in a low voice, so he could not hear and interrupt. I don't know why I did not want to get involved. He looked clean and tidy and respectable enough. I normally always talk to strangers, quiz them on who they are, where they live, how they came here. Till they run away screaming – or decide I am their new best friend for life. Little knowing I am just soaking them up, getting their essence for my own amusement. I do get bored very quickly – and then quickly forget whatever it is they have told me.

But this time we were just popping in for a quick drink, checking out a local pub, on our way home, with no intention of staying long.

Without looking at the man on his own at the middle table, I went to the bar to order our two drinks.

'Stand back there!' barked the barmaid. I had not seen lines chalked on the floor – Covid restrictions about social distancing, presumably.

'Sorree,' I said, apologetically.

I got our drinks and sat down again with Claire in the corner. The barmaid came across and talked to the man in the middle, idle chat about some part of Ryde I did not know but they did.

The garden room door opened and in came a rather burly man in overalls, as if he had just finished some sort of building work. He strode across the room in a very determined manner and sat down at the little table where the talkative man was sitting. The barmaid went back to the bar, ready for the new order.

'I didn't know you were here,' said the talkative man, mumbling a bit and I didn't catch the end of his sentence.

The burly man grunted. The two men clearly must have known each other. There was some more chat, none of which I could hear, but it all sounded amicable.

Claire and I were discussing the Needles and what we had seen or not seen. The talkative man had stopped eavesdropping on us, now he had a friend to talk to.

Suddenly, the burly man stood up – and threw a punch at the talkative man. Who fell off his chair, then got up and started throwing punches back.

Bottles and glasses started flying, smashing onto the floor. The table was overturned, the chairs crashing about, both men were going at each other like prize fighters, trying to knock each other out.

The barmaid was yelling at them to stop, with no success. I could see her ringing a bell for help. A few minutes later, the door opened and into the room came a rather old man in his slippers, possibly the landlord, who had been resting upstairs.

I grabbed Claire's hand and pulled her out of her seat, 'Leave your drink,' I said, 'we are getting out of here now.' I led her straight to the front door. Then we ran home.

We never found out what happened in the end. Did the manager chuck them out? Were the police called? And most of all, who were they and what had caused it?

It had all erupted so suddenly, in an otherwise peaceful and placid bar, which had appeared so attractive and welcoming, with quiet respectable, friendly drinkers.

Back at home I tried to remember what exactly had been the first words of the talkative man to the newcomer. It might have been, 'I didn't know you were out', rather than 'I didn't know you were here'. Which might suggest the other man had been away somewhere – in prison, a hospital, some institution. Perhaps he had tracked down the other man to exact revenge for some slight or wrong, perhaps sleeping with his wife, or having given evidence against him or having double-crossed him.

We never found out. We have still not been back to that pub. We will never know.

And yet the Isle of Wight, so we were told, was such a safe place, few robberies, few crimes, few incidents. The police must know the handful of likely offenders who can hardly escape in a hurry from an island

In the town, I had seen a few dodgy-looking elderly blokes, some almost my age, hanging around the High Street outside Poundland, but just smoking and drinking, mainly talking to themselves. On the seats near the pier there were often some homeless-looking people, sitting around. Along the promenade in the summer there were often little gaggles of teenagers sitting on the sea wall, smoking, but none of them at all threatening.

Obviously, the Isle of Wight is nothing like London, with someone stabbed to death every night of the year, but even so, with a population of 140,000, I suppose you are bound to get the occasional 'incident'.

It didn't worry us at all or make us change our mind about moving here. It didn't make us feel at all unsafe. We still walked round the streets and along the promenade in the dark, not at all worried or hesitant. It was just a surprise, a shock, observing that pub fight. It demonstrated that life on a paradise island can be like life anywhere else on the planet, when there are humans around.

After all, had I not given Claire a slight push to let me get at that stupid sink when it had got blocked? And had she not called me a few choice names? Well, then...

Early next morning, Claire put out the rubbish in the bins

at the front of the house. And came back pale.

'You look ashen,' I said. 'Have you been putting out the ashes from the fire? Har-har...'

'This is not funny,' she said. 'Come and look.'

I couldn't see much at first. The two bins looked much the same as the night before. Then she pointed to something in our little front garden. In the middle of it we have a large cactus that has grown taller than our front window in the parlour. One day it will probably reach up to the height of our bedroom window. I love it dearly and will never cut it down. It means no passersby can see directly into our house through the windows. The glass reflects the cactus.

'Can't see now,' I said.

'Look under the bush...'

I looked. And there was a dead cat, stretched out. Sort of black, with white paws. But definitely dead.

Claire was visibly upset, so I managed a few soothing noises. Claire is an animal lover, any animals really, so naturally she was upset at the death of a living creature.

I never allowed my children any pets when they were growing up, except the tortoise. Looking after kids is hard enough, without having pets to worry about as well.

When I was young, and we were living in Dumfries during the war, we did have a cat. It was called Peter – not really a cat name, is it? There were fields at the back of our house on the Annan Road, where Peter would roam at night, hunting down mice and rats and anything else.

Once he disappeared for about a week and we were convinced he was a gonner. Then one morning we spotted him in the distance, right in the middle of the field, staggering and falling over, clearly in pain. Peter eventually reached our garden fence – and we saw the reason he was staggering. He was dragging a large metal trap clamped over one of his hind legs – some sort of rat or fox trap left by a farmer, which Peter had accidently set off.

He had to go to the vet and had half of his leg amputated to release the trap. For the rest of Peter's life, we could hear him at night going round the house... patter, patter, patter, thump... patter, patter, patter, thump... as he dragged his peg leg.

Claire stood for a long time staring at the dead cat in our front garden.

'Yes, it does look dead,' I said. 'Poor cat. Very sad. Let's go in, I want my breakfast...'

I was not feeling all that sad, nor imagining what sort of awful death the cat had had to endure, as Claire appeared to be. I was thinking, Oh God, how are we going to get rid of this horrible, dead, smelly cat?

After breakfast I went for my morning walk along the beach front, saying I would ring the council when I got back, see if they could suggest what to do with a dead cat. Didn't there use to be a cartoon strip about a hundred uses for a dead cat?

'It's not funny,' she said.

I headed along the promenade for the boating lake, which I do every morning – and, at the far end, I noticed a gaggle of police. Oh no, has there been an incident in the night? They were putting up red-and-white tape barricades to stop all the early morning walkers going around the lake.

One of the police had just pinned up a rather neat-looking notice. When he had moved on, I took a photo. I do like public notices. I like the tone, the typography, the information. It is social history after all. When all this Covid nonsense is over, I intend to come out in the night and steal – sorry, 'liberate' – some pandemic notices. Archive stuff.

IMPORTANT
PUBLIC RIGHT OF WAY CLOSED.
AVIAN FLU OUTBREAK

The public right of way has been closed to prevent the spread of the disease. Notice by Isle of Wight council.

PLEASE DO NOT REMOVE OR DEFACE THIS NOTICE

I wondered if the dreaded Covid had mutated and was now attacking birds as well as humans. A woman walker with a dog came up and studied the notice. She said, 'It's the swans; they've found seven dead swans. The police are roping off the whole of the boating lake.' A shame, she said, as she loved walking round it every morning.

Since we arrived at Ryde, I have yet to see any rowing boats on the boating lake. But on Sunday mornings I have seen little huddles of happy, awfully preoccupied men with remote controls racing their little model yachts up and down the lake. I always stop to watch them. They can manoeuvre their craft so swiftly and cleverly, racing them up and down the lake, round various marker buoys and obstacles.

When we first moved to our London house in 1963, the boating lake on Hampstead Heath hosted lots of model boats. At the weekends they held races and regattas. The practice died out and for decades I didn't see any model boats, although the lake is still called the Boating Lake, by old residents, such as me.

Our local lake in Ryde is officially called the Boating Lake but its main occupants, ever since we have arrived, have been swans. I once counted forty of them. They pad or paddle around as if they own the place, then get out and prance and preen, striding about the paths, waddling about on the grass verges, sometimes wandering onto the road and ignoring the traffic. It is a wonderful sight when they suddenly start flapping their huge wings, showing off like mad. Their wings are enormous and could well give you a nasty injury. Now and again they fly off in little groups and zoom out over the sea, just about half a mile out. They fly so gracefully, purposefully, up and down the coast, moving as smoothly and powerfully and sleekly as a flight of Concorde aeroplanes.

It was a few weeks after moving in, passing the lake each day, that we realised that among all the white swans there was just one black swan. At first the black swan seemed to be all alone, sitting at the edge of the little island, but later we saw her mingling with the white swans, proving she was part of their gang.

I tried to count as many swans as I could, without trespassing on the path beside the lake, which was roped off. I calculated that today there were only about thirteen swans. About half the normal amount. So, goodness, this is serious. Perhaps more than seven have died. Or been taken away. I rushed home to tell Claire the sad news.

Naturally, she was very upset. And she too worried that the black swan was one of the victims. In the three months since we had taken over the cottage, she had snapped endless photos of the swans flapping their wings or striding about, including the black swan. She had sent the pix to her youngest grandchild Lucas, then aged ten. Till he started complaining. Please grandma, send me something different for a change, no more swans – something interesting, such as cars.

We discussed the dead cat again, what to do about it, fearing it would soon begin to smell. We could put it in our dustbin, I said, but I am sure that is not allowed. Perhaps in the middle of the night I will go down the street and dump it into someone else's garden, such as that empty house nearby, the one for sale? Claire said, 'Certainly not, that would be appalling.' Sounding just like my wife when I suggested something gross.

Claire was most worried about the poor owner of the missing cat. We could see a collar, but not read any details. He or she must be grieving for their missing cat,

I then had a horrible thought which I decided not to share with Claire. What if the dead cat had been deliberately dumped in our front garden, a symbol, to warn us, yet more Londoners, putting up the house prices, making it hard for locals to buy anything?

In Broadstairs, I took a photo of some white graffiti on the beach wall, 'DFL – fuck off home.' 'DFL' stands for 'Down From London'.

One of our new friends in Ryde, Jonathan, who lives in Vernon Square, told me how he used to have two cottages in Cornwall, one he lived and one he rented. He sold both as the locals were giving him such grief. But here on the island, he felt no resentment at all. I honestly had not felt animosity either and I had talked to lots of locals, openly telling them we had just arrived from London and bought a cottage. The locals don't seem to feel under threat. We are part of their livelihood.

I did not share my silly thought with Claire about what the dead cat might mean. Did not want to alarm her. Or suggest that the next stage might be the local mafia putting a pig's head through our door.

'OK, then,' I said, 'I'll go down the street and find out who are the local cat owners, ask them if they have a cat missing.'

Most people did not answer. Suggesting their properties might be holiday homes or holiday rentals. Eventually someone did come to the door. I asked if they knew of anyone who might have lost a black cat with white paws. He directed me to a neighbouring street where he said an old woman lived with about ten cats. Her curtains were pulled, the house looked dilapidated. I knocked, but got no reply.

I tried once again to get through to the council to see if they could help. After an hour of waiting, I got referred to the environmental health department. Which took another half-hour of waiting.

They didn't sound interested in our dead cat. So I said, 'What if this new strain of avian flu, you know, which has killed seven of our local swans, you must have heard about it, has already been passed on to cats? All the cats in Ryde might be wiped out. Then it will be passed on to dogs as well... and babies. You could have a proper crisis.'

The environmental health person sighed. Another busybody wasting their time. But he said he would consult a colleague. He returned to say, 'Sorry, the virus affecting the swans will not affect cats, other animals or humans.'

'But what about our dead cat? It will be stinking soon. Won't it then become an environmental hazard?'

'Sorry, the council does not take away dead animals. Try one of the animal charities.'

Oh God, more phone calls. I went online and started looking for likely sounding animal charities on the Isle of Wight.

I found one called Pets at Rest, based in Newport, which appeared to specialise in cremating dead, loved pets. Never heard of a pet crematorium before. I explained our problem, how we loved all animals, blah, blah, especially cats, and were so worried about this poor, dead feline which had appeared overnight in our front garden. Could they help or advise us what to do? 'It is not our cat,' I added. 'It's an unknown cat. Now a very dead cat. We don't have a cat, alas. We are just feeling sorry for it and want it to have decent burial.'

I was worried they might try to sell me a cat's funeral, complete with coffin and pall bearers and solemn music suitable for deceased cats.

The lady at Pets at Rest said, 'Please don't worry. We will send someone round to your house in the next two hours.'

Wow, I thought, that is service. Though I hardly believed it would happen. They might just be getting me off the line.

Two hours later, on the dot, a rather pleasant gentleman called Andy Marshall arrived. He was carrying a pillow. We showed him the cat and he said, 'Oh, yes, poor thing. I think it has died of natural causes. Look, there are no signs of it being attacked or hit by a car. Poor thing.'

He then put the cat in the pillow and put it into the boot of his car. He said they would photograph the dead cat and put the image on Facebook. That way the grieving owner might spot it and might want to give the poor cat a decent funeral. If no one claimed it, Pets at Rest would cremate it. It would then have been given a decent send-off.

Phew, what a relief. Well done, Pets at Rest. I might put a few bob in their collecting tin, if I ever see one. I am kind that way. And do love animals, sometimes.

CHAPTER 11

History lessons

Ryde, circa 1855, as depicted
by George Brannon

Where did the Isle of Wight come from? Obviously, the island has always been there in some form, since the first syllable of recorded time, though it probably was not always an island, till it slipped away from the mainland. You can see from the map two extensive incursions of the sea going rather far inland, from Cowes down to Newport in the middle of the island, and another one on the west side, from Yarmouth.

I mean the name, what is the origin of that? It could be a bad spelling of 'White', so named because of all that chalk. The Isle of Wight is also a 'white' island in that it has few immigrants, whether settlers or tourists. Could that be the reason for the name? Unlikely.

Various clever academics have suggested the name is Celtic and was originally 'Wit'. Or possibly the Old English word 'Wiht'. Or it all goes back to the Norman Conquest when it was ruled by a local king called Wiht and was known as the kingdom of Wihtwara. Whatever.

'Wight' is not a version of its Roman name. The Romans did come, and conquer, but moved smartly on to the mainland without building any towns, forts or roads. All they did on the island was farm, though they did leave seven villas. The Romans knew the island as Vectis – which is a long way, by any linguistic contortion, to the word Wight.

The local bus company is called Vectis. When we first arrived, new to the island, not knowing the history, I was intrigued by the name. I wondered at first it was an acronym: Very Efficient Coaches To Interesting Seasides. Then I was told that was what the Romans called the island. Having passed O-level Latin and read Tacitus, I should have known that. Other little businesses and firms also have the Vectis name. The islanders are clearly quite proud of their ancient history.

There is a simmering patriotic feeling at present, bubbling quietly away on the island, with a Patriotic Party. The island has an annual Isle of Wight Day – on 11 September. Officially, it has acquired its own flag and, since 1974, it has been a separate county and no longer part of Hampshire. It has an MP, but is a bit aggrieved as it feels it should have two. Its population of 140,000 is double that of many mainland constituencies.

But on the whole, judging by my long experience of the island – i.e. six months now – walking up and down the beach at Ryde and around the town, I would say there is no serious attempt to turn the Isle of Wight into a separate, independent state with its own borders, tax laws and monarch. If that did happen, the king would probably be Alan Titchmarsh. He is very popular locally and has been high sheriff.

The island was used as remote farming land for most of its long history, with not much population, no towns, no industries. It could well have been in the Outer Hebrides. Except, of course, in times of war. Goodness, did they not panic, did they not start shaking in London and in our seats of national government and power at a possible sea invasion by our horrible enemies. Just look at the map again. If Old Boney was going to invade or, later, the Nazzies, one way would be to silently sail up the Solent, probably pitch their tents on the Isle of Wight, bombard us with cannon, and that would be it. We would become part of France or Germany.

The French Revolution and the wars with France gave England about twenty years of paranoia. Spies were suspected everywhere. You could be shot for wearing a beret and having a string of onions round your neck. OK, I made that bit up, but the fear of spies was widespread. Wordsworth and Coleridge, when they were young hippies and living down in the west country, were overheard one day to be talking about 'Spy Noza'. Some local busybody shopped them and a heavy was sent down from London to apprehend them. Turned out they were talking about the Dutch philosopher, Spinoza.

But the fear was real, and the reaction was dramatic. And you can still see some of the consequences today.

As you travel on the ferry or hovercraft or fast cat towards Ryde from Portsmouth, you will pass and can clearly see, even in poor weather, two strange, rather menacing, mysterious, circular, fortified islands out in the middle of the Solent. Are they real islands or jumped-up chunks of rock?

They are part of a chain of fortifications built out at sea to defend us against the French, should they ever dare land. They are sometimes known as Palmerston's Follies – after the foreign secretary, later PM, Lord Palmerston, who originally ordered their construction.

The two nearest to Ryde are called No Man's Land and Horse Sand Fort. Like the other forts elsewhere in the Solent, they had to be created from scratch. Complicated, pressurised caves were hollowed out on the sea bottom, then built up. God knows how they did it. And God knows what the cost would be today. No Man's Land Fort cost £462,000 to build in the 1860s. It has been estimated that, in relative budgetary terms, the Palmerston Follies cost the largest amount of public money ever spent by a British government. Well, until Covid came along. The follies were only finally completed long after the danger from France was all over. So, a bit of a waste all round.

But it was seen at the time as a justified military and patriotic gesture. After all, the British Navy was our pride and joy, it ruled the waves, ruled the world. The main naval bases were nearby, at Portsmouth, Southampton and Plymouth. They had to be securely protected. It was not just protecting folks on the mainland from invasion but protecting our navy.

During the last war they were used again for military purposes, just in case the Germans invaded. The soldiers who were stationed there were chosen because they could not swim – and therefore could not desert back to the mainland, or, at least, across to the delights of Ryde.

Horse Sand Fort remains uninhabited, though news emerged in October 2021 that the derelict fort had been sold to an unidentified buyer. In 2015, No Man's Land Fort had opened as a luxury hotel, with four floors, swimming pool and heliport, but I was unable to find a phone number for it, and later discovered that it has been put up for sale. A shame. Claire and I had plans to go there some time.

It was Queen Victoria and Dear Albert buying Osborne House, near Cowes, in 1845, which put the Isle of Wight on the tourist map. A rather exclusive, upper-class, officer-class map. More Pall Mall and Whitehall on the Monopoly board rather than the Old Kent Road.

Immediately, there was a royal entourage, servants and lackeys on the island, along with services and suppliers, local businesses, hotels and yacht clubs competing to have 'royal' added to their name.

After all, had we not stayed at the Royal Esplanade hotel, Ryde, and had lunch at one royal yacht club already? I don't think, in the whole of Carlisle, any hotel or club had the prefix 'royal'. Oh, hold on, Carr's of Carlisle – the world's first biscuit-makers, they were allowed to have the royal coat of arms on their famous Carr's water biscuits for many years, though they lost that honour in 2012, alas.

Royal naval officers from across the water in Portsmouth had their family home in the Isle of Wight and, if not their family, an indulgent mistress. When they retired, they often stayed on, pillars of the yacht clubs, especially the pillars of the bars.

By the end of the Victorian era, happy, over-excited families were arriving each summer for their hols, cramming on the steam ferries and rushing off at the various piers to check into their digs, go straight to the beach to swim or sunbathe and then on to the funfairs and souvenir shops, buying saucy postcards for the poor old folks stuck back home in the Old Kent Road.

A lot of the piers have now gone, fallen into decay, but Ryde Pier, said to be the oldest and longest of the remaining wooden piers in the whole of Britain, is still standing. The big car ferries don't dock there any more, just the fast catamarans and the hovercraft. The car ferry itself lands a couple of miles away, at Fishbourne. A shame they can't manage to dock at the pier.

There are lots of old, pre-war photos of steamers embarking at Ryde Pier in all the antique shops. I love looking at the faces of the passengers, their happy smiles, their clothes and their bags, wondering where they are going to stay. Many of them could have been heading for our street, even our house. Bless them. Happy days.

Thanks to the regular ferries, the island became an important tourist resort, with hotels, cafes and restaurants, museums and funfairs, displays and performances, music halls and cinemas, all created to attract the visiting crowds.

It wasn't just the working classes – the great unwashed from London and the north. The quality came too, headed for the posh enclaves, such as Seaview and Bembridge, hidden-away hamlets on the south coast or deep in the countryside.

A lot of writers visited, with holiday homes at first, often staying for several months, or settling there for years. Looking down the lists of famous people associated with the island, they do not include many artists. Paintings of the Isle of Wight don't fetch large amounts of money and nor were they done by the best painters of the day, unlike images of the Lake District or Scotland. I suppose grand magnificent mountains, deep valleys and large lakes do inspire artists. Seaside views, as in the Isle of Wight, can be found in lots of places.

Lewis Carroll lived on the island for a while. J. B. Priestley lived at Brook, in the south, very discreet and away from the tourist hordes. Today, Benedict Cumberbatch has a holiday home at Brook. The poet Alfred Swinburne lived at Bonchurch. Alfred Lord Tennyson spent many years at Freshwater (and we'll hear much more about the Victorian Poet Laureate in Chapter 24). Keats made a visit in 1819 and stayed in Shanklin. Dickens lived in Bonchurch for three months in 1849 and worked on *David Copperfield*. Charles Kingsley is known to have stayed on the island.

Karl Marx lived at Ventnor in the 1880s and also lodged for a time in Ryde. Mrs Thatcher rented a holiday home at Seaview (very tasteful). Ken Dodd also had a holiday home in the village, but not the same house, though I am sure Margaret would have enjoyed his tickling stick. The actor David Niven also lived there for a while.

Among the well-knowns actually born on the island are Dr Arnold of Rugby School, actress Sheila Hancock, actor Jeremy Irons, and film director Anthony Minghella. His family had an ice cream parlour in Ryde, still going, and I have sampled their cones, well, Claire has. She likes ice cream more than I do. In 2016, Ryde town council unveiled a plaque in honour of Anthony Minghella.

There have been a surprising number of technical types connected with the island – boffins and inventors – which is strange, considering the lack of industries or even a university or technical college on the island today.

On 14 January 1878, Alexander Graham Bell demonstrated his amazing new telephone invention to Queen Victoria at Osborne House. They made calls to Cowes, not far away, of course, but also Southampton and London. Nineteen years later, in 1897, the Italian inventor Guglielmo Marconi set up an experimental radio station at Alum Bay and transmitted from the Needles to Bournemouth. Another inventor, Barnes Wallis, creator of the bouncing bomb used in the successful 'Dam Busters' raid on the Ruhr Valley in 1943, was a resident of Cowes.

Another denizen of Cowes, Sir Christopher Cockerell, inventor of the hovercraft, developed his first prototype on the island. I am hoping to make contact with a hovercraft pilot to let me ride in his cockpit one day. Or is it a cabin? And is it a boat or a plane? Just asking.

One of the best-known manufacturers of aeroplanes and flying boats, world-famous for many years, was Saunders-Roe, based at Cowes. It was founded in 1929 but ceased trading in 1964. Its hangars and works are still in use today, mainly by the Red Funnel ferry line company. They built the *Princess* flying boat which could carry 105 passengers and was the world's largest flying boat. Saunders-Roe was also the company which, in 1959, built the first hovercraft. It was a hugely successful aeronautical and naval engineering and design works for many decades. At its peak, it employed hundreds of engineers.

A woman I know, who lived in the next street to us in London, worked for some years as a marketing consultant to Saunders-Roe, spending two days a week on the island when they were launching new planes or boats. She said that one of the remarkable things about the firm was that almost all the employees, engineers and designers, were local people, not imported from the mainland, as she had been.

The space industry at one time also employed several hundred people, some based at the Needles. The Black Knight and Black Arrow carrier rockets were developed there by Saunders-Roe in the 1950s and 1960s. The actual firing tests were carried out at Woomera, in Australia.

There also used to be a radar station at Ventnor, in the early days of radar.

Today, slowly exploring the island, I have seen few signs of industry; no factories or plants, which makes it hard to believe that at one time there were so many successful and high-tech engineering works. Visiting places like the Needles, you would imagine that farming or yachting are the only activities that have ever been pursued here.

Today, the tourist industry is, by far, the main employer on the island. Even this suffered for a while from the 1960s, when cheap, packaged hols to Spain came in. One effect of Covid and all the restrictions on travelling abroad, was an increase in the number of Brits taking holidays at home. The Isle of Wight never had mass tourism on the scale of Blackpool, Brighton or the Lake District, but it always appealed to the discerning.

The island boasts of its mild weather, milder than the mainland, so they say, though so far I had not felt it was any hotter, sunnier or drier than London. In fact, friends who live over at Yarmouth in the west say that high seas in the winter can make it cold and wet, both there and on the south-west coast. Ventnor, according to the tourist people, is supposed to have the greatest number of sunny days and has its own micro-climate. Snow is very rare. That I can believe. Looking through the fifty or so old books about the island which I have bought so far, there are very few snaps of buildings or promenades under snow.

There are two vineyards on the island, which traditionally used to be a sign of a Mediterranean climate, but these days you can find vineyards in southern England and Wales.

By chance, in buying our house in Ryde, on the north-east coast of the island, I think we have probably chosen the most sheltered coast. You can tell, by all the cacti, palm trees, banana trees and other tropical plants in our local gardens and along the promenade, that the weather must generally be pretty mild all year round. Otherwise the frosts would kill them. I've not seen any bougainvillea yet. I actually managed to grow it in my London garden, although I had to bring it into the conservatory in the winter.

No wonder there are so many retired people on the island. The over-sixty-fives make up 24 per cent of the population, compared with only 16 per cent on the mainland. They like the peace and quiet, the space, calmness and sense of community. At the same time, there are fewer children. Sounds good to me. Keeps the noise down for we elderly folk.

It used to be often said that you could fit the entire population of the world on the Isle of Wight. Standing up, presumably. This idea became something of an accepted truth, and, as such, it pleased those who denied the world was becoming over-populated. An expert, known as the 'Isle of Wight guru', who has a podcast and does lots of island lists online, has recently investigated whether or not this was even theoretically possible. He concluded it was certainly pretty true back in 1980, when the global population was four billion.

He divided the area of the island by four billion and reckoned it meant twelve people would have to stand in every square metre of the Isle of Wight to get them all in. Which was roughly possible – if you included a few children, not too many fatties and squashed all twelve up together. Now the global population is almost double that, over seven billion, which means you would have to accommodate twenty people per square metre. No chance of that. Even if they are all very small, very thin and very intimate. So, the received idea that the Isle of Wight can accommodate all the people in the world is, alas, no longer valid.

There used to be a perception of the island as being full of lazy folks, an image repeated in many pre-war books. Not that these days you would ever say anything like that about anyone anywhere. These national slurs were and are, of course, commonplace, believed by those in big cities about isolated communities in faraway regions. The Irish, for example, were always portrayed as being slow on the uptake. Aberdonians were mean. The slur directed at the inhabitants of the Isle of Wight was that they were indolent.

In response, various Isle of Wight villages started their own Lazy Club. It was a good joke, inviting all local 'lerrups' to join. In the local dialect, 'lerrup' is a lazy person. Can't say that so far I have noticed any local dialects or even local accents. To my ears, they all sound, well, English. The middle classes in Seaview or Bembridge speak BBC English. The long-established ordinary folk sound cockney to me or maybe south London.

I might, in due course, be more aware of subtle differences. Perhaps rural and town people do speak slightly differently. Can a Ryde person, born and bred, identify someone from Cowes the minute they open their mouths? The middle classes are easier to spot. Red or pink corduroy trousers are a clue.

On such a small island, it can be hard to believe the locals really see significant differences between people living in different areas. When I lived on Gozo, one of the Maltese islands (just nine miles across and so a lot smaller than the Isle of Wight), people in Victoria, the only town, looked upon rural people as country bumpkins. It always amused me that families in Victoria would make a big performance of decamping each summer to their seaside holiday home – all of three miles away.

True-born natives of the Isle of Wight refer to themselves as 'caulkheads', which was originally a sneer applied to them by the people on the mainland, but one they are proud to claim. It dates back to the time when shipbuilding was the main occupation on the island, and refers to 'caulking' – or sealing – a boat's hull to make it watertight. If they went over to Portsmouth for seasonal work in their shipyards, they were always referred to rudely as 'caulkheads'.

Caulkheads refer to newcomers as 'overners'; the term 'grockets', meaning tourists, is not quite as polite. I have heard them talk about going to the 'north island' – meaning the mainland – with a smile.

It's a shame some of the older dialect words, mentioned in pre-war books about the island, seem to be dying out. I have still to hear any local talking about a 'gallybagger', meaning a scarecrow, 'mullisheg' for a caterpillar, 'gurt' meaning large and 'nommix' for a morning snack.

I hope I have spelled these words properly. I might bring them into the conversation some time, to impress the caulkheads in the queue at the Co-op in Ryde, but I am not sure how to pronounce them.

My wife and I often used Carlisle slang from the fifties when our children, all born in London, were growing up. Just so they did not know what we were saying. These days, when I go back to Carlisle, to visit my brother or old friends, when I come out with these local words and phrases that we all used at school, they have no idea what I am on about. They think I am raj.

First time I have used the word 'raj' for about seventy years. It meant daft or mad. Spot on, really…

CHAPTER 12

Domestic dramas and duties

Thatched cottages in the Old Village,
Shanklin, 1920s

There were two things I had worried about – well, at least wondered about – lurking at the back of my mind, when we first decided to up sticks and acquire a home in the Isle of Wight.

Firstly, at my age, how will I cope with things going wrong? It is one thing to have an exciting new project but, in old age, will I be able to sort and solve unforeseen problems without despairing, becoming depressed and regretting the whole thing? When you are young, you are full of mental and physical energy. You will have a go at solving most problems. I was for ever clambering up on the roof to fix a tile and stop a leak. Now I can hardly get up the stairs to bed, far less climb into the loft.

Secondly, how will we get on, me and Claire, living properly together for the first time? Weekends and exotic holidays in the Caribbean are all very well. Living cheek-by-jowl, day after day, all warts and wrinkles and annoying habits fully exposed, might well result in some unpleasant discoveries.

To begin with we were, like the whole nation, further cloistered together, thanks to the effects of lockdown. When the government issued area-specific regulations in the form of tiers, the Isle of Wight had been one of the few lucky places remaining under the lightest restrictions in tier one. But on New Year's Eve 2020 we too joined most of the rest of England under the strictest level, tier four, and social intercourse disappeared. Claire and I both love drinks with friends, gatherings and gossip. Thrown totally upon each other, would we now become bored and frustrated and annoy the hell out of each other?

Well, I am eighty-five. Come on. Can't radically change much now. Nor do I think I want to. Which could turn out to be a worse condition. My marriage did last fifty-five years, I am proud of that, but I did rather get spoiled and allowed a lot of selfish and unthinking behaviour.

I came in from one of my morning beach walks, having left Claire to let in a workman who was going to lay a new bathroom floor. She wanted him to take up a carpet which I rather liked, personally. A carpet always feels comfortable in bare feet, but she had said, no, not in a bathroom, it was unhealthy; you should have wood in a bathroom, so much easier to clean and keep dry. Not real wood, of course, but those strips of vinyl stuff which look very like wood and are supposedly easy to put down and don't cost much.

We had been using a handyman, Rob, for a few jobs. He seemed affable and smiley, good enough for boring tasks such as hanging up mirrors and siliconing gaps. Rob appeared to have no particular basic skills or training, such as carpentry or plumbing. He had been a chef but had lost his job – reasons not given – and had been in the army at one time. Been twice married. Claire thought he was wonderful, always willing to try anything; she ahhed and oohed over everything he did, however piddling.

He was not young, possibly fifty-five, rather overweight, but was pleasant enough, did not turn on the radio, did not demand cups of tea with three sugars all the time, and he charged only ten pounds an hour. When I heard his rates I had agreed straight away. Yes, darling, he sounds perfect.

I had left him at it, with Claire fluttering round as if he was Barry Bucknell.

On my return, I opened the front door and shouted up for Claire. That has always been my habit, to shout, 'Hi, honey, I'm home,' even if I have just been two minutes away round the corner for a paper. I also always leave a note on the hall shelf when I go. I know it annoys Claire when I call out, especially if she is busy at the back of the house, in our south wing, as she can't hear. I do wish she would shout back when I shout up to her, but she never does, which in turn annoys me. Means I come home and don't know if she is in or out.

I decided she must have gone somewhere else and wondered if Rob was still working in the bathroom. I trudged slowly upstairs and heard a lot of awful shouting and swearing; fuck this, fucking that, oh God, oh shit, oh fuck. There was so much shouting I wondered if there were two people in the bathroom. Perhaps another pub fight had broken out, this time in our house. I opened the door slowly and Rob was on his knees, sweat pouring from his brow, his vast belly hanging over his trousers, which were falling down to reveal his white, builder's bum. He got up with such an effort I thought he was going to have a heart attack.

He apologised and sat down on a chair. He had not realised the new flooring had to be hammered into place. He had forgotten his hammer and so was using his hands, which was clearly a tremendous effort. I sympathised with his physical struggles, but it was his angry swearing which had surprised me. He had seemed such a calm, pleasant, reasonable bloke. But he had now turned manic. He said, 'Sorry,' about the bad language, explaining he had got so frustrated and in such a temper. I said, 'When I am on my computer and things go wrong, you should hear my language.'

I went downstairs just as Claire returned. I said, 'Don't go in the bathroom. I think Rob could be having a fit. You might have to drive him to casualty at the hospital.' Wherever that was. We had not discovered it yet and, touch wood, we won't ever have to.

She took Rob tea, mopped his brow, said what a lovely job he had done, he was so clever, blah, blah. I think she always overdoes this buttering-up of builders and handyman, even if they are just putting in a screw. Having lived on her own for many years she has had to rely on charming all the workmen.

It took him several more hours to finish – which he managed without another breakdown. I had to admit it looked quite good, making the bathroom cleaner, lighter, more modern. But I did not tell Claire this. I am not buttering her up. It would just encourage her to get more jobs done.

Then we hit two really serious problems. When Claire had moved the Welsh dresser a few weeks ago, nasty dark patches were revealed on the wall where it had previously stood. At first, I thought it was just lack of light that had made it a funny colour. Then one day we noticed the wall was wet. Dripping wet, in fact. And the plaster had started to crumble. Oh God, we have rising damp.

When we had the survey done, six months earlier, we had been told there was some damp in the outside wall, but that it did not need immediate attention. So we did nothing. All the walls looked fine to me. I could smell some damp, but only in my little study at the back of the house.

Now I went online and contacted a firm with a suitable-sounding name: the Isle of Wight Damp Proof Company. Dave Barker, the man in charge, took ages to come as he had so much work. When he did appear, he took out his little testing thing, checked the walls, and said the whole dining room had serious damp. His estimate for doing the worst two walls was £2,500. I practically collapsed. Plus VAT. Oh, God! All of which I would have to pay...

I rang the house insurer who said that if the damp was caused by a leak, then I would be covered, but not rising damp, no chance *rising damp* – that would mean it had always been in the house; it would be a pre-existing condition.

Dave agreed. It was an old house, dating back to 1832 or thereabouts, and they did not use damp-proofing in those days. It had to be properly treated – ripping the walls to pieces, back to the brick, silicone inserted into holes in the brick, then all plastered up again. Yes, he could do it – but not for another month. Up to us.

Claire said I could afford it – after all, we had gained a bit on the stamp duty which had been reduced at the time we had bought the house. So I gritted my teeth and said, 'Yes, we will have it done.'

Dave, who was about fifty, small, muscular and heavily tattooed with a very intense stare, did manage a brief, tight smile, then left, promising to give us a starting date in due course.

While we were waiting, something else went wrong – the bloody drains. The sink, which had blocked a few weeks ago, but we seemed to have sorted, started playing up again. We got two firms to come and look at it. They put a camera down a manhole in the courtyard. They both agreed a soil pipe was the cause, something was blocking it and they could not get their cameras round the bend. It could be a leak but, more likely, the cause was some poor workmanship, many years ago, putting in the wrong sort of joint. The whole yard would have to be dug up and the pipes going into the main drain ripped up. Probably even needed a new manhole. It was going to cost another £1,200 – plus VAT.

Did I swear and moan! The insurance agreed, at least, that I was covered for this, but only for 70 per cent of the final costs. And again, the drainage firm in question could not do it for another month. We were beginning to think that nothing ever happens quickly in the Isle of Wight.

The damp and the drains turned out only to be the start of it. The oven started playing up, then the washing machine and the dishwasher – all of which we'd inherited. Over the years, the kitchen must have taken a hammering from all the holidays lets, although the applicances had seemed to be OK. I said, 'Can't you manage, pet? They are still working – after a fashion.'

Claire got some kitchen experts in, who charged £95 just for the call-out. They showed her what was wrong with the oven, but said the dishwasher and washing machine were ancient; new ones would be cheaper than repairs.

I said her standards were too high. We are on a separate little island now, not London. Anyway, you don't need to wash clothes every day when there are just the two us. You can easily wash up our few dishes by hand. You're a big, strong girl.

But both the washing machine and dishwasher did pack up completely and Claire ordered replacements from Currys. They had, of course, to be fitted, which meant more complications and expense and waiting in. The old dishwasher had been integrated – don't ask me what that means – so a handyman had to be found to do some magic on the woodwork before the new one could be installed.

One evening I went into what we were calling her office, otherwise our spare bedroom. She was on her computer about to order a new fridge.

'The fridge is fine,' I said. 'It always keeps my sauvignon blanc chilled, so what more do we want it for?'

'The fridge light,' she said. 'It doesn't go on when I open the fridge. I have tried to replace it, but they don't make them anymore.'

'Give me strength,' I said. Bloody manufacturers of domestic products – and mobiles and computers; in fact, everything today. They do this all the time, just to make you upgrade.

She insisted she needed a light in the fridge. Now it was getting into winter, she wanted to see exactly what she had inside.

'Use a torch,' I said.

'Don't be stupid.'

'I'm not. This is becoming pure indulgence…'

She was furious at this, and stormed off. I took it back, realising I had gone too far.

Claire – like my wife before her – thinks I am potty, not

just tight, pointlessly saving a few pennies. I used to say it was because I was brought up during the Second World War, when we had to waste nothing, turn off all the lights, drink our own bath water and boil our old clogs for supper.

But this is not quite logical. My wife was also brought up in the war, but did not turn out to be a penny-pincher. With Claire, I can go on about the blackouts and rationing, scrimping and saving without her pointing that out. Not that she is a spendthrift – I must say that or I will be for it. It is just that if she is buying something, she doesn't want the shoddy or the shabby, the ugly or the nasty, and certainly not the cheap. Unlike me. When Claire makes a smoked salmon sandwich, I shudder at how much salmon she uses. She can use two whole packs, just on a simple lunchtime sandwich for each of us. Dear God, if ever I did splash out on smoked salmon myself, which was rare – have you seen the prices? – I would spin out one pack for a whole week.

When she treats me, going off to buy me a new T-shirt, she comes back with five, in different colours. I am amazed anyone can wilfully buy so many of the same items at once. I rarely buy her anything. I might get the colour wrong or the style or the make. That's my excuse, anyway.

I try to bite my tongue and not make too many comments when she buys new things for the house. But as we spend longer alone together, just the two of us, I seem to be upsetting her more often. I think I am simply making a helpful suggestion. Such as why does she not make a list and just go to Tesco once a week instead of every day? Or, does she really have to use so much weedkiller on the back terrace? I can see no weeds at all, so why is she bothering? Bleach, why does she keep buying bleach? Is she drinking it?

She gets things into her head which often seem to me to be dopey, such as spending ages online trying to add her name to our ferry pass. Residents, which we now are, get concession rates, but the car was just put in my name. Even though it is her car. It seemed convenient at the time and I said the ferry people don't care. They know the registration, they don't need to know the names of both people. They have had the money. We are not trying to cheat them. But she would not be told and at last she finally got it altered.

'You are always criticising me,' she said, flouncing upstairs to her room.

I was not criticising her. Well, I didn't think I was.

I always try to have two walks a day, in the morning and afternoon. She always says she will come, so I stand at the door, waiting patiently.

'Stop hustling me,' she says. 'I have to finish the cleaning. It won't do itself.' Or she decides at the front door to send an email to her son Miles or to order something online which had to be done now. I moan at her as I wait impatiently. 'You can't wait, can you? For anything. Always the same. Go on, you go...'

I will then go off on my own, sulking. Hoping of course that my walk along Ryde beach and the sands will clear my head and I will come back all happy and cheerful. Which is how I usually am.

That, of course, is my image of myself. It's probably bollocks. I am beginning to realise I can be a bit of a pain. In a long marriage, one party often gives up complaining and simply switches off, or decides to ignore the other's annoying habits. My wife was certainly annoyed by my continual rabbiting on. 'Do me a favour,' she would say. 'Don't talk for the next half hour.'

She also used to say that, even though I struck people as being relaxed and agreeable, I could be bossy and dominating. In the end, she said, I always got what I wanted. I denied all that. But now, I can see the same thing happening again. Claire now asks me not to talk when she is busy doing something.

I always like to read the paper at the same time every evening, with a drink, of course. No talking, as I concentrate on *The Times* each day, reading every word. So if Claire asks me something, the chances are I will just grunt, my mind miles away. I can see that must be annoying.

In her bath each morning, she always has Classic FM on the radio. I prefer Radio 4 for the *Today* programme, so I have to change it. Then she has to change it back next morning.

These were real differences emerging between us, piddling though they were. None of it seemed serious, so far – at least, I did not think so. Just normal, married life, accepting passing irritations, which all couples go through. After one particularly fraught week, getting on each other's nerves, we had to go back to London for a few days. I am sure I had been tiring her out, chuntering on, making stupid comments, being a bit of a pain. She probably did need a break from me. And me from her.

We wanted to see our respective houses, check if our lodgers had trashed them, attend to various domestic matters, but most of all we wanted to see our dear families. We had both missed our children and grandchildren. One of the reasons for trying to get the damp proof and the drain sorted as soon as possible was wanting the house to be perfect for when our families came to stay, for their first visit, during the next school hols.

Oh, God, we had words about that as well. I insisted that when my daughter Flora and her family came for a long weekend, I wanted to be here, in the house, to welcome them. I would explain to them how things worked, then take them to the beach, to the town, introduce them to all the delights. I was sure Claire would want to do the same when her son Miles and his family came.

'Certainly not,' she said. 'Neither of us is going to be here when they come. We just give them the keys and let them get on with it. It is their hol. Not ours. You just don't understand.'

'But I want to see their smiling faces when they look round our house.'

'You want to show off, you mean!'

Behind Claire's back, while we were in London, I asked both Miles and Flora if they would like us to be there when they came to stay, to help them understand how the house works.

They both said – not really, thanks. They would rather be left on their own to explore. But they were looking forward to it so much. It would be a big adventure, coming on the ferry, and the children were so excited about having a seaside holiday.

I gave in. We arranged not to be in residence when they came. In this case I did not get my own way. See, it's not true that I always do. So there.

Back home in London, after one night away from Claire, alone in my house, I was so lonely. After another night I was desperate to see her, I was missing her so much. I realised how much I needed her, wanted her, loved her. Despite the silly petty little aggravations, all of them piddling.

It was such a relief, after our short sojourn in London in our respective houses, to be returning together to the island.

I vowed to myself to try to mend my ways and say nothing that might smack of criticism. I am so grateful, all the time, for everything she does for me, for us, for the house.

When we got into bed on our first night back, in our little love nest, I told her about The Beatles, how John and Paul used to have awful arguments over their company Apple, all about how it should be run, and by whom. It led to the lawyers being brought in, to the band suing each other, shouting and screaming.

During one day at the Apple offices, with their respective advisors, having yet more awful rows, John and Paul happened to go to the lavatory at the same time.

As they were standing there, in silence, exhausted, John

turned to Paul, pushed his specs up high on his forehead, and said, 'Paul, it's only me.'

Then they returned to the boardroom and continued arguing with each other.

I said to Claire, 'When I do piss you off in the future, we must never go to bed on an argument. We must recite this mantra: "WE ARE SO LUCKY!"'

Which, of course, we are. Having a new home, a new project, on a new island, and most of all having each other.

CHAPTER 13

Osborne House

The Italianate towers and gardens of
Osborne House, in an old postcard

We are not the first couple, nor will we be the last, to create a love nest on the Isle of Wight, somewhere to get away from it all and be together. I wonder if, like us, these other couples bickered over piddling things, tried to knock their new houses into shape but struggled to find workmen to do all the jobs that needed doing and then had to wait for ages for the work to be done, argued about style and design – about the bedrooms, the kitchen, the gardens, the south wing? If they have one, that is.

And I also wonder if, in due course, they began to find it irritating, being constantly together, if they got on each other's nerves, and ended up wanting a bit of peace and quiet and some time alone? It's only natural, whatever age or however well-off you may be.

I'm thinking now of another couple who created their dream house on the Isle of Wight, but who did so a very long time ago – 175 years ago, to be precise. Yes, I'm talking about Victoria and Albert. I see some similarities between us, honestly. Albert, for example, had a rather dinky moustache, a bit like mine.

Queen Victoria married her first cousin Prince Albert of Saxe-Coburg in 1840, and they had nine children together. At the time, she had three large houses to live in – Windsor Castle, Buckingham Palace and the Royal Pavilion at Brighton.

But there was something missing from each of them. Windsor had little private space for the children to play in. Buckingham Palace did have a private garden but, come on, right in the middle of a stinking, throbbing metropolis. Step outside and it was a nightmare, everyone staring at you. The Royal Pavilion at Brighton, that was a joke, really, totally unsuitable for either private or family life, with no gardens and no nurseries, bang-slap in the middle of a busy street. Yes, it was near a beach and the sea, unlike Windsor or Buckingham Palace, but a boring, pebbly, public beach.

Claire and I, when we began this odyssey had – on paper, at least – four houses, one more than V & A! How do I come to that conclusion? We both had a three-storey house in London and I'm also counting here my access to my family's house in Broadstairs and oh, yeah, almost forgot, a house in Portugal, which I gave over long ago to my children. Unlike poor Victoria, we could have retreated to any of these together, at any moment.

The Queen and Albert were a lot younger than us – both aged twenty when they married – and immediately started having children. Victoria wrote how she longed for 'a place of one's own, quiet and retired'.

As a girl she had twice visited the Isle of Wight, once to lay the foundations of East Cowes church, and had fond memories of it. In the mid-1840s, Victoria and Albert made a trip to the island and fell in love with Osborne House, a Georgian house close to the sea, not far from Cowes. 'It is impossible to imagine a prettier spot – we have a charming beach to ourselves, we can walk anywhere without being followed or mobbed.'

The house came with a thousand acres of land, jolly handy for quiet walks. The prime minister of the day, Sir Robert Peel, gave her his blessing, agreeing that the Isle of Wight was not too remote for a hands-on monarch to continue to reign and not too cut off for him and his ministers to visit. It's interesting that, all of 175 years ago, they did not consider the Isle of Wight to be remote or rather out of reach. Only last week, I had a photographer from a magazine coming to the Isle of Wight to snap me and Claire for a feature – and they cancelled. Too far and too difficult to get to, apparently, much too complicated to work out the ferries.

The only snags with Osborne House were that it was owned

by someone else and was a bit small for their growing family. In 1845, Victoria and Albert bought the property for £28,000 – and proceeded to knock it down. That's the way to do it. Don't mess around. Do it the way you want it, right from the beginning, no messing about. Lucky them. There were no things like Grade II listings to worry about. We wanted to put a window in our downstairs lavatory, but everyone said, no chance, you won't get planning permission. Grade II listed, don't you know.

Prince Albert, who was awfully clever, good with his hands and with anything mechanical, designed the new mansion with Thomas Cubitt – one of the most celebrated architects of the time – in the style of an Italian Renaissance palazzo.

On 23 June 1845, the Queen and Prince Albert laid the first foundation stone. They took up residence in September 1846.

What? A house that size was completed in just over a year? It was true that two eastern wings were not yet finished; these would provide additional accommodation for the royal household when they all arrived, but the main house was indeed ready in just a year, with a hundred or so rooms, massive courtyards and Tuscan-style towers. The local builders and local tradesmen must have been miracle workers, back in the early years of Victoria's reign.

Our cottage in Ryde is roughly the same vintage. The first reference in the deeds is 1832, but I think this was when the land was first purchased. Proof of a house being on the site, with an eight-hundred-year lease, has survived since around 1850. If Isle of Wight builders in Ryde in the 1840s and 1850s had been as smart and efficient as those over at Cowes, our little cottage house could probably have been put up in ten minutes, half an hour max, counting tea breaks.

From then on, the Queen and Albert spent as much of their spare time as possible at Osborne. They still had a summer holiday at Balmoral in Scotland (which they acquired in 1852), and spent Christmas at Windsor, but Osborne was clearly their happiest home, the place where they spent their happiest days together. They always celebrated the Queen's birthday in the house, the day starting at seven in the morning with a band playing below her bedroom window. Often the tune was one of the hymns Albert had composed. Goodness, he was a man of so many talents.

Alas, Albert's life was cut short by typhoid fever in 1861, when he was aged just forty-two. They had had fifteen wonderful, productive years together at Osborne House. The Queen was heartbroken, spending most of her life from then on in black and in mourning. Over the next forty years of her widowhood, she returned to Osborne House as often as she could, considering it a sacred place, filling it with relics of her husband and the life they had led together. And it was here that she died, on 22 January 1901, just making it into the twentieth century.

Now owned and run by English Heritage, Osborne House remains by far the grandest and most historic property on the island. It is a place that everyone should visit – not just the people who live on the island, but everyone in the UK and across the English-speaking world. I don't know why it took Claire and me so long to visit. Oh, yes, I remember now... The Covid pandemic and the resulting lockdowns meant that it was shut for about a year.

Once the house had reopened, albeit with restricted visiting times, we made an appointment to see the curator, on 24 May 2021. As we were queueing to get in, there was a rather precocious girl of about ten talking to one of the guides. 'Do you know what colour Queen Victoria always wore?' asked the young girl.

'Tell me,' said the guide indulgently.

'Black, she always wore black.'

'Why was that?' he asked. I never heard the girl's answer because at that moment, the curator appeared and kindly escorted us through the ticket barrier.

The curator of Osborne House is a Scotsman called Michael Hunter with luxuriant grey hair and a good tan. How apt, as John Brown, Victoria's good and faithful servant after the death of Dear Albert, was a very smart, well-dressed Scotsman. John Brown moved into Osborne House in 1864, three years after Albert died. Did she ever sleep with him? Perish the thought. I believe the Queen only ever slept with Albert, but she adored John Brown and was buried with a lock of Brown's hair, his photograph and Brown's mother's wedding ring, given to her by Brown, along with several of his letters. Some intimate material was destroyed by Victoria's family after her death, as they resented the influence which the Scotsman had upon the Queen.

Michael Hunter was wearing a tartan tie, which he said was the Hunter tartan. Goodness, I have come all this way to the Isle of Wight to discover there is a Hunter tartan. Must get some. He was born in Arbroath, went to Arbroath High School and then to Edinburgh University and studied fine art. His first job was at Dublin's Abbey Theatre, as a set designer. He did a variety of other jobs at the theatre and then one day he saw an advert in *The Stage* for a job at Castle Howard in Yorkshire. He knew that the stage jobs were getting harder to find so he quite fancied a change of career.

His job at Castle Howard was curator of costumes. He worked in the rooms which were used to film *Brideshead Revisited*. He worked in a number of curatorial roles in other stately homes until 1998, when he saw an advert in the *Museums Journal* for a curator of contents at Osborne. Previously the role had been part-time, but English Heritage had just started a five-year renovation of the whole house and contents at a cost of some five million pounds.

One of his many tasks was tracking down original furniture, paintings and ornaments that had once been in the house or, where they couldn't be traced, making modern reproductions based on photographs of the contents when Victoria and Albert were in residence. He spent a lot of time with the royal collection identifying items that had originally been at Osborne.

Reproduction chandeliers were commissioned from David Wilkinson, a third-generation chandelier-maker. Material had to be found for the carpets which had originally been handwoven. When all the work was completed in 2003 our present Queen came to reopen the house. 'I had the honour of taking her round and she planted a tree,' said Michael Hunter.

He led me and Claire through the grounds and around part of the house and we admired the sparkling condition of the towers, windows and buildings. The whole building is painted in one colour which looked sort of yellow to me – but could possibly have been white or even grey.

'It is Naples yellow,' said Mr Hunter. 'Prince Albert chose it to reflect the Italian nature of the architecture.'

He congratulated us for choosing such an auspicious day to visit Osborne House. Which confused me. Did he know that 24 May was my son's birthday? I had sent him a card. I'd never forget the actual day either, in 1966. It was a home birth and I had to cut the cord as he came out with it around his neck, silly boy, and the midwife had not turned up.

But how could English Heritage or Mr Hunter possibly know that?

He explained everything. Queen Victoria's birthday is also 24 May, as I am sure that little girl at the front door was well aware. Bad research on my part. The Queen was always here for her birthday.

I very much wanted to know how Queen Victoria got to Osborne House. Mr Hunter explained that she took the royal train from London, arriving at Gosport, on the Hampshire coast, where she had her own railway station. One of the smaller royal yachts, *Alberta*, was there to meet her and take her to Cowes. Her coach and horses would then drive her on to Osborne House. There was a period when the royal yacht, instead of sailing to Cowes, went directly to Osborne Bay, beside her little private beach; but it is very shallow there and it meant that the Queen and the royal party had to disembark off-shore and be rowed to the landing stage at Osborne House. This could be pretty uncomfortable in bad weather. According to Michael, her door-to-door train, boat and coach ride from London probably took three-and-a-half hours. That's about the same as it takes most people today.

I wanted first of all to go round the grounds and visit the beach, while the sun was out, which suited Michael, as he had some work to do. He promised to meet us later for a cup of coffee – and, all being well, he would open up the Queen's bedroom especially for us. It was currently closed to the public, being in a part of the house that was yet to reopen owing to the pandemic.

The walk to the beach, along a tree-lined route and through lush gardens, took longer than I expected. One of Prince Albert's many passions was nature: trees and woods. He could not quite do what he wanted at Buckingham Palace or Windsor, as the grounds there were under the control of the Commissioners of Woods, but Osborne was private property, bought by the Queen out of her own money, so he could indulge himself. He planted thousands of English trees, such as oak, elm and beech, in the grounds, while introducing foreign trees nearer the house.

As an old lady, I expect the Queen mostly went down to the beach in a little coach. If she was going to swim, it would be handy for carrying her togs. She was a regular wild swimmer – as they did not call it in those days – and had her own bathing hut. She first used it on 30 July 1847, the summer after they moved in, and made the following entry in her diary:

Drove down to the beach with my maids and went into the bathing machine where I undressed and bathed in the sea (for the first time in my life), a very nice bathing woman attending me. I thought it delightful, till I put my head under the water when I thought I would be stifled.

The beach hut is still there, beside the little sandy beach, a very pretty, nicely painted caravan on four large black wheels. There are some steps leading up to it, so you can peep in, but not enter. It even had a lavatory inside – jolly handy, lucky thing – which, by staring through a window, I could just make out.

The ever-so-clever and handy Albert also created a floating swimming pool out at sea for his children. The pool has long gone, but there's a photograph of it in which it looks like a large paddling pool, floating a few yards out in the sea. It's big enough to have a proper swim in. You can see the royal children splashing around, attendants on hand, ready to rescue them if need be. What fun.

Also in the grounds is the Swiss Cottage, a large and handsome alpine chalet. It was erected in 1853 for Victoria and Albert's children; here they learned carpentry, gardening and cookery, entertained their parents for tea, and sold them produce they had grown themselves in their little garden. You can see their individual garden tools and wheelbarrows with their initials on. So sweet. So very like idyllic, colour-supplement family life today, among right-thinking, enlightened, middle-class, affluent families.

We then walked back to the main house and had coffee on the terrace with Michael, outside his office, before he took us on a tour of the interior. But not all of it, thank goodness. I think we would be still there, if we had attempted to visit every room, corridor and closet. Michael was not even sure how many rooms there are in the whole house but he estimated two hundred. Quite a lot of them are empty – rooms left over when the Convalescent Hospital for Officers, which occupied the household and main wings from 1904, was closed. The poet and novelist Robert Graves was one of its inmates during the First World War, as was the writer A. A. Milne. Graves was president of a humorous society, the Royal Albert Society. One day on the Osborne beach he found an old ship's fender some of whose knotted ropes had frayed so much they looked like human hair. Graves dressed it in some trousers and a discarded boot he found further along the beach, decorated the whole thing with seaweed, then alerted a passing coastguard to the presence of a dead body. The coastguard stopped a few yards short of the 'corpse' and exclaimed, holding his nose, 'Pooh, don't he 'alf stink.' The hoax was reported in the local papers.

The hospital closed in 2000 and seems to have been empty ever since, while English Heritage make up their mind what to do with the space. Flats or a hotel have been discussed, but not deemed suitable for such a historic and royal site.

During lockdown, only Michael and four other members of staff stayed on duty. Michael busied himself updating the catalogue of contents. 'We have ten thousand items in the house, all of which have been catalogued, but I had to update them and check them.'

In a normal year Osborne House receives 360,000 visitors, making it one of the most popular of English Heritage's attractions. There is a staff of around a hundred, including gardeners, which is roughly the same number of staff as when Queen Victoria lived there.

I said how much we had loved the beach and all the gardens and the trees and walks. Where was the best view of them from the house? Michael got out his keys and took us up some hidden stairs, bare and empty, and on to the roof – which is not accessible to the public.

The views were stunning, down into the formal gardens, then to the wooded path to the beach, and beyond over the Solent, alive as ever with yachts, tankers and cruise liners.

Victoria and Albert often came up on the roof in the evening after dinner, to watch the moonlight. That is, of course, when they were not having petty rows and sulking, which they did, like all couples.

Then we went downstairs and began a tour of the state rooms – at least the ones which were open. The Durbar Room reminds you that Queen Victoria was also Empress of India, and had two Indian servants on her staff at Osborne. It is a large dining room but, decor-wise, a bit mad and mixed up. One half is in traditional Tudor style, with a minstrels' gallery. The other half is Indian, like a temple, very ornate.

The formal dining table was set for twenty people. It was going to be a sumptuous meal, by the look of it, each guest with their own menu and lots of cutlery and glasses. It was all, of course, a staged setting. I examined the sparkling glasses which seemed a bit modern for the surroundings.

'I bought them in Jenners in Edinburgh,' said Michael. 'They are brand-new but they are of an antique style. I thought they would suit our dining room tableau. The Jenners assistant asked me how many glasses I would be needing and I said two hundred. They were very surprised – and delighted.' One of the advantages of going contemporary is that, should any light-fingered visitor – perish the thought – try to slip a crystal tumbler into their pocket, it would be pretty cheap to replace.

But it seems that visitors to Osborne are generally well behaved, consisting as they do of very well brought-up family parties or academic researchers – practically all of them British. 'We don't get many foreign visitors. Perhaps they think the Isle of Wight is hard to get to and they haven't heard about Queen Victoria and Osborne House.'

During Victoria's time, Osborne had many famous visitors. Most of her children married into other European royal families, just as she had done, and an assortment of kings, queens, princes and princesses descended on the Isle of Wight at one time or another. Kaiser Wilhelm II – Victoria's grandson and a keen yachtsman – was a frequent guest.

Parties and musical evenings were arranged for these distinguished visitors. Jenny Lind, known as the Swedish nightingale, gave a recital. In 1878 Alexander Graham Bell gave a demonstration of his new invention – the telephone – which he had patented just two years earlier. 'It is rather faint and one must hold the tube rather close to one's ear,' reported the Queen. Other innovations included a lift and an early version of central heating.

Queen Victoria worked on state papers while she was in residence. In the Queen's sitting room, you can see the two desks where she and Albert sat, side by side, looking out of the window, working away. There was a bell push powered by electricity which could be pressed to summon staff. Prince Albert's desk is slightly smaller than the Queen's – he being in effect her secretary and PA. This was where they conducted affairs of state and received visiting ministers from London.

'From this little room,' said Michael, 'Queen Victoria was controlling the whole of the British empire.'

One of the notable features you spot as you wander round the staterooms and halls and corridors, is the amount of naked flesh on show – all in the best possible taste. Massive paintings of classical scenes, which just happen to contain beautiful, bare-breasted young women, throwing out their arms, displaying and preening themselves. Also quite a few bare male bums on a staircase, firm and solid and athletic. The Victorians were very keen on naked flesh, as long as it was either allegorical or classical.

At last Michael took us to the Queen's private quarters,

unlocking the door. The Queen's dressing room featured her own bath and shower. I examined the bath, which was in a sort of cupboard, very dark and cramped, not a proper room. Michael told us the bath was made of mahogany and copper, pointing out that despite appearances, it was very modern thanks to the hot and cold running water which Albert had organised. Victoria didn't need maids running up and down stairs with buckets of water. She could fill the bath herself by turning on the taps unless, of course, Dear Albert did it for her.

Albert's bedroom is about twenty yards away, across a landing, and he also had his own bath and shower. In his case, the bath is in a proper, spacious room with a window. Just a few feet away there is a twenty-foot-high, classical painting of a stunning naked woman. It must have been disconcerting for Albert to be looking at her every morning. Michael pointed out that the painting is allegorical. Hercules is standing looking at the naked woman. So Albert may have liked the painting not just for the nudity but because of the symbolic role reversal – that Hercules is really being subservient to the Queen, just as Albert was in real life.

For forty years after Albert's death, a servant still brought hot water into his dressing room every morning. Was Victoria attempting to maintain their private quarters as they had been, long after he died? It is thought she had forgotten to cancel the order for hot water.

I asked Michael if he thought the royal couple slept mainly in separate bedrooms. Which was the fashion among royalty and aristocracy – and still happens today. We presume, of course, said Michael, as they had nine children, they were sleeping together a good part of the night, with Albert perhaps going back to his quarters in the morning to have a bath and get dressed.

Finally, we were taken into the Queen's actual bedroom. It was a bit eerie and creepy, as there were ghostly sheets and coverings over her bed and the furniture. This was to preserve them during the period that the house had been closed to the public. The bedroom was not quite ready yet to be reopened, so we were jolly lucky to get in.

The Queen's bed is a tall four-poster with drapes and a commemorative plaque at the top put up by one of her daughters. Beside this bed, sleeping alone for the next forty years, she kept her favourite portrait of Albert – looking very manly as a knight in armour.

Michael also told us, although we couldn't see for ourselves, because the bed itself was roped off, that there is a silver plaque at the bottom of the headboard, with two dates inscribed, 1846 and 1861. It took Michael and other researchers some time to work out their significance.

'We think one date marks the first night they slept together in this bed and the second date was the last time they slept together in this bed.'

That evening, back in our cottage in Ryde, I decided I would get a plaque made for our bed. It would have the date of 20 September 2020 inscribed on it – the first night Claire and I had slept together in our own home. Just one plaque, one date. After all, who knows what is yet to come...

CHAPTER 14

Music men

Festival-goers in the Isle of Wight, 1969

f you had to ask the average Brit what they know about the Isle of Wight, I wonder what they would say? They know roughly where it is – sort of bottom of the map of England, in the middle, sticking out a bit into the sea, but that is about all. They would have to think hard to conjure up images or places.

Osborne House perhaps or the Needles. Cowes Week, with all the yachts. Parkhurst prison, that is well-known – or, at least, was when it had its famous inmates and the name might still register. There again, some folks might well suggest it is in Devon, confusing it with Dartmoor prison, also the residence of some infamous offenders.

Among the younger generation, the Isle of Wight Festival would get a lot of name recognition because of the legendary bands and stars who once played there, long before most younger pop fans were born. When we moved to the island, I too struggled to recall what little I ever knew or had read about. I could remember Bob Dylan playing, though I was not sure which year, or if a music festival of any form still took place on the island (it does). It turns out it was 1969 when Dylan appeared. Stories, photographs and films and the chaos and dramas associated with that particular festival still appear in books and the press – the year when 150,000 turned up to listen to him, including John Lennon, George Harrison, Ringo Starr, Keith Richards, Jane Fonda and, according to rumour, Elizabeth Taylor and Richard Burton.

The 1970 festival was even bigger, attracting – take this slowly – 600,000. That is at least five times the size of the island's population. How on earth did they all get there? Today the ferries seem full all the time anyway. There are contemporary photographs showing the 1970 crowds and it is hard to believe they are not a fiddle, a montage perhaps, photoshopped, faked photos. The 1970 festival was the largest outdoor pop festival the world had ever known until that point, bigger even than Woodstock. It featured The Who, The Doors, Miles Davis, Joni Mitchell. The star attraction was Jimmy Hendrix, who died just a few months later.

And yet it all began with three local brothers called Foulk – one a printer, one an estate agent, one an art student – who had grown up on the island and had no connections with the pop world or the music industry. They had held their first concert in 1968, attracting eight thousand to listen to Jefferson Airplane, The Pretty Things and others. Their original aim was to raise funds to build an indoor swimming pool.

After the success of 1969, the 1970 festival grew into a monster. Although well-organised for its time, it ended up losing money, despite all those hundreds of thousands attending. The three mega-festivals on the trot, growing more enormous every year, were enough. There was no 1971 festival and none again on the island for the next thirty years.

By chance, just a month or so ago, I met Ray Foulk in Ryde at an event, talking about his book, *Stealing Dylan from Woodstock* (Medina Publishing, 2015). He was a rather distinguished gentleman, academic looking, who today lives in Oxford and works as an architect, author and environmentalist. Back in the 1960s, he was a printer on the Isle of Wight with hippie leanings. It was later, after his heady years as a festival promoter, that he resumed full-time education and got a place at Cambridge to study architecture.

He has written several books about those three amazing Isle of Wight festivals, and appeared in films and documentaries. People still ask him how he did it, how – with no experience or connections – did he attract Dylan, the most famous pop star in the world, to the Isle of Wight of all places?

'Actually, I didn't really know who he was,' he smiled. 'OK... I had heard his name, but I had no connections with him. It was just luck and timing, I suppose. I told him that Tennyson had lived on the Isle of Wight, having heard that Tennyson was Dylan's favourite poet. Dylan then decided not to go to Woodstock and instead decided to come three thousand miles to appear somewhere he had never been to before, the Isle of Wight.'

The total cost of bringing Dylan to the island was $87,000 – a bargain, even at the time. In the one press conference he gave, when asked why he had come to the Isle of Wight, Dylan did confirm he wanted to see the home of Tennyson. Alas, it was owned at the time by Fred Pontin, of holiday camp fame, who was against all these hippie types invading the island and lowering the tone. But Dylan did get to visit Osborne House.

So what happened in 1971 to bring it all to an end on the Isle of Wight?

The island was always a strange choice of venue to host hippie-style pop festivals – not just geographically but because the population was not a natural fit. The established citizens tended to be rather old-fashioned and behind the times, while newcomers were – on the whole – retired middle-class professionals, posh 'county' types or sailing enthusiasts. After the mass invasion of festival-goers in 1970, when bad behaviour by the vast crowds caused considerable disruption to life on the island, there was something of a local uprising. They said, never again, we don't want any more pop festivals. The cry was taken up by the local MP, local councils and other notables, leading to an addition to the Isle of Wight County Council Act of 1971. It banned all public events on the island with crowds of more than five thousand people. And that was it. Peace at last. Well, for a while at least, until the festival was revived in 2002. But more about that in a moment.

During the summer of 2021, despite the island having been

through the ravages of Covid and lockdown still lingering with us, massive posters and billboards announcing the line-up for the latest festival started to appear. There were also plenty of references to the Isle of Wight festival in the national newspapers, which mentioned the stars who were coming and also how much the tickets would be; apparently they started at £70. Young people must have so much money these days. But then all pop festivals cost a fortune today. Perhaps the Isle of Wight attracts the more mature music fans, couples in their thirties, bringing their families, making a holiday of it?

Then I wondered who organises it. The council? Or some private promoter?

I did not know that the man in charge of it was living not far away from us. Not quite a local, in fact; a global pop music legend who has organised pop concerts on a vast scale for many years and been an agent or promoter for all the biggest bands in the world these last fifty years. Step forward John Giddings.

I invited him for a drink in our little hideaway. He arrived looking ever so smooth and cosmopolitan – in a real leather jacket, black pullover, tight black trousers and highly polished black shoes, fit and ageless, with fashionably short grey hair and a tan. Not quite one of the holidaymakers you normally see getting off the hovercraft. I had never spotted him before – not on the beach or in the Co-op or Sainsbury's or any of the caffs and shops. Yet he has a home not far from us, near Ryde Pier.

His main property is in Barnes and he has been frightfully busy this year, running Solo, his music promotion business in Fulham. John is sixty-seven and was born in St Albans, Herts, where his father worked for the council. He went to the private St Albans school, but was never considered academic. 'In my year, thirty-three boys went to Oxbridge. No teacher suggested I should try. I did do A-levels, but just scraped through. There are two forms of intelligence in life. One is academic and the other is what I call "suss intelligence" – street intelligence, knowing how to survive on the streets. You couldn't give an academic person a piece of string and an old oil drum and tell them to make a raft – but suss people would have a go.'

John's passion as a boy was playing the guitar and watching bands playing. 'I loved it, but once you see professional musicians perform, you realise how poor you are. I knew I could never make a living from playing, but I got it into my head very early what I wanted do – promote the latest music in pop concerts.

'I remember one event I put on in Harpenden and a skinhead came up and said, "If you don't stop playing that fucking shit music I will kick your fucking head in." But I loved it and was not put off. All my friends at school had no idea what they wanted to do in life, but I always knew, long before I even went to university. I went to Exeter University, purely because I wanted to become social secretary and book all the bands.'

Which he did. This was a period in the early seventies when a lot of bands – who were later world-famous – played early gigs on college campuses. The bigger, well-organised universities could pay groups just as much money as the smaller commercial venues and attract just as large crowds. While he was at Exeter, organising concerts for the students, John booked The Kinks, Procul Harum and Genesis: 'We had to pay Genesis six hundred pounds – and all they demanded as extras was cups of tea.'

John ended up with a pass degree in philosophy and sociology, but as social secretary he was a big fish in a little pond, and he made the most of it, finding out how the music industry worked, making contacts. He joined a promotion firm straight away and eventually set up on his own. 'I did have a partner but he let me down so I called the company Solo from then on.'

He went on to promote concerts with David Bowie, The Rolling Stones, The Police, Lady Gaga, Madonna and many others, winning several awards for being promoter of the year.

'Then, in 2001, we were asked if we were interested in promoting the Isle of Wight Festival, which was being re-formed. There was a girl in our office from the Isle of Wight and she was keen we should see the council and discuss it. I had a meeting with them, told them my proposal. I was interviewed with a colleague in front of fifteen councillors. They didn't seem to know much about festivals and didn't really seem interested in the future of festivals on the island. They voted in front of us and the vote went 8-7 in our favour. I discovered later that they had broken their own protocol. They should not have had the vote in front of us, while we were still there. Anyway, I was offered the job and took it. I thought it would be fun.

'I had organised so many concerts at various festivals over the years for other people. I thought it would be amusing and interesting to run my own festival for a change. In that first year, it lost £350k. In the second year, the loss was around £500k. But the council did not give up on the festivals. They could see the economic and publicity benefits to the island with so many thousands coming.'

John reckons that, in the twenty years since he started running the festival, it has generated around ten million pounds annually for the island. How? The answer is in the number of visitors. Between 50,000 and 60,000 music fans come each year, so the ferries get a lot of extra income for a start. Then there are the hotels, bed-and-breakfast places and campsites, as well as pubs and restaurants, that make money from the festival-goers.

'Now we do, more or less, break even, but pop festivals are not cheap.' There was no festival in 2020, because of Covid, but for their 2021 festival, they attracted headliners such as Liam Gallagher, Duran Duran and Snow Patrol. 'By April we had sold 35,000 of the tickets. We have also started taking bookings for 2022 – and that is going well.' Were audiences nervous about shelling out for tickets in times of Covid. John said, 'They are paying up front, but if we have to cancel or change the date for any reason, they get their money back. I am sure we will do well this year. And that there won't be another lockdown. People do say my middle name is "Lucky". I suppose I have always been pretty lucky.'

In 2018, he sold 75 per cent of the festival to one of the world's biggest concert promoters, US firm Live Nation, but he has remained managing director.

'I look upon the Isle of Wight as my hobby. I run it for fun. My main business is still running Solo, where I have a full-time staff of ten.' His definition of 'fun' is perhaps different to most. 'It is a worrying business, running an open-air music festival, so it is best to have the backing of a much bigger company. You don't know what worry is until the day it begins and you look out at a field of mud with the rain pissing down and realise that today you could lose two million pounds.

'One year we paid £100,000 to erect a "B-stage" where the Rolling Stones could rehearse. That was all it was for. I remember thinking that, if I get knocked down by a car tomorrow, I will have brought the Stones to the Isle of Wight. In 2012 it poured down for four weeks – before and also during the concerts. The ferries got stuck as well. Oh God, we had so many problems. But then we always do... You can supply fifty thousand urinals, but blokes will still go and pee in a hedge. So, locals will complain. I have thought of erecting plastic hedges and putting up signs saying "Piss here".'

The festival is today held every year near Newport, in Seaclose Park, land owned by the council. His partner in the venture, who is mostly responsible these days for running the festival, is his wife Caroline, a Durham graduate who trained as a lawyer. She was working in a firm of solicitors and was called in to advise his company when they were involved in a legal battle with a local authority over ticket sales. 'I first talked to her when I was in a taxi, driving across London. I was getting bored. I noted she had a very posh voice. During the call, I said, "Call yourself a fucking solicitor? Have you read the fucking contract?"'

'She replied, "It would have helped if you had read the contract before signing it."'

Despite this unpromising start, they married in 2007 in Cliveden House, a grand country mansion on the Thames in Berkshire. He has three children and four grandchildren from a previous marriage. She has one daughter, now also a student at Durham. He owns a property in Portugal, where he and Caroline eventually plan to spend three months of every year, and they have the house in Ryde, a stunning Victorian mansion. 'I used to stay at the Premier Inn in Newport in the early years, but decided I needed a place of my own on the island. I didn't want any more people accusing me of being a rich bastard from London who comes over once a year, takes all their money, and just walks away.' Their home has a long garden going down to the sea and a slipway to the beach running down the side of the house, but he didn't own the whole property at first.

'In 2006, I bought a large flat in the house, then realised I did not have the garden. The woman who owned the garden and the rest of the house said she was selling it. I said, "I will buy it from you, if you sell it to me – now." And she did. So we got the whole house. At the moment it is nightmare as we have rising damp.'

Don't tell me, I said. We have been through that. I think the Isle of Wight has damp basements everywhere. It must be the result of being a small island, with the sea all around.

John's accent is hard to place. Not posh, considering he went to a fee-paying school and good university. It's more a London suburban accent, sounding a bit like a Hertfordshire version of Mick Jagger.

He seems to have had quite a few disagreements over the years with the local council and with the police. 'They just don't understand what we are doing, what our problems are and, of course, don't appreciate enough just how much we contribute to the local economy. The other year there were about 35,000 people one day trying to get into the field at the same time. The roads were totally blocked, all the way to Ryde. People were stuck for so long that some were falling asleep in the cars. The police were doing nothing, did not know how to solve the problem, just standing there, doing nothing. I walked along the road and opened a gate into a field. I said to the drivers of the stationary vehicles; there you are, you can park here in this field and then walk to the show ground.

'I didn't own the field. I didn't know who did. When the field had eventually filled up with cars, I went to the farmhouse, knocked at the door and said, "Excuse me, I would like to rent your field." We then agreed a deal.'

The logistics of getting fifty thousand people across the Solent from the mainland is not his problem – he leaves that to the ferries. 'There are at least 180 crossings a day during the festival – counting the two car ferries, the catamaran and the hovercraft. They must make a fortune out of our festival. I did once do a deal with Red Funnel. I hired one of their ferries especially to take Amy Winehouse and her entourage across the Solent. That was a scene. I am surprised the ferry ever arrived on the island. When we had Bryan Ferry playing, I got him and his lot to take the ferry. I organised some publicity photos of Ferry on the ferry.

'There are always unforeseen problems each year which have to be solved on the day – and, of course, the rain is a permanent worry. But so far, since I have been involved, the big names have always turned up. No one has let us down.'

I wished him luck for this year and freedom from new Covid variants and new quarantine regulations. It was scheduled for

September 2021, which was going to be exactly a year since Claire and I moved onto the island. Would we be able to go and celebrate our arrival, bless our project, and ourselves?

CHAPTER 15

Wayne and Father Stephen

The Esplanade at Ryde, early twentieth century

On my morning walk along the front I always stop and chat to Wayne opening up his café, The Big Kahuna. Strange name for a café – and Wayne is a rather strange person himself. Always cheerful, handsome, tanned, with excellent teeth, in his fifties, always full of old chat, but I never realised at first why he was so well-known, with all those people waiting to talk to him. And I did not know, till the day he told me about his background.

'I am a bit of an anomaly on this island. I come from a family of showmen, travellers, gypsies – whatever you want to call them. I was brought up in a caravan in a family of travellers and we went round the country with a travelling fair. My family had done it for generations. At one time they had a travelling menagerie but that had gone by the time I was born.

'Most of my family cannot read or write, but I was sent to school, now and again, in the winter-time when the fair was closed. Then Harold Wilson and the socialists came along and started a social experiment to educate the travelling community. I was one of six who were chosen to go to a private prep school – Yateley Manor in Surrey. I saw two sides of racial prejudice. At school I would get bullied as a gyppo and then when I came home in my red blazer and gray flannel shorts they all thought I was posh and gave me a hard time too. My little brother later joined me but he was bullied by a school teacher who forced him to have a cold water shower because we were dropped off late at the start of term. My father heard his screams, ran in and thumped the teacher and pulled us out of there. I left school at fourteen for good.

'I didn't really want to follow my family into the fairground business, but I worked on the fairground as a showman for a while. In fact, I invented a stall. It was called "Shoot Saddam". If you shot and got near his nose on a superimposed target, you got a prize.'

This, of course, is a reference to Saddam Hussein, president and dictator of Iraq, who invaded Kuwait in 1990 and was finally executed in 2006. Wayne tells stories at such a lick it is hard to stop him and get him to explain everything.

So, how did you end up here in Ryde, Wayne, after your fairground years?

'I eventually started printing the Saddam targets and made quite a bit of money. In fact, I used to go to Stringfellows and The Hippodrome up the West End. But before that, in the early eighties, a posh girl used to follow me around the fairs and said that she had grandparents in Miami, so let's go out there for the winter while the fairs are closed. I ended up living there for five years. She worked as a model and I managed a reggae bar in Coconut Grove. The Americans couldn't really understand my accent, unless I slowed my speech down but when they heard I was British they would say, "Do you know George Michael or James Bond?"

'I then started a packaged snack food business, buying the ingredients and making little, red-hot snacks from chickpeas that me and my partner Donald from Trinidad sold to local bars. We did so well we got a contract with Eastern Airlines to provide miniature-size snacks for passengers on their planes. The US government wanted to deport me so my girlfriend said, "Let's get married." She had dual nationality so I would become a citizen and we could remain in Florida.

'The Eastern Airlines contract later doubled in size because we were asked to supply more flights and we had to borrow money to get larger premises to meet the demand, producing lots more of the channa chickpea snacks. Then, one day I returned home, switched on the news to hear that Eastern Airlines had gone bankrupt. That was the beginning of the end really. I soon ran out of money and Chrissie, my wife, left me. I eventually came back to the UK, where I discovered I was just in time for the summer of love. Acid house festivals had become a big thing in the late eighties and I started taking my family fairground rides and equipment to them. Acid parties were illegal but very busy, so at first I made quite a bit of money. Once they became legal, they were not as popular.

'I always wanted to work by the seaside so, about 1991, I decided to come to the Isle of Wight. There were already some showmen on the island. Travellers who trade at the seaside are known as "sandscratchers" – because they scratch a living on the sand. They tend to look down upon the travelling showman. I worked in the Peter Pan fairground for a while, here in Ryde along the front, and then I bought a bar and named it Atlantis Sports Bar. I took over Sandy Slip kiosk in 1995... Eventually, we got planning permission and turned it into a larger Wimpy Bar and traded it as a Wimpy for thirteen years.

'I decided to convert it and make it more modern. I decided it should also have a modern name – The Big Kahuna. It was my son, Lloyd, who thought of the name. It comes from the film *Pulp Fiction*, when they are talking about a fictional hamburger joint... I have since acquired a few other outlets along the Ryde front...'

Phew, well done, Wayne, that was some story. He was clearly quite an entrepreneur. I had admired his Ryde Pier café, not knowing he owned it, for its stylised 1930s' lettering – very fitting for a seaside resort. 'It's Romany sign lettering,' he said. Which was news to me; I never knew gypsies had their own fonts. I have also bought stuff at his souvenir shop nearby (again not knowing it was his) because of the excellent prices. But that's not all: he's involved in island politics as well.

'Yeah, for the last twenty years I have been a local councillor.

When I first started, Ryde was not a town council. We had what was called the "forum" and I was a representative of the beach-front community. Eventually I became mayor. I moved on to the county council. I am still doing both.

'I began as an independent because I am not really political. I didn't want to get mixed up in a party. I just wanted to help the community. But the Tories are the dominant Isle of Wight party and held most of the power at the time and asked me to join them. In 2012, I joined the Tories and got elected in 2013 as a Tory councillor. My friends said, "It's the rat joining a sinking ship." I felt I was selling my soul but it seemed a sensible trade-off as I wanted to improve tourism. I could not have joined Labour. Showmen never do. And, anyway, I have been a victim of Labour social experimentation.

'I have now got several council portfolios on the island. I look after regeneration, business development, tourism, events and leisure. In normal times I am attending between nine and seventeen meetings a week. I do get paid. I get £7.5k a year as a councillor and another £7.5k because of my portfolios. Sounds a lot, but I have to pay two people to look after this place when I am at council meetings.'

Wayne's wife, Iso, also works in The Big Kahuna, and sharp-eyed readers may recall that I met her back in Chapter 7. She was brought up in Namibia and christened Isobel, but this was always shortened to Iso. She later moved to South Africa, where she worked in security, as a bodyguard and eventually ended up in the state prosecutions department.

'I first heard about Iso,' said Wayne, 'through my cousin Alfred, who had moved to Pretoria and opened a gun shop. One day he told me that he had a friend who wanted to leave the country after a contract was taken out on them. This person was none other than Iso, who worked as a witness protection officer during the Mandela years. My cousin knew I had a couple of flats in Ryde and might be able to put her up. I was getting divorced and my two sons were quite young at the time; I wondered if she could help me look after them. So she moved in. We are now married and have a daughter aged thirteen.

'There is nothing much happening here on the island in the winter – no tourists or seaside attractions open. Our fantasy retirement, me and Iso, is that we will buy a property abroad in the southern hemisphere – a shop or a stall on the beach, perhaps in Australia or South Africa. So we will be living in the sun in the summer and by a beach all the year round. But we won't, of course, give up the Isle of Wight. We think it is the best place in the world. It is only five miles across the Solent to the mainland, but really it is like five hundred miles away. The countryside is so different here and so spacious. And we love the community. Not many communities in the whole of England would elect a traveller as a councillor, would they?

'What I don't like about the Isle of Wight is the sometimes negative mentality. A lot of people think they are being hard done by. It really is because they don't realise what they've got. The old local families have probably never or rarely travelled to the mainland in their lives and don't know what life can be like over there, as I do, after living in various places. I also realise that tourism is vital to the island.

'I have been asked to become a Tory MP. In fact, I went through the selection process, passed and was put on the official selected candidates list. But I am not going to stand. It was just to see if I could get selected. I couldn't stand going to Westminster. I love it so much on the island. And I have my family and my businesses to attend to.

'We go to my Romany family weddings and funerals now and again, but I've mostly lost touch with them. They are only really interested in their own community and don't listen much when you go on about what you're doing. They are not really interested in what goes on outside show-land. They would probably take more interest in me if I had failed. Then they could say I should never have left. Frank Sinatra sang everyone loves a winner – but the truth is, most prefer a loser. It makes them feel better. Showmen say, "Any fool can make money but it takes a wise man to hold on to it."'

Very true. Thanks for all that, Wayne. I had to sit down and have a coffee at his stall, after all that torrent of talk.

Before I left, I asked Councillor Wayne Whittle for a little help on purely personal matters. No, not about me and Claire. Though he is clearly a man of the world. In his capacity as a councillor, I wondered, could he give me the names and contacts of council officials I can write to about my drainage problem? See if I can put some of the blame on them...

Our conversation concluded, I continued my normal, daily promenade on the promenade. I came across a parked vehicle I had not seen recently. I had been wondering if the occupant had been ill, though I had never talked to him so far. His vehicle was hard to miss – an ancient, VW camper van painted bright orange. On the outside are lots of stickers and hand-painted messages, such as 'Wight Trash' and 'This urinal is not in use to enable social distancing'.

I peered through the window at a bed, a stove, a TV, lots of boxes and ornaments, posters, old rugs and old sacks, but all of them very colourful. It looked like the inside of a leftover hippies' den from the 1960s. Then I sensed I was being watched. By the sea wall stood the man who must have been the owner of the van, a tall, straggly-bearded person with a woolly hat. He was sitting over what looked like an upturned tin can in which there was a wood fire burning. He had obviously been cooking sausages for his breakfast.

When we first arrived on the island, he and his colourfully painted vehicle had been parked in exactly the same place for months. I did nod and say hello to him when passing, being awfully friendly, but he was usually nattering to a lady friend or holding his dog. I imagined he was looking at me a bit suspiciously, as if I might be spying on him. Then suddenly he just disappeared. For months, his van was not in its usual place, just yards along from The Big Kahuna.

Now I went over to the wall and said, 'Hi, haven't seen you or your dog for several months. How are you?'

He explained that his dog had died. She was very old and very blind and one reason he always parked in the same spot was so that the dog could jump straight down on to the beach and not get run down by other cars. As for him, he had had a stroke. Three months ago, he said, he collapsed while getting out of his van but managed to drag himself inside, start the car and drive home to his room in Ryde. He collapsed again in his room and was unconscious for a while.

I had assumed he lived permanently in his van, as it looked so well-equipped for occupation. I didn't realise he had a place in the town. His friends realised there must be something wrong with him; one of them gained entry to his flat and took him to hospital. He lost the use of his right side for several months but now, so he said, he was back to normal. And back to his normal habits – driving most days in his van to this part of the beach, then sitting all day, making himself meals, talking to passers-by, or just looking at the sea.

He said I could call him Father Stephen; most people did. He was brought up in Wexford, Ireland, and for a time attended a seminary for priests. He then came to England.

'People call me "Father" because so many people talk to me and I talk to them. I take confessions and I give penances. I often see a couple walking along not talking to one another. I talk to both of them, hear their stories and their worries and try to help. That is why I am Father Stephen.'

His full name is Stephen Reed-Enerstad and he is fifty-six, much younger than I imagined from his straggly beard and worn clothes. He worked for many years as a school caretaker at Richard Taunton College, Southampton.

'You've not heard of it? It is very famous. Benny Hill went there.'

He has been married and has two children but has lived alone for the last twenty-odd years and still sees himself as a bit of a hippy. Until his stroke he was still skateboarding and windsurfing. He has travelled much of the world, often living in vans.

His present vehicle, the distinctive orange VW, is twenty-nine years old and is a VW T4. He invited me inside and showed me his bed, his chemical lavatory, his TV, his heater and a stove. He calls the van Fanny and pointed to a notice which he got from a junk shop in the USA which says, 'Fanny's Rest Stop. Eat here and get gassed.'

He lived solely in the van for two years, until the winters drove him to his room. He can afford the rent as he has got a decent pension from his years as a caretaker.

'Sometimes I drive off into the woods in the middle of the island, often with a friend who also has a mobile home. We park side by side in the wood. Then we'll sit there for a few weeks, just looking at nature, gathering wood for the fire, cooking our own meals. I can be very sociable but I also like being on my own, enjoying my own company. I do a bit of reading. My favourite author is Bill Bryson.' He has made his own roof rack out of an old iron bedstead. On it was a water tank and on top of that he keeps what he calls his pitfire – a large metal pot with holes in it which he uses for cooking. 'This van is unique. It is going to die with me. I am not going to leave it to my children or my ex-wife. I have arranged with the lifeguards and given them some money and they will tow the van out onto the sands, about three miles out, till they get to the red pole, can you see it? And then burn the van.'

Won't that be an environmental hazard?

'I don't care, I won't be there. I will be dead. The lifeguards will scatter my ashes in the sea at the same time. It will be a Viking funeral. I have got Viking blood in me. I used to have red hair when I was young – until I went bald.'

I wished him good luck and said that I would see him again soon, I hoped.

I walked on to the Dell café and had one of their coffees, which are excellent. I love sitting there, looking back at the curve of the beach to Ryde, at the tower and the pier in the background. The coffee does cost £2.90, almost twice as much as it does at my halfway point, the Lifeboat station shop. But their coffee is instant.

When I eventually got home, I was too tired to explain to Claire my two encounters on the Ryde promenade, which I normally would. I wanted to have a lie-down.

CHAPTER 16

Words of warning

The seafront at Ryde, with All Saints'
Church on the right

Would Claire and I still be speaking by September? Still be chums and still have the house? Oh God, I hoped so, but we did seem to be having trivial rows and piddling disagreements.

Nothing serious, nothing worrying so far, just the usual boring silly irritations which always crop up in long relationships.

Nothing irritated me about Claire during our first rapturous months of living together. Oh no. I was just so thrilled to be with her, to have a companion for life, I hoped, or what's left of it. And I was so thrilled by our project, that we had found this house together, were creating a new life together, getting to know a new place and getting to know each other.

Now, after nine months, I was becoming too aware of some of her little ways. Just as I am sure she was finding some of my habits not as amusing as she once did.

She has a passion for washing clothes. I am messy – I am always dropping things down my front – but alone in my own house I was able to make T-shirts and trousers last three days. Underpants and socks I always change every day; I do have some standards.

She also seems to shop every day. I keep saying, 'Why don't you plan meals for a whole week, as my wife did, then you never have to think each day about what you are going to make?' That was a mistake, of course. I vowed never to go on about my wife when I first met Claire, but sometimes it slips out.

She pointed out, quite rightly, she was doing all the shopping and cooking, not me. And, anyway, since we arrived, the bulk of the shopping has been domestic items for the house – new sheets, new rugs, bathroom things, new tiles, new chairs. She can't trust me to buy curtains or carpets. I have no taste. By which she means I have not got her taste.

When we go for a walk and I insist on taking with me two pieces of fruit – usually a pear and an orange, which I eat as we walk – she shudders at the sight of me peeling the orange. Strangely enough, my wife also used to complain about me eating fruit in the street. 'Your hands will now be all sticky,' she would complain. I blame it on the sort of old-fashioned girls' high schools they went to. Girls eating in the street was a hanging offence.

Now, what are the other ways that I irritate her? Obviously, I am totally rational, sensible, caring and considerate, so what can she possibly object to?

I love arrangements, I am always trying to get her to commit to going somewhere at a certain time so I can put it in my diary – then I go mad if it gets changed. My excuse is I am still working, unlike her, so I need to be organised, meet my deadlines.

I am naturally pretty scruffy; I wear pullies with stains and holes, which really does upset her. I have tried to mend my ways – if not the holes. But she has smartened me up these last three years. She is so generous, when she does not have a great deal of money herself, lavishing presents and food and drinks on her friends, and on me.

Her cleaning is intense, hoovering, washing the floors. I come in from the beach, all ready to tell her some saga, about someone I have just met. I walk straight into the house, my mind elsewhere – and she goes mad. 'Take your shoes off! Now. There is sand everywhere! Oh God, I have just done it as well. You always seem to choose the wrong time.'

Behind her back I always break one of her golden rules – which is never to go to bed for my rest with my socks and trousers on. I lie, of course, say I never did, what an outrageous suggestion.

She says I am very demanding; goodness, what can she mean? I want her attention, cuddles and affection all the time. Sounds reasonable to me.

She also says I boss her around, criticising her, not appreciating all the huge amount of work she does in the house. I deny it; perish the thought. Am I not good-natured, cheerful, placid old Hunter with no real opinions or arrogance? Someone who never gets bad-tempered? Or so I think.

One of the things about living with a new person is that you suddenly become aware that your self-image is not always how the other person sees you. With age, you have become set in your ways, till you believe that how you behave is normal and sensible and socially acceptable. But Claire has got it into her head that I can be bossy. She says my children probably think the same, as probably Margaret did. 'Rubbish,' I always say.

I have at various times been a real boss, of just a few people, but I am sure I was not bossy. Just ever so friendly. I was the editor of my student newspaper at Durham, then later editor of the *Sunday Times* women's pages, and then editor of the *Sunday Times Magazine*, which was a much bigger job, as it was the heyday of the colour mags. All of these jobs were many years ago and I didn't do them for very long and I can hardly remember them. But she maintains I still have a tendency to tell people what to do. I say I am only helping them, making suggestions, offering advice based on my many years of experience.

But, alas, I am beginning to think Claire might be right. I have become a Bossy Betty, as we used to say in Carlisle, which I never thought I would. Claire has recently said something Margaret used to say: 'You always get what you want.' I wish. If only I did get my way.

One of the things which rather upset me after Margaret died was reading something in her diaries. She wrote a diary throughout her life – it amounted to about two million words. She wrote about both personal and professional matters, about her work as well as her domestic life. I found the diaries fascinating and have passed them all over to the British Library.

In her 1986 diary, she suddenly says, out of the blue, something which totally surprised me: 'I wonder when it was that Hunter became a hustler.'

The word 'hustler' upset me. It makes me sound so dodgy, as if I'm a con man. If she had said I was 'pushy' I might have found it more acceptable.

I thought about it a lot. I had changed so much over the years since we first met at school, when I was a nervous, hesitant, self-conscious, shy, little weedy boy – with so many chips on my shoulder – whereas she seemed born confident and middle class, even though we were from exactly the same background. Over the years, I picked up some of her confidence, and perhaps over-did it. I rarely take 'No' for an answer, always pushing and pulling, trying again when things don't work. Margaret believed in luck being something that happened to you – both good luck and bad luck. I believe you make your own luck; keep putting up ideas and one of them might stick; keep the balls in the air, some might land the right way. She maintained that when bad luck came, you could do nothing about it. Just prepare your mind and accept, be stoical. Which is what happened when she got cancer. From which she died in 2016.

We also had the trivial rows, the domestic squabbles, which Claire and I are experiencing, now we are living together. In the early stages of my relationship with Margaret, when we were courting, both still living in Carlisle, with me as a student and Margaret still at school in the upper sixth, trying the Oxbridge entrance exams, we had the most appalling rows.

'It'll never work,' she used to say. 'I will just make you unhappy. I am not good for you. We had better split now. Goodbye...'

This often happened out of the blue, when we were walking and talking, apparently happily, then it would all pour out. She said we were just too different. I was outgoing and optimistic and sociable, thought the best of everyone, whereas she was clinical and pessimistic and anti-social, saw things far too clearly and darkly.

'Don't be daft, lass,' I would say. 'I love you, that's all that matters, so stop twining on.'

Then she would take me through the sort of person she really was, analyse herself, so coldly and realistically, that I half began to think it was true, that we were totally unsuited. She said she never wanted to get married and never wanted children.

'The world is a horrible enough place as it is, without bringing more children into it.'

'Who's asking you, lass?' I would reply.

Sometimes her angst would lead to a most awful outburst and I would wonder about her mental condition. She was so much cleverer and analytical then me, brilliant at arguing. I could never change her mind, make her see sense. She would often storm off, marching ahead on her own. I would plod behind her, made miserable for a moment by what she had said, thinking it might be true. Then I would recover, tell her not to be so silly, she was imagining things, and give her a hug.

'You don't have to,' she would say.

But after a few years, when we knew without saying it that we were together for ever, her outbursts lessened. Marriage and children calmed her, deflected her demons. She also found success in her career and seemed content in the end – with me and with life.

Those early rows worried me at the time, her shouting at me for being stupid and not understanding her. But just as quickly they faded and, after a few days, I forgot she had ever thought or said such things. That is how I always cope. Put nasty things to the back of my mind, tell myself they never happen. That's what happened after she had her first operation for cancer – a double mastectomy, when she was young, aged around forty. Once she recovered, I wiped it from my mind. We never talked about it.

In the last decades of our marriage, I don't remember any rows at all. I know I annoyed her by doing various little things. I irritated her at breakfast by loudly scraping every last morsel from my muesli bowl, then wiping the bowl with my fingers and licking them. She went mad, saying it was disgusting. I was never even aware I was doing it. I am sure Claire would be equally furious if I did that today. But I cured myself.

With Claire, I am still, alas, transgressing, doing things which I know will lead to her being really annoyed.

The other day, after lunch, I went to bed for my afternoon rest. I had had two glasses of sauvingnon blanc, which was a mistake. I am trying to cut down, as I am putting on weight but, being together in our cottage, it does seem like being permanently on holiday. We both over-indulge. I closed the bedroom curtains, got into bed and was straight off, snoring away, when suddenly I felt the sheet and duvet being furiously pulled off me. I woke up with a start, wondering if I was having a nightmare. It was dark, with the curtains closed. I did not know if it was night or day. I often feel this, after my afternoon sleep, not knowing what day or time it is, or even where I am.

Still half-asleep, and in the dark, I imagined there was a figure in the room. Was it an intruder? Then I realised it was Claire. She was shouting at me. I eventually regained enough consciousness to understand I had been discovered wearing trousers in bed. She had pulled the duvet down to reveal my secret. With a furious tug, she pulled the duvet and sheets entirely off the bed, so I was fully revealed, lying on a bare mattress in trousers and socks. Oh God. That was the worst offence, proof of my appalling standards and disgusting behaviour. She stormed out of the bedroom, still shouting, and slammed the door.

I got up, a bit befuddled by the sudden storm, thinking, Why does she get so upset over such silly things? I decided I had better steer clear of her for a while, so I went straight out for a long walk along the beach, getting all the way to the Dell. But I walked too quickly and my back began to hurt, so I rested for a while, before limping back, moaning and feeling very sorry for myself. Claire was attentive and concerned, as she always is when I am complaining about my health. After all, during these last four years she has been with me through my triple heart bypass and my hernia op. But I could tell she was still furious.

After a good supper and yet more wine, we were chums again. I knew I had sinned during the day and did not want to raise the topic again. Being shouted at once was enough. If Claire is in a huff with me, or me with her, we try to make up before bedtime – or at least become civilised with one another. Obviously, I am always hoping for more, that she will allow me a cuddle even though I can see she is still in a mood. I know now it's best not to push it. That would only make things worse... I have learned a few things about Claire, after four years. I turned over, gave her the smallest, chastest peck on the cheek, muttered, 'Goodnight, darling, sleep tight, don't let the bugs bite.' Then I said, 'Sorry.'

I added, 'I don't mean sorry for mentioning bugs,' knowing she has a phobia about fleas or insects and dirt of any sort. 'I mean sorry about today, sleeping in my trousers and socks. I promise to mend my ways...'

She grunted, already asleep, or pretending to be.

'Don't forget our mantra,' I said. The mantra I had created which we each have to say out loud every night before we go to sleep, especially if there has been, er, any sort of atmosphere.

'WE ARE SO LUCKY!'

There was a pause, and then I heard her mutter it, her head under the duvet, her eyes already closed...

CHAPTER 17

Up the workers

RACING OFF RYDE

A poster produced for British Railways, promoting
their services to the Isle of Wight, 1950s

do know, of course, that Claire and I are not alone in bickering. When it is to do with domestic life, a common cause of irritation – what to do in the house, what needs replacing, and in what colour – one thing always helps: take it out on the workers. It does unite you, being able to blame everything on the workers.

And where the hell are they? They promised. Oh God.

Workmen not turning up when they said they would happens everywhere, in all parts of the country. But it seemed to be worse in the Isle of Wight, or so everyone had been telling us. Being on an island, tradespeople don't have a lot of competition. The half-decent ones are always fully booked. You can't really bring alternatives in from Portsmouth, near enough though it is as the crow flies, as the extra cost of the ferry would be enormous.

No wonder so many of our new friends, especially those in that very pukka enclave in Vernon Square – who, like us, have moved from London – all made the same joke: don't forget, this is the 'Isle of Wait'.

After months of waiting, both sets of workmen, with whom we had agreed estimates, promised they would come this very week. They would be there, definitely. Oh bliss.

The Damp Proof Company and DARES (which stands for Dial A Rod Engineering Services, an anagram I could never remember, informed us they would be delighting us with their presence first thing on Monday morning. We never expected them to coincide, but decided it would be a good thing. I suppose if you are going to have two separate jobs done in your house, both of which will produce dirt and noise and chaos – inside as well as outside – it makes sense to have both sets of workmen in at the same time and get the hell over with quickly. And – at least in theory – one lot, the damp proofers, would be inside, while the drainage people would be outside. Would we have enough tea and sugar to cope?

Claire was dreading the mess. But then she dreads any mess. The day before she was already fretting about the dirt to come, going to bed early, on her own, as she said she would have to be up at the crack of dawn to get ready. Claire insisted we had to be up and ready by eight. I said, 'Don't be daft. I bet none of them will be here before nine.' So it meant no tea in bed. Oh gawd, it is going to be so awful, she moaned. I can't bear it, I hate all mess, just when I have got the house so clean and nice.

Personally, I was rather looking forward to meeting all these real islanders. Be nice to talk to some locals, born and bred caulkheads, to see how they like living here. Dave the damp proofer arrived on his own at 9.30 a.m., which was pretty good. He was very efficient and organised looking and began unloading his gear.

Claire had already taken down all our touching family photos from the walls of the dining room and removed any soft furnishings, so Dave was able to start at once putting up sheets, covering the floor and sealing the doors with tape, so no dust would escape.

We waited and waited, but there was no sign of the drains people. I eventually picked up a voicemail (which I always forget to check and anyway my mobile signal is rubbish in this house – it only works in certain rooms). A female voice said that Martin, the boss of the drains firm, had been delayed on the mainland and could not get back in time.

We had not yet met Martin. A few weeks earlier, when we were arranging for him to come and inspect the problem, it turned out he could only make a time when both Claire and I were over in Cowes, so we gave our house keys to David and Jason who live along the street. They waited an hour for him, but he never turned up. Oh God, it's so embarrassing when you ask a favour of people and they end up being messed around.

I then received another voicemail message from the assistant, 'Sorry, Martin has had to go to Parkhurst prison.' No, he had not been locked up. They had an urgent drains problem which he had gone to sort out. But he would be with us soon. In the end, he never turned up at all that day. But Dave the damp-proofing man got straight to work, stripping off the plaster up to about a metre high on two walls. Then, with an enormous drill, he started to bore holes in the brickwork. The noise could probably be heard two streets away.

Dave worked all day, without a rest, even refused tea and coffee, had no awful music on, so that was good. It was a bit hard to talk to him, with all the noise, and with him being completely masked up and wearing protective clothing. And anyway, Claire had said I was not to disturb him – there was to be no asking of cheeky personal questions. He was here to work, not to be cross-examined.

On arrival, he had explained he was on his own today because the wife of his usual assistant had been kicked by a horse. Unusual excuse, I thought, though I did believe him. In London, when workmen let you down or turn up late, they rarely bother to apologise or give an explanation. You know the real reason. They are balancing several jobs at the same time and yours is the least lucrative.

The noise and dust and grime was appalling all day, as Dave worked non-stop, not even taking a lunch break. At four he suddenly said he had to pack up and leave, as he had to pick up his two kids from school. So we gained a small insight into his personal life, but I hoped there was more to come. I am so nosey about everyone I ever meet, asking them intimate questions which they don't have to answer. Within a few weeks, I have usually forgotten all the answers.

On leaving, Dave also forewarned us he might be late starting the next day. Some mixture he needed for the injections had not come yet but should be on the ferry. It made me realise that, while locals might moan about workmen, they are dependent on so many of their supplies coming from the mainland. And if they are one-man bands, as Dave appeared to be, they can get stuck when deliveries fail to arrive.

The drains men turned up the following day. They worked in the yard, so I had little chance to chat them up and keep them from their task. But Dave was inside all the time. Behind Claire's back, while she was out shopping, I managed to have manly chats with him. I started with football but, alas, that got me nowhere. He did not follow the sport. But he did seem to soften a bit – he was not as remote as he had appeared at first and eventually accepted the odd cup of tea. He even put his radio on for a bit, though he could not possibly hear it with all his drilling.

Dave was rather clipped and taciturn. He would stare at me blankly when I asked him some crass question, half-smiling, as if he was thinking, we've got a right idiot here. I wondered if he might once have been in the army or some similar institution.

Eventually, one lunchtime, when Claire and I were sitting in the sun in our courtyard, scoffing smoked salmon and drinking a glass of sauvignon blanc, he agreed to join us for a short break. He refused any wine but accepted a cup of coffee and a chocolate biscuit.

He said he did not smoke, drink or take drugs and had recently become a vegan. He had been up that morning at 5.30 a.m. to do his yoga and meditation. After that he had given his two children their breakfast and taken them to school. Blimey. I felt like a real slob, totally self-indulgent.

Once we had had that initial chat, he was more forthcoming and each day in his lunch break I got a bit more from him. Claire said I was being pushy and told him to ignore me and not to answer my questions, but he said, no, it was part of his therapy not to conceal what had happened to him. He did not mind taking about himself. And, eventually, it all came out. He was born in Peckham, London, before his family moved to the White City. 'It was a dysfunctional family, which explains a lot of what I have done in life...'

'My parents were permanently in debt and the bailiffs were always knocking at the door, wanting the rent, wanting the milk money, whatever. We would all hide or do a runner. I remember once crouching at the top of the stairs with my mother. I must have been five or six. I had been singing a song I had just heard on the radio, "Someone's knocking at the door, someone's ringing my bell". I think it was a Paul McCartney song. My mother told me to shut up singing at once or they would hear us outside.'

Spot on. It was 'Let 'Em In' from Paul's *Wings at the Speed of Sound*, released in 1976. So if Dave is around fifty now, the dates fit.

'I left school with no qualifications. The only job I could find was as a labourer to a plasterer. I used to go to lots of raves when I was a teenager, around the White City, take lots of dope when I could afford it. One of the dealers took a fancy to me. He told me I should try being a dealer, I could make a lot of money out of it. I thought, I'm not fit for much else in life. From my background, I'm never going to have a proper job, so I thought I would have go. I was a drug dealer for twenty-five years.'

What? That must be about half your whole life. Did you get caught? Did it pay?

'I didn't make a lot, not a fortune, not really. But I earned enough to get married and have two kids. Then a little miracle came along, another daughter. I bought a house and had nice holidays – but I didn't save anything. I bought the drugs from a main dealer – cannabis, cocaine, ecstasy. Then sold them to my regular clients I built up over time. I wasn't threatened by any of the main dealers I used or any of my clients or another dealer whose territory I happened to step on. But I can't say I always slept peacefully at night. I was always well aware there were dangers. I managed to avoid getting mixed up with the hardened criminals or big gangs. I did have a few clients who cheated on me and never paid up.'

In the end, after twenty-five years of full-time dealing, Dave did get caught for growing prescribed drugs. He was arrested, stood trial and was convicted.

'Fortunately, my sentence was suspended.' By this time, his marriage had already collapsed. And he had been having mental and physical difficulties. 'Then my daughter suffered a severe head injury. I felt I had to get her away and I moved to the Isle of Wight in 1999.

'During those twenty-five years, I had always told myself this was the only job I was suitable for. Selling drugs was all I was capable of. I had such a low opinion of myself. During all that time, I did everything to excess – too many drugs, too much food, too much alcohol, too much sex; weight shot up to seventeen stone. I was in a terrible state. So, I saw moving to the island as a new beginning. I went for help this time, which I had never done before. I decided to get sober. And followed the advice I was given.'

He found a new girlfriend, whose family came from the island. He went on to have two other children, those he is now bringing up.

'I had to look for work, so I went back to what I had done all those years ago, working as a plasterer's labourer. This time I went to college to learn plastering properly. I did well enough to buy a house on the island, but my second marriage collapsed. I got custody of our two children, who are now nine and seven. They live with me full-time but they see their mother once every two weeks.

'I had to have damp proofing done in the house I bought. I watched him doing it, and I asked if I could work with him, as his plasterer. That's how I learned to do damp proofing.'

Dave has now been doing damp proofing on his own for five years, with his own firm, the Isle of Wight Damp Proof Company. He has two vans with his firm's name and two regular workers for big jobs. 'My business is now a limited company and I am waiting for a new van to arrive.'

When he gave an estimate, I was impressed by his headed notepaper, the detail and wording in his professional estimate, explaining what exactly he would be doing and the guarantees. He had made it clear he could not do it for two months, as he was fully booked up, which was also impressive. During our chats, I asked who did all his paperwork – did he have a girlfriend or some sort of office help? No. These days, one-man bands can use a specialist online agency who will create all the paperwork and post it out to the customer. All in all, he has done really well in his life, to reinvent himself with his own successful, legal business.

'If only I could meet myself now, when I was six and sitting on those stairs with my mum. What a surprise I would get. I like to think I have turned myself round. I have had help. And follow what I am supposed to do. I don't go round telling people all this as soon as I meet them, which is why I didn't really want to talk to you. But I don't mind admitting it. When it comes out, I tell them the truth.

'I am great fan of Gazza – Paul Gascoigne. I think he had all the problems I had when he was young: OCD, bipolar, doing things to excess. He brought himself round and is still alive and seems healthy, at least, when I have seen recent photos of him. He has been an inspiration to me.'

Dave did not know that I was a writer and had ghosted Gazza's memoirs. I also did his second book, which was about his mental health problems and the treatment he had. So, we discussed Gazza for quite a while. I said Gazza always maintained he did not actually like drinking and would often empty his glass into plant pots. It was only when he got really low and depressed and felt suicidal that he would drink or take drugs to excess – just to escape himself.

'The thing is, you have to keep it up. You can always slip back, as I am sure Gazza knows. I try to keep myself as healthy and fit as possible, mentally and physically, not abuse my body or my mind the way I used to.' Today Dave lives alone, without a partner, just him with his two kids. 'No, I haven't got a girlfriend, nor am looking for one. When my second marriage collapsed, I went out and had six or seven girls on the trot in about a year, but the relationships were not good. Now I am concentrating on trying to bring up my kids properly. I don't want them to have the sort of life I had as a kid.

'They take it in their stride, seem to accept that they see their mother once a fortnight. I have had to learn to cook for them, which I had never done before. During lockdown, that was the toughest part. They were at home such a lot and I tried to help them with their school lessons online. But they were too quick and clever for me.

'My kids are a triumph. I have turned round my life now. I didn't think I could live this way. It's not easy, but the rewards are great. Anyway, who would want to go out with me? I don't drink, smoke, take drugs, go out to raves, go out anywhere, really. I just work. All I want to do is build up the company and look after the kids. Really, I am very boring. I don't think anyone would fancy me now. I'm no fun anymore.'

It took Dave the whole week, working full-time, to strip down and inject the two walls, then plaster it all up again. On the last day, one of his helpers, Orlando, did the woodwork, repaired or replaced the skirting boards, a bit of filling in the gaps. Dave told me the day before that he was coming to help him. Orlando was very chatty, cheerful and open. He said his father came from Mozambique and had moved to Southampton to work in the docks. There he met a woman from the island and moved here. Since the Isle of Wight seems like a very 'white' island, I was interested to know what Orlando's experiences had been growing up here.

'Yeah, at school there was only one other black kid. What with that and being called Orlando, I did rather stand out. But, really, I never had much abuse. I was not aware of being prejudiced against. I suppose I was not a threat as most of the kids at school had never met anyone my colour. I like to think I am the handsomest black man on the island. Mind you, there's not a lot of competition...'

The drainage company, DARES, proved to be almost as interesting. I chatted from time to time with the main drainage work man, John, who spent the next four days digging up our courtyard. He was just as efficient and clean and tidy as Dave, but he was more laid back and took all his breaks. He always went out to his van and sat with the *Daily Mirror*, doing the crossword. If Claire or I ever offered him a cup of tea, he always said the same thing, with great emphasis: 'I would LOVE a cup of tea!'

I do like people with enthusiasm. I hate workmen who just grunt when you offer them tea or coffee, then leave it to go cold.

John was tall and long-haired, about fifty, and I suspected had been something of a hippie in his youth. One day he arrived on a vintage motorbike, which he was very proud of. It came out that for fifteen years of his life he had lived and worked in Spain. I asked if he had learned Spanish.

'Not a word. I only did drainage work for English people; then, after work, I went to an English pub. So I never had to speak a word of Spanish. The Costa Brava is full of English expats. But about nine years ago there was a recession in Spain, the work dried up, so I had to come home to the island. I've got two kids, grown up, who are still out there. Oh, I wish I was there now. I do miss the sun.'

His boss, Martin, eventually did turn up, to inspect progress on the drains. In his youth he had been a speedway champion, riding in competitions round the world. His personal email address begins with 'Maddog', in memory of his past. He had built up his own rather big drainage firm, for the island, with fifteen men and two women in the office. Like Dave the damp proofer, he always seemed to have more than enough work. I managed a quick chat and he revealed he nearly did not go into drains at all.

'Do you remember the film *That'll Be the Day*?'

I said, of course I did. Ringo was in it and my equally dear friend Ray Connolly wrote the script. It was a sort of coming-of-age film, set in the 1950s.

'Well, it was shot here on the island, did you know that?'

Nope, I didn't.

'It was shot here because this island looked as if it was still the 1950s, but it was in fact 1973. I had just left school and had quite a good job working in a butcher's. The film people were working on the island for about seven weeks and were looking for extras for crowd scenes. I applied, got a job, and immediately left the butcher's. I went on to do more than just crowd parts. Look at the film and you will see me, driving people around. I often went after the day's shooting to the local pub with Ringo and the other star, David Essex. I was even invited to the world premiere in London at the Odeon, Leicester Square. I went to London and really liked the film, and everything to do with it. I had enjoyed the whole experience so much that I thought, I could do this, I would like to work in films, full-time, sod it being a butcher.

'I applied for an Equity card – the union card, which everyone needed in those days. But I was turned down. I didn't really have the right experience or contacts. Just think, I might have spent my whole life in films as an actor... instead of unblocking drains.'

After the workmen had all gone, taking their tools and their memories with them, carting away their life stories, I could hardly believe they had been here. During that mad week, they had made such a noise and mess, caused such upheaval, took over the house and our life. And then they were gone.

Both of the firms, the Isle of Wight Damp Proofing Company and DARES, the drainage firm, whose arrival we had been dreading, turned out to be well-organised, efficient and professional. And they cleared up beautifully.

So I will no longer speak ill of island workmen.

CHAPTER 18

Garlic and gin

The Isle of Wight Garlic Farm,
nirvana for the garlic-lover

The next week we had a grand day out together. Claire and I went out into the country to observe some unusual rural activities.

Firstly, we visited a farm. Nothing unusual about visiting a farm, but this is not your normal, everyday farm. It is a garlic farm. Amazing, that one small vegetable – once considered by Brits to be foreign and rather unattractive, not to say smelly – should have led a farmer to create a family empire which attracts a quarter of a million visitors a year, just to look at his garlic. I had heard it was one of the island's most popular attractions, but could hardly believe it, though Steve, an electrician we had had in the house the day before, had raved about it, said it was his favourite day out for him and his family.

The Garlic Farm is roughly in the middle of the island, about four miles from Newport, down little roads we had not previously driven. So far I had not been all that impressed by the inland landscape, which the natives are always boasting about. It just seems like normal English countryside, full of the sort of rolling fields and woods you see all over the south, nothing like the Lake District or Scotland in terms of grandeur or beauty. I do rate the beaches, though. They rarely make the top tens when the *Sunday Times* and other papers do their annual round-ups, but I reckon they are up there with the finest in England.

As we approached the farm, I realised we had entered a hidden valley, with hills and pretty views. I began to think I might have to change my mind about the interior of the island being boring. But when we reached the farm's car park – good gracious, I could not believe there were so many cars on the island, let alone in one place. And there were queues, real queues, with folks patiently waiting. There seemed to be a lot of youngish couples, thirty-somethings, rather than the family parties I had expected. It was a Sunday and the nation was getting back to having its traditional weekend day out in the country. It seemed we were mostly among native islanders. A day out for them is easy. They only have to drive ten miles – twenty max.

We had been invited for Sunday lunch with the owners and founders of the farm, but I was not sure where to report. I wandered into a large shop, jammed with jostling customers and dozens of garlic-related goodies. All over the island, you see Isle of Wight Garlic Farm goods on sale in most of the better delis. I have even seen their produce further afield. For several years, near my London house, at the weekly farmers' market at Parliament Hill Fields on Hampstead Heath, there has been an Isle of Wight garlic stall. Very popular with the Hampstead types in their Barbours and Hunter wellies. I had always wondered if the people on the garlic stall had really come all the way over from the Isle of Wight with garlic grown on the island.

Now I was in their shop at the front, where I counted about a hundred different items on sale – garlic in jars, garlic in pots and garlic in packets. There was also garlic bread, garlic rolls, garlic soup, garlic mayonnaise, garlic pickles and bottles of garlic beer. Or you could lash out on a massive hamper and gorge yourself on a selection of garlicky delights.

I wandered outside, and found myself in a sort of farmyard. There was a huge marquee set up where people were eating, with tables spread out around the lawns. Watching all the humans were assorted cows and sheep. Right in the middle, among the crowd of people, was a bird that I didn't quite recognise – it looked something like a massive peacock, or perhaps a turkey; whatever it was, it was strutting around as if it owned the place. Kids were lying flat on the grass nearby staring, fascinated, but fearful of getting too near this unusual creature. It looked unreal, a stuffed giant of a bird, with enormous fluffy, frilly legs and wings, like a fur coat which had grown too big for itself.

It turned out to be a giant Brahma, an unusual type of chicken, developed in America from birds imported from China. Children are captivated by them – not really afraid; just in awe, hence the kids observing while prostrate, almost in worship.

Beyond a wall I glimpsed a rather attractive-looking period farmhouse. I peered through the slats in a wooden door and in the front garden I could see an assortment of kids' toys and bikes. As I peeped, being very nosey, the gate suddenly opened and out came our hosts, Colin and Jenny Boswell, owners of the farm and presumably grandparents of the owners of those toys and bikes.

They had already booked us a table, which was lucky, as the place was full, so the four of us sat down together on wooden benches and studied the menu. For an open-air caff on a farm, it was surprisingly imaginative. I had seafood pasta, which was delicious, and Claire had a salad, which she pronounced excellent. Yes, there was garlic in my seafood pasta. What did I expect? But I do like garlic, having long got over the post-war phobia about it being smelly.

Colin was tanned and healthy-looking and wore a tweed jacket. He was also well-spoken, polite and charming; I estimated his age to be about seventy, and Jenny's the same. Colin's father bought the farm when Colin was about nine years old. Until then, his father had been farming in Kent. Colin went away to Bryanston boarding school in Dorset and then on to Nottingham University, where he read politics. It was there he met Jenny, a doctor's daughter from Childwall, near Liverpool, who was reading Russian. She was attracted not just by his good looks but the fact he was from the Isle of Wight. 'I thought he would be bound to take me sailing.'

They got married and worked in London at first, Colin in marketing and Jenny in the City. When he was about twenty-five,

Colin returned to the island to take over the family farm. It was not doing all that brilliantly. It was the mid-1960s and farmers, who were having a hard time, were being urged by the government to diversify. His father had started to specialise in sweetcorn, which Colin continued when he took over – he even managed to land a big order from a supermarket. They had also, by chance, been growing some garlic, for their own domestic use.

'My mother, Norah, had a kitchen garden and loved growing garlic. She used a lot in her cooking, which was pretty unusual at the time in England.' It was Elizabeth David's cookbooks that introduced many members of Britain's middle classes to garlic. Hitherto, eating garlic had been frowned on as a nasty habit indulged in by funny foreigners, who had bad breath as a result. When Mrs Thatcher opened the Channel Tunnel, she was said to have remarked, 'I can smell the garlic from here.'

Colin and Jenny decided to go into garlic properly and professionally. Colin researched its history, which he says stretches back five thousand years – all the way to Ancient Egypt. He travelled to places like Kazakhstan to observe their garlic-growing methods.

'The first reports of it being grown on the Isle of Wight date back to wartime, to 1942. Some French officers were stationed in Cowes and grew to hate the English food. They managed to persuade two secret agents who were making clandestine flights to France to bring back some garlic bulbs in their plane. The local innkeeper agreed to grow them in his back garden.'

On the farm, Colin was the ideas person, the marketing man, thinking of ways to promote and sell their garlic. Jenny made it all happen – creating and trying out recipes, using garlic in her own kitchen. They progressed to filling jars and bottles with their own garlic-based food products on the farm, with their own bottling and packaging plant. The farm secured a massive order from a supermarket – and then it all went wrong; they fell out with them. Colin tried to explain the full drama but I got a bit lost in the complexities of the story. The long and short of it was that the farm immediately lost a lot of money and they had to sell some of their fields. 'We had to downsize drastically from employing 350 staff. It was a big struggle. It took us time to recover and find a way to start all over again. We decided we would go direct to independent shops, restaurants and farmers markets. But these days we do also supply a few supermarkets.'

'All supermarkets consider they own you,' said Jenny. 'They think they can do anything with their suppliers, dictate any sorts of terms, cut your margins, just because they are giving you a big order. These days, when I see two-for-one in any supermarket, I think, Oh God, the poor farmers and suppliers, they will be the ones losing money because of this offer, not the supermarket.'

Colin and Jenny have five children. As they were growing up, they were roped in to help on the farm and with the selling. 'When they were as young as twelve, we would get up at four in the morning on a Saturday, pack the garlic and the children in the van and catch the first ferry to the mainland. I would then drop the children off at one or two different farmers' markets – perhaps in High Street Ken, Notting Hill, Ally Pally, Stroud Green and at Parliament Hill. I would set up each stall, give them the products to sell that day, and leave the children there. Even as young as twelve, they would be on their own in a strange place, on a pavement or in a playground, running the stall from ten in the morning till I picked them up at two in the afternoon. Then we all came home on the evening ferry. It was an excellent way to find out if your children are going to be entrepreneurs or not. I can recommend it…'

Today, Colin and Jenny are semi-retired – and their children are all directors – even one of them who lives abroad. Natasha, aged thirty-five, the oldest, appears to be the main boss today.

'Well, she is my boss,' says Colin. 'She and her husband make all the big decisions.'

Their son Hugo also works full-time on the farm. He looks after the seven self-catering cottages and the five luxury yurts, originally based on Central Asian design. After lunch, Jenny took us to see them. They are situated in their own little rural enclave, complete with tennis court, football pitch and a communal meeting place. I had never been in a yurt before – and I was most impressed. We met some people who were packing up, who said they were going to book again for next year, so when they finally left, we had a look round.

From the outside the yurts looked like big tents; they were circular and made entirely from canvas, but inside they were spacious, ingenious, fully equipped holiday homes, with kitchen, bathroom and three bedrooms. The self-catering cottages themselves are mainly old farm buildings and barns which have been converted.

Today, the garlic farm extends to some three hundred acres and they employ thirty staff to cover the farm, shop, restaurant and the self-catering. Canning and packaging of the garlic itself is now done elsewhere. They supply five hundred different outlets across the UK and Europe, even selling their products in the spiritual home of garlic, France.

They also hold a lot of events, such as walks and talks. There is a farm trail with a professional guide. They show films and put on shows. Colin plays the guitar in a group. And they have created a local garlic festival which attracts crowds of five thousand people.

'This was really just to help the local village festival, in Newchurch. It had become a bit run-down and they were looking for new ideas. I was at the meeting and heard myself proposing a garlic festival. They suggested in that case I should run it. I came home and told Jenny – and she was not exactly thrilled. We are supposed to be retired. I just do it to help the village, not the garlic farm.'

There was so much to see on the farm, with all its various activities and attractions, that I quite forgot we had not actually seen any garlic being grown. Colin explained that the garlic fields were scattered around the three hundred acres. The fields have to be rotated every seven years, so they rarely have a mass display of garlic-growing. You have to walk round and find a garlic field. At any one time they have twenty acres totally devoted to garlic growing, producing a hundred tons of garlic a year, which amounts to several million bulbs.

Jenny took us to a small field not far from the café where visitors can see a display of the twelve different varieties of garlic which they grow on the farm. I noticed that one of the varieties was a Ukranian garlic chosen by Jenny. It is a strongly flavoured garlic called Lubasha. Jenny explained that in Russian this means 'Little loved one'. So, despite forty years building up their thriving, multi-faceted family garlic business, getting a degree in Russian all those years ago was not totally wasted...

Jenny's likes

- Sailing, which was one of the things that attracted me to Colin and to the island in the first place.
- The independent minds and outlook which the locals have. You come across a lot of quirky, unusual people living on the island who go their own way, ignoring conventional life.

Colin's likes

- I like getting up in the morning and knowing it will be all lovely, with no awful surprises. I walk around, knowing everything, knowing all the people. That does please me. It is a lovely island to live on.
- Brading Roman Villa. I visit it often. In another life I would like to have been an archaeologist.
- The Isle of Wight people. They always surprise, with their original minds and natural wisdom.

Jenny's dislikes

- Travel: getting anywhere on the island these days is becoming a lot harder, with all the traffic. Getting to the mainland is not too hard, but getting back, at a time you want to come back, that is always a struggle.
- Schools: that does not personally concern me now, as my children are grown up, though we do have eight grandchildren. But it did when my five children were growing up. The educational choices on the island are limited. There is no university or college on the island where you can study for a degree.

Colin's dislikes

- I was so disappointed when in the Brexit referendum 67 per cent of the island's population voted to leave Europe. Our whole island life, our whole future and that of our children to come, is tied up with the continent. We should never have left.
- I am personally contented here, but it would be good to have more young people, with young families. There are a lot of retired people here – and of course I am now one of them.

On the way home we visited another local enterprise originally connected with farming. It's surprising how many of them there are here, hidden away in rural enclaves – and surprising also how many people start off in one direction and then end up taking another.

Conrad Gauntlett was brought up across the Solent in Southampton, although he was actually born in Singapore where his father was in the services. After school in Southampton, Conrad joined the RAF, where he stayed for a few years specialising in radar systems. He also bought and did up houses, selling three in total at a good profit. He came to the Isle of Wight in 1985, working on radar systems for Plessey, based in Cowes. Then he noticed how cheap land was on the Isle of Wight.

'I suddenly decided I would like to create a vineyard. Quite a few people were doing it in the 1980s in England and I thought I would have a go.'

In 1986, he bought the Rosemary Riding School which covered about twenty acres, not far from Ryde, already planning to turn it into what became the Rosemary Vineyard. While still working on radar, he visited between twenty and thirty vineyards around the UK, finding out how to do it, asking them for any tips.

Vineyards were established in the south of England by the Romans about two thousand years go, but then interest faded and Britons decided that really, it was best to leave making wine to folks in better climates. In the 1950s several types of vine were developed that could resist the British winter. In the last three decades, there has been a wave of vine planting in the UK; mainly in the south of England but also in some northern countries – and even in Scotland. Today, there are thought to be five hundred vineyards in the UK. And English wine often wins awards on the world stage.

Conrad made a few mistakes at first, such as planting the

wrong sort of vine, but after three years he had his first crop producing decent wine. He built up the business over the next twenty years or so, turning it into a tourist attraction and employing about twenty people – all of them local. He stood for the Isle of Wight council and Ryde town council and served for several years. 'Councillors come in two forms. Those interested in politics – which I was not – and those who wanted to put something back into the community, which is my aim.'

By chance, the council wanted to take some of his land for a new through-road and said that, if he agreed to it, they would allow him to have building permission for 140 new houses on his land. 'The bypass was never built and I didn't build any houses – but I still have the planning permission – which runs out soon.'

In 2014 he woke up one day and thought, Gin. 'The vineyard was doing well enough, but there are two easy ways of losing money. Buying a yacht or creating an English vineyard with our damp climate. The thing about a vineyard is that it takes you three years, at least – if you are starting from scratch – before you can start selling any wine. And then one year in seven you lose your whole crop – the spring frost often catches you out. I have loved having a vineyard but it was stressful. I thought gin would be an easier and more rewarding way of life.'

He set up the Isle of Wight Distillery with a partner, Xavier Barker, who had great experience with the brewing industry. They bought a long lease on a well-known country pub, the Wishing Well, in Pondwell, Ryde, which owned a large caravan park that was not making much money. They rechristened the venue the Mermaid Bar and it is now the home of the Isle of Wight Distillery: the first – and still the only – gin distillery on the island. Claire and I had driven past it several times while heading down the coast, but we had never been in.

On the way home, we decided to pop in for a drink. Even

though we don't like gin. It just looks like a rural pub from the outside, but inside it is much larger than it appears. The distillery itself is at the rear and you can ogle the stills and the gleaming pipes through a large glass screen. They sell bottles of gin, both full-size and miniature bottles. A couple in their seventies were buying two bottles of gin at thirty-eight pounds each and three small miniature bottles. His bill was £109. I couldn't believe it. He said he was from Nottingham and he and his wife were staying in a local caravan park. He was a retired headmaster who had become a Church of England priest and was helping out at six local parishes.

I asked how he could afford to spend so much on gin – though I have heard headmasters can retire on a good pension. 'Yeah, I heard that as well,' he said and smiled. 'You can pay twenty pounds for a bottle of rubbish gin in a supermarket. We like to try speciality gins and I have heard about Mermaid Gin and how good it is. I can't wait to taste it.'

When I met Conrad, I told him about the priest buying gin, spending what seemed to me like a fortune. Personally, I would never pay thirty-eight pounds for a bottle of anything. Not even Chanel No. 5, which I know is Claire's fave. Hard cheese, pet. Conrad pointed out that his bottles are very distinctive and expensive to produce. They are made in Italy and then painted in Yorkshire or Poland. It costs roughly £2.80 every bottle – even when ordering ten thousand units. The glass is crafted to look as if it is covered in mermaid scales, all very subtle and artistic. On the bottom is their mermaid logo. The cork is biodegradable and the plastic-looking capsule is in reality made of very clever starch material that is dissolvable.

'The bottles themselves have proved one of the most popular features,' says Conrad. 'People now collect them all over the world. I have seen them being sold on eBay for up to twenty-five pounds.'

I suddenly remembered – when we go to our favourite supper

place, the Dell Café, the tap water on the table is served in empty Mermaid Gin bottles. Very trendy. I wonder how many get nicked?

When they started, just seven years ago, all their gin was sold on the Isle of Wight. Three years ago, 50 per cent was sold in the rest of the UK. Now at least half of their production each year is sold worldwide, particularly in Europe, and they have won awards everywhere.

But it hasn't all been straightforward. 'I came into gin thinking I would have a quieter life than I had with the vineyard, but I never knew about all the problems.' Tax is one. Gin is much cheaper and easier to make than wine in production terms, but then excise duty has to be paid, as is the case with all spirits. The tax on a bottle of wine is roughly two pounds – but on a bottle of gin it is five times that.

'If I sell ten thousand bottles of Mermaid Gin to a customer on the 30th of the month, the next day – on the 31st, I have to hand over excise duty tax of £100k. I have to pay it there and then, whereas a customer or any other outlet I provide gin to, has up to ninety days to pay. So balancing the cash flow can be very difficult and it can end up being very problematic.'

However, the distillery is doing excellent business. So much so that they currently have plans to move it to new premises. The Rosemary Vineyard may be moved into the fields behind the Mermaid Bar. Conrad had in fact hoped to have a go at planting vines in these fields some time ago. But the lockdowns conspired against him, making it impossible to transport vines bought in Germany to the Isle of Wight. He seems to have wasted quite a lot of money as a result.

'The thing about a distillery, just like the vineyard, is you are always making mistakes. You rarely get it right the first time.'

I complimented Conrad on his advertising and marketing; the copy featured all the right-on phrases and was written in environmentally sound prose. He said they did it all themselves.

All thirty staff were local islanders, including the marketing people, though they had used a London designer for the bottles.

Despite not drinking gin, I splashed out on a presentation box containing three miniature bottles – two of gin and one of vodka. Price £16. What a spendthrift I can sometimes be. I intend to offer a sip to my children and to Claire's family when they come to stay. Young folks today, eh? They all seem to be going mad on designer gin. But I did enjoy the packaging and admired the purple prose:

Mermaid Gin is handcrafted using ten ethically sourced botanicals. A smooth yet complex blend of fresh, organic lemon zest, the peppery notes in grains of paradise and a hint of sea air from fragrant rock samphire. Mermaid salt vodka is shot through with a pinch of locally sourced island sea salt, enhancing its smoothness and accentuating its subtle flavour, like the gentle kiss of a mermaid. Mermaid Pink Gin infuses the flavour and aromatics of island strawberries with the smooth yet complex taste of our award-winning gin.

Conrad's likes

- The beaches. I have two grandchildren. Having so many beaches is wonderful.
- The slowness of the island, I do like that even when it sometimes drives me mad.

Conrad's dislikes

- The ferry service. It is so expensive and I am sure it deters visitors.

CHAPTER 19

The Royal Yacht Squadron

The headquarters of the
Royal Yacht Squadron, 1903

The current secretary of the Royal Yacht Squadron is a woman, and she has been secretary since 2003. However, the Royal Yacht Squadron voted to allow women members only in 2013, just two years before the club's bicentenary.

Women are becoming more prominent in gentlemen's clubs. The Garrick and Athenaeum clubs in London now also have female secretaries and the Garrick looks at long last as if it will allow female members. At Henley Royal Regatta, women can wear trousers. Goodness, what changes.

The Royal Yacht Squadron secretary joined the club many years ago in the events department. She is efficient and approachable, but rather quiet and has not acquired the airs and graces which long-term members of staff at gentlemen's clubs often acquire. Today, the club has 535 full members and a waiting list of both male and female candidates. Serving and retired Royal Navy officers can also be proposed for membership. Then there are associate members. Finally, there are honorary members – including members of the royal family. Altogether, they have around a thousand people in a variety of categories.

Becoming a full member – my goodness, what a complicated business it is. The whole membership votes on whether to accept you, a process that can take about three years as you go into the candidates' book and slowly progress through various stages. There is a vote held twice a year; each member used to have to put a white ball or a black ball into a box – hence the word 'blackball' meaning to reject someone's candidacy for a club. Balls are still used in the voting today, but they are all identical and made of cork and are placed into one of two boxes – a 'nay' box or a 'yes' box. So 'blackballing' never happens...

The secretary says membership fees are not as enormous as

some people assume – though she would not reveal how much. There is a full-time staff of twenty, plus an army of seasonal staff in the sailing season. You don't have to have a boat to join but you have to have an interest in yachting.

The vast majority of members do not live on the island. They live in London or New York or elsewhere. However, quite a lot of the British members have holiday homes on the island.

'We in the office love and hate Cowes Week,' she said of the island's vast yearly regatta. 'It is great to see both Cowes and the club really busy but it is the most stressful week of the year. There is the matter of not just the enormous amount of extra people and staff to worry about, but things like the unpredictability of the weather. Very windy and a lot of yachts cannot go out. No wind at all and they cannot sail. If it is very wet, a lot of people don't like that either.'

The secretary herself does not sail, but she says it is not really such an elitist sport as some people assume and they welcome all types in the club. She would like to see younger members, as the average age is probably mid-sixties. Despite the image of the club as traditional and old-fashioned, the Royal Yacht Squadron likes to think of itself as forward-looking. They have made lots of changes and improvements, such as the pavilion – for viewing the races – and the Haven, their own private mooring outside the club.

The club building is Grade II listed, housed in a Tudor castle that dates back to Henry VIII, one of two fortifications built in Cowes to protect against invasion by the French or the Spanish. It's thought to be the oldest occupied castle in the whole of England – though never once in its long history did it ever have to fire its guns in anger. The other castle, which also helped to defend the entrance to Cowes, has long gone.

The origins of yachting in England date back to 1660. The Dutch East India Company presented to King Charles II a decked sailing boat known as a *jacht* – in Dutch the word originally meant a hunt or a chase and came also to describe a light, fast sailing vessel. The king's brother, the Duke of York, was so delighted by the boat that he had one made for himself. He and the king used to race their yachts up and down the Thames. Other aristocratic enthusiasts soon followed the royal example and more yachts began to appear on the Thames. Samuel Pepys was most impressed. 'One of the finest things ever I saw for neatness and room in so small a vessel.'

The origin of the Royal Yacht Squadron dates back to 1815, which makes it one of the five oldest yacht clubs in Britain and Ireland. The others are the Royal Cork, Co. Cork; the Lough Ree, Athlone; the Starcross, in the Exe estuary; and the Royal Thames, London.

The original members of the Royal Yacht Squadron did not have any permanent premises. They were just forty gentlemen interested in yachting who met in a London pub and decided to call themselves a club. Almost from the beginning, they did their actual sailing in Cowes.

The club became the Royal Yacht Club in 1820, when the Prince Regent (a member since 1817) became king. Racing in Cowes began in 1825 and the club acquired its present name in 1833 by order of King William IV. Other eminent members over the last two hundred years or so have included Sir Ernest Shackleton, the Antarctic explorer, and Robert Stephenson, the railway engineer and the son of George Stephenson. It would have been hard to imagine George, a horny-handed Geordie who never went to school and was mocked for his accent, being a member. But his only son was well-educated and became an MP.

The club moved into their present premises in 1858. Members of the Squadron are allowed to fly the White Ensign on their boats which no other yacht club is allowed to do. The use of the word 'squadron' reflects the club's association from its earliest days with the Royal Navy. In addition to an interest in all things yachting, the original club deeds mentioned 'cordiality' as one of the club's objects. It is true to say that enjoying themselves still appears to be one of the aims of all the club members.

The Royal Yacht Squadron also prides itself on being at the forefront of racing and encouraging developments in yachting around the world, which helps to provide work on the Isle of Wight for shipbuilders, sail-makers and yachtsmen.

Yachting at Cowes has always been one of the highlights of the society season, attended by aristocrats, the wealthy and the influential, both men and attractive young women. For many years, a lot of them were American. During the years 1880 to 1910, it is reckoned that three hundred very well-off American ladies married into the British aristocracy. One of them was Jennie Jerome, an American heiress, who married Lord Randolph Churchill – and became the mother of Winston.

Claire and I then went on a tour of the club. Gosh, she was excited. Claire is a yachtie, but I had denied her any sailing at all – except to watch the model yachts on the lake beside our house in Ryde. I maintain the best thing about all boats is looking at them rather than sailing in them. They do complete a view of the sea.

We were taken round the club under the expert guidance of a steward who has been working at the club for over thirty years. On the way through the stately reception rooms, the steward made comments on all the paintings. He was particularly amusing on a large painting showing some racing yachts very near the shore, painted by a well-known naval painter called William John Huggins.

'Look at the flags. Flags don't fly that way. When a yacht is racing, the flags fly backward. He has some of them flying forward – just because he wanted to paint them that way. You can see how fast the boats were going, and he does capture their speed very well, but they are far too near the shore. They are obviously about to crash into the shore and get wrecked. All those sailors pictured, who had climbed up on the rigging, were about to fall off and probably get drowned...'

The painting I was most fascinated by was a huge one which showed all the members in 1895 standing outside the club. The steward pointed out how all of them were wearing brown shoes – gentlemen in the nineteenth century wore brown shoes when they went to the country. Most of them seemed to be smoking cigarettes. Some members of our royal family were present, plus Kaiser Wilhelm II of Germany, who was a very keen yachtsman.

'You will notice there is a big gap beside the Kaiser. This is because the member who was standing beside him was painted out. I think he was not very popular with the members and considered a bit pushy. But he managed to get himself painted in on the other side of the painting – look there he is, over there.'

There was a key to the painting, which I studied carefully and discovered the man standing on his own was Lord Lonsdale.

'Poor old Lordie,' I said. 'What a shame. Don't you know who he was?'

It was my turn to show off my knowledge as a Cumbrian, which of course I never do. Hugh Lowther (1857–1944) was the 5th Earl of Lowther and inherited practically half of Cumberland. He was known as the Yellow Earl because he dressed his hundreds of staff and the soldiers in his own little regiment in that colour. He was a keen sportsman and was one of the early motorcar enthusiasts. The AA's colour to this day is also yellow, thanks to Lord Lonsdale. The Lonsdale Belt for boxing is also named after him.

Then I remembered another fact about him – that he was visited at his stately home, Lowther Castle, by the Kaiser himself and given a Prussian medal. This was in 1895, the same year the painting was done. So come on, he and the Kaiser must have been reasonable friends. No wonder he wanted to stand beside him in this painting. If the story that he was painted out and then repainted standing on his own is true, then it must have been done afterwards, once he had gone home to Cumberland. Perhaps he had made enemies in the club – he was an eccentric figure, even in Cumberland. Perhaps he failed to pay his mess bill.

I noticed that the steward was wearing an all-black tie. We happened to be in the mourning room, in which there was a painting of Admiral Nelson. The tradition in the club is that they are still in mourning for Nelson, more than two hundred years after his death at Trafalgar in 1805.

'That is why all the staff wear plain black ties. Club members also wear a black tie and they wear it with a tie pin in the shape of the club's emblem; lady members wear a brooch in the shape of the emblem.'

The club has two dining rooms. One is called the 'dining room' and the other the 'ladies' dining room' – because, for many years, that was the only place where women guests could eat. The grand table was ready for dinner that evening and looked almost as posh as the setting we had seen at Osborne House. The silver was gleaming, masses of glasses were lined up, yet it was only set for six people. There still seemed enough cutlery and glasses to serve a regiment. That evening, apparently, they were to have a tasting menu.

We finished off our tour in the glass-fronted racing platform at the front of the club, looking over the Haven and the sea. It was empty that day, but on a racing day there can be forty judges and officials with binoculars and an army of techies working computers and radios to register the progress and speed of the competitors out on the ocean.

The platform has its origins in a panic caused by a whim of Queen Victoria. Her son, the Prince of Wales, was a keen yachtsman and member of the club. One day the Queen said,

'Oh, I would like to see your club.' The club knew they had to entertain the Queen, but no women were allowed at all, even as guests. And so the platform was built, jutting out, so it was not actually inside the premises, ready for Her Majesty's appearance.

But as far as we know, the Queen never did make it to the Royal Yacht Squadron in Cowes. Not even on to the platform. Shame. She could have been its first female visitor.

CHAPTER 20

Arts at the bottom of our yard

A view from St John's, near Ryde, looking
towards Spithead and Portsmouth,
by William Turner (1789–1862)

We didn't know when we first moved that we had an arts centre right behind our house. The back wall of our little courtyard is also the wall of the Monkton Arts, as the centre is called. At some stage in the long-distant past I think we must have lost half our garden to the building that now houses the centre.

The reason it took us so long to realise this is because to reach it you have to go round the back of the block, down an unattractive-looking cul-de-sac which contains a builders yard, a garage and a workshop. Each time we left the house we went the other way, straight across the road and onto the beach. Or we turned left and headed for the pier and the High Street.

People began to tell us about the arts centre, including Cathy, the previous owner of our house; that it was run by two women, a mother and daughter, has become a kind of arty-crafty focus for the local community, and puts on a lot of exhibitions and performances.

It was not until November 2020 that we went to our first event there – a harvest festival. Gosh, it was fun. About thirty neighbours sat in the main gallery to be served a lovely, three-course meal, all homemade – goats' cheese and onion tart to start with, then a vegetarian curry, followed by a pudding – it was, they said, a Samhain harvest supper.

We were entertained throughout by Irish music – two blokes, one on the fiddle and one on the guitar. The fiddler turned out to be in real life a local vet, an Irishman called Donal, while the guitarist was a professional musician.

The whole evening, music and the meal (bring your own wine), cost only twenty-five pounds, which I thought was a bargain. We were seated at a table with another local couple of roughly our age, who lived just a few streets away. What an enjoyable evening it was, and what a worthwhile contribution to the local community. But soon afterwards lockdown was reimposed. The island lost its tier one status and joined the rest of England in tier three.

I met the younger of the two women who run the centre, walking with her children on the beach one day, smiley as ever, but she said they were having a hard time. The centre was closed, they could claim nothing for being self-employed, as they did not yet have a year of self-employed taxes to show, but still had rent and costs. They were receiving some government grants, though, which were helping them get through.

In the new year, as Covid receded and restrictions began to be relaxed, they were able to open up, albeit slowly at first. Coffee and cakes were served on tables in their little courtyard and soon the place was bustling with locals. And then they started putting on events again.

It must be such a busy life, running a café and arts centre with so much going on – especially if you have a family to take care of. But both mother and daughter seemed to take it all cheerfully in their stride. It was quite hard to pin them down for a moment and get them to talk about themselves. But eventually, after the centre had closed for the day, I sat down with Jenna and her mother Dawn, while Jenna's two young children, Daisy and Joseph, rushed around, making things and painting posters.

'It was challenging, having no income,' said Jenna, 'but in many ways it has been a blessed relief to have such a long rest. I think otherwise I might have had a nervous breakdown. We had only been open a year when Covid came along and yet we had proved much more popular than we had ever dreamed of.'

I was surprised they had only been open for a year – the centre felt so well-established and well-organised, with its impressive programme of events. This timeframe also suggested they had moved in just six months or so before Claire and myself had arrived. So were they newcomers to the island as well? Not quite, it turned out.

Dawn, who is a very young-looking sixty, was born in Sheffield and studied at Rotherham Art College, where she met her husband Duncan. ' I really loved lettering. That was my favourite subject.' She and her husband started a little printing firm in Rotherham, most of their work being connected directly or indirectly with the coal mines. When the mines started closing, the whole community suffered, including their business. In 1990 they decided to sell their house and move to the Isle of Wight. They had enjoyed some great holidays on the island over the years, so they set off blithely – with nothing planned, no accommodation or jobs lined up – taking their six-year-old daughter Jenna and Dawn's parents and renting a house in Binstead, near Ryde.

'Back in the 1990s, the island really was so behind the times,' says Dawn. 'It was almost like the 1930s. Which was why we loved it so much. There were none of the big supermarkets we have these days. Today, you can buy anything you want on the island. Back in 1990, if you wanted to go supermarket shopping you had to go to Portsmouth or Southampton for the day.'

They bought a truck and decided to sell soft drinks round the island – a venture that does sound ancient, very like the 1950s. They sold door-to-door, not to shops.

'Looking back today, I can hardly believe the changes which have happened in just thirty years. I remember the excitement when the island got its first escalator. In the winter, the roads were empty. Today, there is no real difference in traffic throughout the whole year. You can't really tell the season by the number of cars.'

They then moved into making hand-sculpted, porcelain *Thunderbirds* dolls as collectors' items. Each doll was certified by creator Sylvia Anderson. Eventually, they were able to buy a house in Shanklin – with the money saved from the sale of their Yorkshire house – and went on to have two more children. Dawn began working in a local school, helping children with special needs. She became so interested in the subject that, aged forty, she decided to go to university in Portsmouth to study psychology, graduating with a first-class degree.

It so happened she was a student at the same time as her older daughter, Jenna, who had been to school on the island and then took a degree in textile design at Galashiels in the Scottish Borders, moving on to Winchester School of Art at the University of Southampton. Jenna met her future husband, Alex, there – by chance he had also moved at the age of six and grown up on the Isle of Wight. Alex went on to become a lecturer in child development at the University of Portsmouth, where he still works. He commutes each day by bike, from the house where they live in Ryde, to catch the catamaran on Ryde Pier, then cycles on the other side to the university.

'The whole trip takes him only thirty minutes and he loves the journey. It can take me longer than that just to drive from Ryde to Newport to do some shopping.'

Meanwhile, Jenna and Dawn heard that an antique and bric-a-brac shop at the corner of Monkton Street was available to rent from its Portuguese owner. They took it over, selling coffee and cakes and exhibiting works by local artists – all of which went so well that soon they were looking for bigger premises. They then heard about a dilapidated printing works around the corner whose owner had failed to get planning permission to build new houses, which meant that it had stood empty for two years.

They both fell in love with the space and agreed a modest rent. The bigger challenge was that they needed to modernise and convert the whole derelict premises at their own expense.

Apparently, the building had at one time been used as a general's stables. They showed me photos as it was when they first moved in. It looked like a bombsite. There were holes in the walls, rubbish on the floor, broken fittings everywhere. It also smelt of damp.

'We worked out that doing it all by ourselves, with our husbands and family helping, it would still need ten thousand pounds, just to make it habitable. We didn't have that sort of money. We were working on how to get a bank loan, and getting nowhere, when a local man, Barry Acons, who had been a customer at the antiques shop, heard what we were doing. He said he would lend us the ten thousand pounds. He would not charge any interest and we could pay it in back in due course. That was why we called the downstairs gallery the Acons Gallery. Sadly, he has just died.'

They opened in 2019 – and were an immediate success. Today, they have three studios upstairs which they rent out to artists. Visitors to the Monkton Arts Centre can watch the artists at work. Downstairs, they have bookings in the Acons gallery for the next eighteen months. The shop also hosts work by local professional artists, and there's a children's gallery exhibiting work from local schools.

In that first year they put on one event per week, with local musicians, artists, sculptors and authors playing or performing. And all this they have done on their own, just the two of them, mum and daughter, with no previous experience of running an art gallery, a restaurant, a coffee bar or hosting art events. They have now taken on some additional staff to operate the centre on Sundays. And they employed one of the musicians, who turned out to be an excellent barista.

I could not have been more impressed at hearing what Dawn and Jenna have achieved. But I am sure that all over the UK, in the unlikeliest of locations, you would find examples of such enterprise: women and mothers creating something from scratch, without any training or funds; people who have a dream – and then work their socks off to make it a reality. They must be permanently exhausted... I asked them how their day had gone today.

'Two things went wrong today,' said Jenna. 'I have a new till on the coffee bar counter and I could not get it to work. Oh God, I was going mad. Then twenty thousand copies of a new leaflet I had ordered from the printers came back all wrong. They will have to go back.'

Generally, on the occasions I have been in the centre for a coffee, Jenna's two children have been around, mucking about, amusing themselves. As her husband works, they spend a lot of time at the centre after school. Suddenly daughter Daisy rushed in, screaming in excitement.

'Princess Anne has landed in the rec! Princess Anne has landed in the rec!'

I thought at first Princess Anne had been involved in some sort of wreck; had there been some sort of accident? What on earth was she doing round here?

Then I realised that by 'rec', Daisy was referring to the Simeon Street recreation ground, a small park behind the gallery. A wall had recently been built round it, as it had suffered from serious flooding some years ago.

Daisy eventually calmed down and slowly explained what she had just seen. Princess Anne had arrived by helicopter on the recreation ground. Only an hour earlier, I had noticed a large black helicopter hovering over our house, but assumed it was a naval aircraft, perhaps on some manoeuvres. It turned out it had arrived to pick up Princess Anne, who had been visiting some of the charities she supports on the island. She had landed by helicopter at Northwood House, where I had given my talk to the literary festival. This is the usual way members of the royal family now arrive on the island. Long gone are the days when Queen Victoria sailed over on the royal yacht. They usually then do something at Cowes, of a yachty nature, then get driven across the island to Ryde, from whence they depart.

On this particular day, so I read later in the local papers, Princess Anne had in fact sailed from Cowes round to the Fishbourne yacht club, and then been driven to Ryde where she visited Ryde School. Well, that was a bit of excitement, Daisy!

I asked Jenna what was wrong with the leaflets, and if I could have a look at them. To my surprise she produced a political leaflet on behalf of a new local political party called 'Our Ryde'. Nine members were standing in the May elections for Ryde town council, including Jenna Sabine. Until then, I had not known her married name.

I told Jenna I thought she must be potty. Why would you want to be a councillor when you have two young children at school and a time-consuming business that has only just got going?

'I have become so fed up having to deal with Ryde council. It is full of old men... nothing wrong with old men, but we need a greater representation and reflection of the demographic of the town. They are not interested in new things happening, just leaving things as they are. Even worse, many are not interested in preserving the wonderful old buildings we have in Ryde, such as Appley Tower – there was a rumour that Isle of Wight council were going to sell the Victorian folly to a councillor to convert into his private beach hut. Luckily, it was prevented by Ryde town council. The building was saved to become a local asset. But I think generally they don't always care for the town enough and do little to promote it. But I was inspired by the town's mayor to join the Our Ryde group. Under his guidance, a group of us with similar views had decided to start our own party – not really political, just a group trying to preserve and regenerate Ryde.'

I asked Dawn what she thought about her daughter becoming a councillor. It would presumably leave her to be mainly responsible for the Monkton Arts Centre. She smiled, followed by a slight grimace and a bit of eye-rolling, then she was back to smiling again.

'Oh, I approve of what she is trying to do. The council needs people like Jenna.'

Do they ever fall out, have words? Mothers and daughters don't always see eye to eye. Anyway, who is the boss? They both said neither of them was. In that case, how do they divvy up the duties? Did one look after the paperwork and the other do front of house? Nope, none of that. They did everything together. There were no demarcations. The meal for thirty people at the harvest festival, for example, was cooked jointly. They decide together which events to put on and then share the organising. It's usually Dawn who books the musicians; she also gets the tickets printed and sold.

'People are always saying they can't believe we never fall out, but we don't, honestly. Obviously I sometimes say, "Mother you are wrong," and she says, "No, Jenna, you are wrong." Then we start laughing, sit down, open a bottle of wine and discuss it all. And we end up coming to a sensible solution we both agree with. I suppose the secret is that we are very alike. We like the same things, want to do the same things. Also, we are both gigglers. We usually both laugh when things go wrong.'

All the same, I am relieved that they are using a bit of outside help at last. And not just a barista: they have hired an accountant to do their tax returns.

'As we have grown, we do realise we need some professional help. Next thing will be to hire staff to help out in the galleries. We are planning lots of new things, but trying not to be as manic as we were at first. We were organising six events a week at one time – we expanded too quickly. Now we are planning to do just one event a week. But the object remains the same – we want to be a community hub, a place for artists to meet and show their work and for locals to come and see their work – but also to get to know each other. We have just started asking everyone in the Monkton Village area to fill in a form online, saying how they came to be living here – then we will turn it into a book.'

Is there no end to their enterprise? I thought I was a busy bee, but I would never in a million years think of standing for a local council when I was doing so much for the community already. Good luck, Dawn and Jenna.

Dawn's likes

- The landscape and the views.
- The spirit of community.
- The sense of belonging.

Jenna's likes

- I love looking out over the Solent towards Portsmouth and feeling grateful that I am not there and that Portsmouth is not here. I only lived on the mainland for a short time. I am so pleased and thankful to be back on the island. I like the feeling of separation from the mainland.
- The beaches, of course – I love them all, and the community.

Dawn's dislikes

- I hate the big housing estates outside Newport. There is one called Pen which they have now changed to calling Open Meadows. It's horrible. They are in fact like pens – people being herded like cattle into such small places.

Jenna's dislikes

- The Isle of Wight council – the county one as well as the town council in Ryde. They are so backward-thinking, don't realise or appreciate what a wonderful island they have got here, that it has to be cherished and protected.
- The plastic tourism attractions which are getting more common. I have nothing against old-fashioned seaside amusements like the sort we have in Ryde – the pirates' den, for example, the crazy golf, the trampoline. But the one at Shanklin on the seafront I think is horrible and nasty and should not have been allowed.

In the May 2021 elections, Jenna was elected to the town council. But she wasn't done yet. Later she also elected deputy mayor of the town. Well done Jenna!

For a while it looked as if I was going to have *two* chums and neighbours on the council, but alas, my friend on the front with The Big Kahuna café, Wayne Whittle, decided not to stand again, after twenty years of service.

CHAPTER 21

Hovering with the hovercraft

The world's largest hovercraft takes to the
sea for the first time, East Cowes, 1968

So much for the arts. But what about science and technology? Here also, the Isle of Wight does not disappoint, for it boasts a unique feature in the form of the world's oldest and – as of 2021 – only known regular hovercraft service, connecting Ryde and Southsea. Beat that, Cornwall or the Lake District.

I remember catching sight of it on our first visit to Ryde. What on earth is it? A beast, a creepy-crawly, a giant snail, slithering and sliding and slipping across the wet sand next to Ryde Pier. Is it a boat? Because it clearly moves on water – no, hold on, is it a plane? It clearly is in the air, hovering just above the waves. Very weird. Human eyes and brains are not used to such an unusual creature.

After they have arrived, and once they have climbed down the dinky steps and over the flapping skirt of this strange craft, almost all passengers – whether first-timers or regulars – turn round and take snaps of it. For the hovercraft is one of the Wight Wonders.

When he was a little boy, Neil Chapman was transfixed by the hovercraft. He lived in Portsmouth, where his dad was in the navy. He has a photo of himself aged two, in 1970, standing in front of the hovercraft, just after it had landed in Ryde. It was his granddad's favourite treat, to take little Neil for a trip on the hovercraft. That's all they did: got on the hovercraft; got off; then got back on again for the return trip. They never ventured into Ryde.

Now, some fifty odd years later, Neil is the managing director of Hovertravel. His dream has come true. 'I still consider it an honour to have this job.' He has spent all his working life in the travel industry, starting when he left school and joined Lunn Poly, the travel agent. For many years he ran a team in a customer services company at Gatwick airport. In 2010, he was invited by the owners of Hovertravel, the Bland Group, to become their MD.

The origins of the Bland Group go back to 1810, when an Englishman named Marcus Henry Bland established a shipping company in Gibraltar. In the 1890s, the company was acquired by the Gaggero family, who expanded its shipping interests and also ventured into air travel and tourism, becoming owners of the Rock Hotel in Gibraltar in 1959. Today, the Bland Group owns not just Hovertravel, the company that runs the hovercraft service, but also Griffon Hoverwork, a company based in Southampton that develops and manufactures hovercraft. The chairman of the Bland Group is James Gaggero, the fourth generation of the family to have chaired the company.

The idea for a vehicle or craft travelling on a cushion of air had been around for a few centuries, but it was Christopher Cockerell, a boat builder and engineer living in Norfolk, who created, and patented, the first successful working model of a hovercraft in 1955. Cockerell discovered the key concept of his design – a wall of moving air around the edge of the craft – when he used a hair dryer to blow hot air into the space between a coffee tin and empty cat food tin placed inside it... Or was it a coffee tin placed inside a cat food tin? I am a bit hazy on the precise details, but Neil, could you be kind enough to explain the physics and how it works?

'My experience is in the running of the company, not explaining how exactly a hovercraft works. But I can arrange for you to talk to one of our experts.'

Cockerell faced similar difficulties of understanding back in the fifties. The government scientists, when he unveiled his invention, suspected they might well have a brilliant new secret weapon on their hands, but the navy said, 'It's not for us – it's not a boat, it's a plane.' And the air force said, 'It's not a plane, it's a boat.' For a year or two it remained classified, but in 1958 it was declassified, and Cockerell was able to persuade the government-funded National Research Development Corporation to develop a full-scale model of his hovercraft. The NRDC then commissioned Saunders-Roe, a firm that had long experience and success in flying boats and aeroplane production – and was based on the Isle of Wight – to make the first hovercraft. So hovercraft history began in the Isle of Wight, and the craft enjoyed its early years and successes here, all of which explains why it is still here today.

The present hovercraft service from Southsea in Portsmouth across to Ryde began in 1965, just in time for little Neil to gaze in wonder and amazement. For a time, it looked as if there would be similar services all over the world, an alternative source of marine transport. For those living in Britain and France, the best-known hovercraft service ran from Dover to Calais for thirty years. The arrival of the Channel Tunnel in 1994 rather finished it off, by providing an easier and more economical service. The hovercraft is a bit expensive to fuel.

Neil, are you really now the only hovercraft service left in the world?

'Hmm, we are a bit careful with the wording. We tend to say, "The longest-running regular hovercaft service." There is some sort of hovercraft in the wilds of Russia which still gets mentioned from time to time, but I don't think it is a regular service, all the year round. Not like ours. I see us as a community service. Yes, it has to be commercial and has to run at a profit, which it does – a small profit – but I like to think it is part of the social and economic fabric of the island.

'During the worst of Covid, the NHS contacted us for help getting people quickly across the Solent to hospital in Portsmouth. We re-fitted the insides to allow wheelchair access and enabled an ambulance to come straight up to our steps – and then an ambulance at the other end to do the same. When Portsmouth FC are at home, we always put on a late hovercaft which leaves Portsmouth at 10.30 p.m. for Ryde. It brings home the Isle of Wight's Pompey Supporters' Club members who have been across the Solent to see the game. Normally, our last trip of the day is at 8.30 p.m., so it is of great use for football fans.'

His fleet of hovercraft – or should it be called a squadron? – numbers just two, the *Solent Flyer* and the *Island Flyer*. But they do a great deal. Each holds seventy-eight passengers and one wheelchair. Between them, they buzz back and forward all day long, making a total of seventy crossings. The number of passengers carried in a normal year is 800,000. This seems like an enormous amount for relatively small craft – and even more so when you consider the total number of visitors each year to the Isle of Wight is only two million. A staff of just seventy – including pilots, engineers and office staff – keep the show on the water.

Today, 10–15 per cent of the passengers each day are islanders, travelling to Portsmouth for shopping, medical or other reasons. About 70–80 per cent of the total are visitors, tourists coming to the island on holiday or to visit friends and relations. Neil reckons that around 10–15 per cent of passengers are regular commuters – not only to Portsmouth, but going on elsewhere in Hampshire and even as far as London. Neil's own home is in Brighton and he goes across some three times a week. He stays at the Royal Esplanade Hotel, Ryde if he has lots of meetings, otherwise he returns the same day to his flat to be with his partner, Graham. The onward train takes around ninety minutes – just bearable, he reckons. Graham works in the airline industry and Brighton is handy for him to get to London's airports.

'We have one regular – a former judge called Richard Price – who calls himself the longest-serving hovercraft commuter passenger. He doesn't need to do it any more – he is just a hovercraft enthusiast.'

By chance, a few weeks later I sat next to Judge Price at a rather boozy lunch party in Seaview and asked him if it was true. 'Certainly,' he said. For fifty years he travelled every day on the hovercraft to Portsmouth, first as an articled clerk at a firm of solicitors, later as a barrister and then as a judge. 'I loved the hovercraft – and loved every crossing.'

The 6.30 p.m. hovercraft into Ryde each evening turns round and becomes a designated Royal Mail craft for parcels. The packages tend to be bulky or breakable items or contain living creatures – they get a lot of baby chicks and unaccompanied pets – which need to get to the mainland quickly and in one piece. Other regular passengers include windscreens and urgent legal documents requiring signatures.

Hovertravel are always willing to hire out a hovercraft for birthday parties or commercial purposes. And apparently there is a small – but possibly growing – market for bereaved passengers who wish to hire the hovercraft as a place from which to scatter the ashes of a loved one.

There is keen competition between the various cross-Solent services. Despite it being a small island, there are four ways of getting to the Isle of Wight. Two car ferries run – the biggest being Wightlink – formerly Sealink – which goes from Portsmouth to Fishbourne. The other car ferry is Wightlink which goes from Lymington to Yarmouth. I've not been on Red Funnel, but I assume it carries a better class of customer, as it serves places like Cowes and Yarmouth. We residents of Ryde can be a rather rough lot. The FastCat service runs catamarans from Portsmouth to the end of Ryde Pier, controlled by Wightlink.

The fares and facilities are hard to understand, let alone compare. For newcomers, booking can be like navigating a labyrinth. Wightlink seems to come in for most criticism from locals in this respect – for expense and delays. It depends, of course, on the time of day and the season and also whether you are a resident, in which case you can buy a batch of of tickets at a cheaper rate.

Mostly, Claire and I have taken the Wightlink car ferry to Fishbourne, as Claire always insists on having her car to carry all her stuff for herself and for the house. It cost us £156 on that very first trip, back in the summer of 2020, which horrified me. Though some people say they have paid over two hundred pounds at really busy times.

Once we settled down and got proof of residency, I bought a book of ten tickets for the car ferry at a cost of £290 – which works out at twenty-nine pounds per trip, for me and Claire and her car. The hovercraft service is not just quicker – ten minutes compared to forty – but also cheaper, usually costing around twelve pounds (although of course it has no room for cars or bikes, and there's not enough time to serve refreshments). But going on the hovercraft is an event in itself, appealing to the small boy in everyone.

Is there a Hovertravel fan club? I wondered. Like the one for Eddie Stobart enthusiasts – the obsessives who spot these familiar lorries on our motorways and write down the female names given to each of them. There were at one time 25,000 Eddie Stobart fans with their own magazine, meetings and outings.

No, they have not quite reached that stage, but they hope to work on it, some day. Neil pointed to a large wooden block inscribed with the letters 'HUG' ('Hovertravel User Group'). It does apparently issue various leaflets and announcements for regular users.

Throughout our conversation, Neil jumped up every fifteen minutes or so – and sometimes went out onto his viewing platform – to look down at the next hovercraft coming in or out. The noise was so shattering that any talk between us would have been impossible. He has one of the best views in all Ryde, right on the shore, beside all the action.

Recent developments in the technology have made the hovercraft engine more economical. The early models had two engines. One produced air with those huge, paddle-like wheels you can see at the rear of the hovercraft, pumped the air under the skirt and lifted up the hovercraft. The other engine was required to propel the craft through the water. Now the same engine – currently fuelled by diesel – serves both purposes.

As I left, Neil promised to include me on a special outing which they have once or twice a year. This year they were going on a jolly for the day across to Lee-on-the-Solent to visit the hovercraft museum. Never knew they had one. How exciting.

Can I sit up top with the pilot?

'Not sure about that – health and safety, you know. But you can talk to the pilot when we land. And on the way across, he will be doing something unusual – figures of eight in the water, which we don't usually do on the normal, cross-Solent service.'

A few weeks later, Claire and I got to the terminal for the trip really early, very excited, though we did not know what to expect. Would it be like a staff outing, a media jolly, nobs from the island or just ordinary punters? Turned out to be the punters – hovercraft lovers who had paid for the trip a year ago, when it was postponed because of the Covid pandemic. There was a long queue round the building – half families with overexcited kids while the other half seemed to be fairly elderly gents with their cameras and notebooks at the ready.

Halfway over we did indeed do a figure of eight. It happened rather slowly at first and I thought the pilot was just trying to avoid some of the yachts. It was a Sunday and the Solent was awash with sails. I realised we were slowly spinning round, full circle. Then we did it again. I didn't feel sick or scared, the way I used to be on the big dipper or the waltzer at the fairground.

It was all smooth and easy – it was just that the horizon was suddenly moving round 180 degrees. It did not seem real. More like a back projection at the movies, when they superimpose different scenes and landscapes behind the actors.

There was a crowd of about a hundred people waiting to greet us when we got to Lee-on-the-Solent, watching and waving, standing on a little grassy knoll beside the slipway. Probably not a lot to do in Lee, I thought. Then I understood they were waiting to get on our hovercraft for their own, half-hour pleasure trip, having been promised, like us, that the pilot would be doing figures of eight.

Neil was on the slipway when we got out, with his fluorescent Hovertravel jacket on, the boss working on a Sunday, which I thought rather admirable. His partner, Graham, was also there, helping passengers. Plus about a dozen other staff.

'These excursions are a great day out,' said Neil. 'And a wonderful promotion of the hovercraft, celebrating its history at the museum.'

The hovercraft museum was right on the shore near the slipway, which was historic in itself, being formerly used to launch seaplanes. It is the only museum of its kind in the world, run by a charity created in 1988, totally staffed by volunteers. It normally opens only on Saturdays in the summer, yet attracts around six thousand visitors a year and is officially a transport heritage site. It looked a bit run-down from the outside, consisting of two very old hangars, but one turned out to be Grade II listed (like our house) and, inside, there were sixty different hovercraft of all shapes and sizes and ages, plus models, photographs, excellent videos and information boards explaining the history of the hovercraft. The hangar dates back to 1917, when it was a naval seaplane training school, run by the Royal Naval Air Service. In the last war, the site contained the busiest airfield in the south of England during the D-Day landings.

Four of the exhibits are officially 'national historic ships', because they are either unique or awfully historic. One of them is the biggest civil (as opposed to military) hovercraft ever built – the SRN4 *Princess Anne*, which used to cross the Channel from Dover to Calais in thirty-five minutes. It carried 418 passengers and sixty cars.

A lot of the hovercraft on show are military or naval vessels, some rather dark and sinister-looking. But there are also fun ones, built for fairgrounds. There's a little hovercraft dating from the 1960s, intended for personal use, that could be carried on top of a Mini. Our guide, Doug Coulson, stopped in front of a rather dinky and pretty little yellow hovercraft which he said was inflatable and belonged to him. He paid £4,000 for it four years ago and takes it out to sea three or four time a year. Apparently these hovercraft are still being made by a company in Sandwich. A new one today will cost you £15,000. Sounds like a bargain to me – that's cheaper than many a yacht.

Several of the hovercraft on show have appeared in films over the years, such as *Murderers' Row*, a 1966 comedy thriller starring Dean Martin. The star attraction is probably the hovercraft which appeared in the James Bond film *Die Another Day* in 2002, starring Pierce Brosnan.

I was surprised how fast some of the craft crossed the Solent back in the 1960s; much faster than today. In 1964, the DRN 3 crossed the Solent in four minutes and fifty-three seconds, reaching a speed of 65 miles per hour. No wonder hovercraft were at one time deemed perfect vessels for naval action. The only trouble was the noise. You could always hear them coming.

Our craft eventually returned to pick us up, and we did some more figures of eight – wow. Back in Ryde I managed to talk to our pilot, Nick Wood. He has thirteen years of experience in the role. Guess how many times he has done the trip between Ryde and Portsmouth? Oh, go on, guess, indulge an old man. And don't rush to the end of this chapter for the answer. That's cheating.

Nick is thirty-nine and was born in Newport, then lived in East Cowes, where his mother was a teacher. His father was in the merchant navy, then became a harbour master and later a Southampton pilot – that's the kind of pilot who takes out a little boat in all weathers to climb up a ladder to pilot a vessel safely into port, not the sort of pilot in a hovercraft who does figures of eight.

It was inevitable that Nick would follow his father and end up at sea. After attending the fee-paying Ryde School, he went to study at Fleetwood Nautical College, Lancashire. For two years, he was an officer of the watch on various tankers, he told me. 'Then I joined our rivals, Wrightlink, and worked for them for three years.'

He had a girlfriend who, like him, lived on the island. The varying shifts and having to start and finish work in Portsmouth each day became tedious so, when he saw an advert for a pilot on Hovertravel, based in Ryde, he applied. The training lasted three months, during which he went from never having set foot on a Hovercraft to being 'let loose' to pilot a craft on his own – albeit initially with strict limitations on what he was permitted to do. He undertook twenty-five hours of training on an empty craft. A further one hundred hours were completed on the route, again under instruction. Then he took another test to become a fully-fledged hovercraft pilot, one of only eight in the company – and in the world, really, unless there are some hovercraft pilots lurking in Russia we don't know about.

On each crossing Hovertravel use one pilot and two members of crew who can take over the controls should the pilot fall ill. They know the basics, but are not trained pilots. One crew member sits with the pilot in his cabin, helping to keep lookout and navigate, while the other remains downstairs, attending to the passengers.

Nick took me round the outside of the craft and explained that, beneath the big black skirt there are strips of the same material hanging down which they call fingers. These wear down and have to be replaced every three months or so. I lifted up the black skirt to have a look, and I could see the floating fingers hanging down.

Because the tide goes out so far on Ryde Sands, the craft usually travels the last hundred yards or so on sand. Is that easier, faster, or does it feel just the same?

'It is different. I could tell with my eyes shut if we were over water or sand. You do have to take extra care on sand, but it is easy enough.' In theory, Nick said, the hovercraft could carry on, after leaving the sands, into town, along the Esplanade, up Union Street, whizz through the town and along the roads. That would startle the shopkeepers and amaze and delight the tourists.

At last, I was allowed into the pilot's cabin. You get into it from the passenger area, climbing up a very steep ladder. I found it hellish at my age, with my dodgy knees. Squeezing through the small gap at the top must also be very difficult if you are overweight. Inside the cabin, it was remarkably spacious, with windows all round.

I said there was as much space as on Concorde. Back in 1986, when my wife and I went to Barbados, we were invited into the pilot's cabin. And we got a certificate afterwards to say we had flown at Mach 2, which is about 1,350 miles per hour. Beat that, Nick.

Hovercraft can fly – yes, Nick did use the word 'fly' – at 50 knots per hour, which is pretty fast over water, but they never do more than 45 knots for safety reasons.

The cabin had a full complement of screens and displays, radar, GPS and two VHF radios. One radio keeps him in constant contact with Hovertravel base while the other allows a harbour master at either end to warn of any dangers or problems, telling him to slow down and wait if, say, there is a monster tanker about the length of the Wembley Stadium approaching or the new HMS *Queen Elizabeth* destroyer is leaving Southampton. This happened recently, so Nick had to wait and give her a clear run.

'There is no steering wheel. And no brakes.'

What? Nick, can you say that again?

'Yeah! People are always surprised by that. They think all we do is turn a steering wheel one way or the other, like the dodgems. There are lots of hovercraft fans out there who think they know better than us. After a trip, they will collar you and say why did you do that, why did you turn that way?' He explained that the pilot steers by operating a rudder located at the back of the hovercraft. 'I have a footbrake I can use to change the rudder, but being a modern pilot – oh, yes – I use a joystick which I find much easier.'

In an emergency, he would have to put the engine into reverse, open flaps on the side of the vessel and drop the skirt – causing his craft to stop within two lengths. Even then, you have to concentrate properly to avoid being smashed to smithereens by a monster tanker.

'The first time I saw one,' he said of these huge ships, 'I could not believe it. It was like a skyscraper looming over me. But you can always see them. I aim to cross half a mile after their stern, to avoid the worst of their wash. But it is the little boats you always have to worry about. I work on the principle that yachts and small boats never know what they are doing or where they are going. So I always veer away from them. The Solent is so busy, all the year round: there are thousands of yachts, people on paddleboards and, of course, swimmers. In the summer I see a windsurfer getting into trouble, or a yacht losing control, every single day.

'One of the other pilots saw a man on a paddleboard drifting towards Ryde Pier, obviously not knowing what he was doing. He slowed down, opened his window and asked the paddleboarder if he was OK. He said, "I am fine." He knew he was not, being aware of the strong currents round the pier. So he warned base on the radio – and ten minutes later the paddleboarder had crashed into the pier. They had to rush out and rescue him.

'I had a mayday call not long ago. The coastguards were telling anyone near Ryde Pier that there was a boat on fire. I stopped and had a look, but could see nothing. It turned out to be two lads in a dingy who were drunk and sitting smoking something. They were just drifting and ended up stranded on a sand bar and had to be rescued by the coast guards.'

Nick says that, after thirteen years, he still loves his job. 'No two days are the same. Each day is different. The sea is always different. The number and types of ships are never the same.'

So, what about the figures of eight, presumably he doesn't do them on service crossings?

'We don't actually call it that. I call it a 360-degree spin. We turn round full circle, usually twice. We could in fact turn on a penny, without moving at all, as the craft can easily turn on itself. But in a 360-degree spin, we do a wider arc, so everyone can see and enjoy all the views changing around them.'

And now the answer to the question I asked earlier: how many crossings has he done?

'I have worked out I have done twelve thousand hours in my thirteen years, based on four full crossings a day. So I make it that, in total, I have done 48,000 crossings.'

Now you know...

CHAPTER 22

Alan Titchmarsh

Yachts on the first leg of
the 2012 Round Island Race

At the ferry terminal in Portsmouth, where you catch the car ferry for the Isle of Wight, they have a gallery on the staircase leading to the little shop and café in which are hung portraits of the great and the good of the Isle of Wight, famous folks who lived here at some time, such as Queen Victoria and Dear Albert, poets and writers like Lord Tennyson and Alfred Noyes. I studied them all carefully as I walked up the stairs.

I noticed only one living person – someone who is greatly loved on the island. He is a poet, among other talents, and an illustrator and a bestselling writer of non-fiction and fiction. He is so well-liked and respected on the island that in 2008 he was appointed High Sheriff of the Isle of Wight, just for a year – an honorary position for which you have to dress up in black velvet knee-breeches and tailcoat and carry a cocked hat and a sword.

Guess who he is? Here's a clue. His best-known claim to fame is as a gardener. Now you know – yes, it is the one and only Alan Titchmarsh. Before we arrived on the island, I never knew he had any connection with the place, but I then noticed his name popping up everywhere in the local media, as a local celebrity. I wondered how someone who had always seemed to be something of a professional Yorkshireman ended up on the Isle of Wight? After all, one of his memoirs was entitled *Nobbut A Lad*…

He was born in Ilkley in 1949, son of Alan, a plumber, and Bessie, a stay-at-home mum who, before she married, worked in the local mill. Alan left school aged fifteen with one O level but he was very lucky – he got a job as an apprentice gardener working for the council.

'I was thrilled. It was all I ever wanted to do. Gardening had been my ambition as a boy. When I was aged ten I built my own greenhouse. My hero in life was Percy Thrower.'

Having served his apprenticeship as a council gardener, he went on to horticultural college and from there moved to the botanical research and educational centre at Kew Gardens, where he did a diploma. 'Kew was the making of him,' said his wife, Alison. 'That is where he first flourished.'

He met Alison when he was living in Kew and attended a meeting of the Barnes and Richmond Operatic Society. She was a dance teacher. They got married in 1975. At Kew he progressed to becoming supervisor of staff training. One day, he was asked by his boss if he knew anyone who had any literary leanings; anyone who saw themselves as a writer. He put up his hand, having loved writing at school and fancying himself as something of a wordsmith. His boss had spotted an advert placed by Hamlyn who were looking for an assistant gardening book editor. Alan got the job. It was difficult, deciding to give up Kew for publishing, but Alison encouraged him to make the jump.

One day, the author of a book they had commissioned on house plants failed to deliver, and Alan volunteered to write it. And so, in 1976, *Starting with House Plants* became his first published book. Since then, he has published more than forty gardening books and, since 1998, twelve novels, several volumes of memoirs and a book of poetry. The total of his published works now comes to more than seventy. Not bad for a lad who started out with only one O level.

He has also had a long radio and TV career. 'I got a regular job on Radio 4's *You and Yours* as their gardening expert. By then I had become deputy editor of *Amateur Gardening* magazine and I heard they needed a gardening expert so I just wrote them a letter. I still have the carbon copy of the very letter I wrote to them in 1977. The first time I was interviewed I had to talk about turf. I was introduced by Derek Cooper who called me Alan Titchfield. At the end of the programme, the producer told him he had got my name wrong. He gave out my correct name and said, "Sorry" for his mistake – adding that although I might be dynamic, I was no thunderbolt. But he was sure that the nation would be hearing more from me in the future.'

Cooper's joke may have aged a little… The *Titfield Thunderbolt* was a popular 1953 British comedy film about a locomotive called the 'Thunderbolt', which a group of villagers acquire for their threatened branch line.

'It was at the time of a greenfly invasion in Margate, in 1979 – swarms of them had blown over from the continent – that I made my first appearance on television. The Radio 4 *Today* programme asked me to come in for a few minutes and talk about it. I was then contacted by *Nationwide*, who wanted me to offer the same advice to TV viewers.'

He has hardly been off the radio or TV ever since – not just doing gardening stuff, such as *Gardeners' World*, *Ground Force* and presenting coverage of the Chelsea Flower Show, but also hosting general magazine programmes such as *Pebble Mill*. He also had spells hosting Songs of Praise and presenting classical music on Radio 2.

Some forty years ago, once his media career was blossoming, he and Alison moved from their first tiny house in Sunningdale, Berkshire (Barnes and Richmond being beyond their means), to Hampshire. Twenty years ago they moved for a second time, into a Georgian farmhouse with four acres not far from Winchester. In the 1990s he bought a boat – a motor cruiser which he kept at Chichester, on the West Sussex coast. It was family trips across the Solent that introduced them to the Isle of Wight. Twenty years ago, he and Alison bought a holiday home on the island, where they now spend around four months of the year. The house is in Cowes and has a stunning situation overlooking the Solent. It's not one of your period gems, it's much more contemporary, the sort of clapboard house you see at Martha's Vineyard or Cape Cod. Claire immediately decided that Alan's house is the one on the island she really, really wants.

It wasn't their first place on the island. They originally had an apartment in a large house along the front – and bought a second apartment when they started having visits from grandchildren. About five years ago their present detached house came up for sale, so they sold the two apartments and bought it. 'It belonged to the harbour master in Cowes. He was downsizing and going to live in Lanzarote.'

It has a lawned garden with trees sloping down towards the sea. At the back is a steep, sub-tropical garden, with palms and tender plants that enjoy the mild climate by the sea, plus a handsome mulberry tree. I wanted to go out and inspect that bit, hoping to find some weeds, but it seemed unlikely. Alan admitted he has two gardeners who come every Tuesday afternoon to tend to the garden, under his direction, of course. Just imagine having Alan Titchmarsh watching you do his garden!

There would be no problems, of course. Alan has the reputation of being one of the nicest chaps in the media. Everyone speaks of his kindness, naturalness and lack of ego or pomposity. And he is supposedly something of a sex symbol. For decades, women of a certain age have been fancying him from afar, longing to get their green fingers all over him.

The house itself is spacious, with gleaming wooden floors and lots of original artworks. In one room there is a massive doll's house in the style of a Georgian manor, which he proudly opened up for me. He did not actually make the structure, but he personally decorated and furnished all the many rooms. It must have taken him ages.

He is 'a bit of a collector', interested in books and other objects. And yet there is no obvious sign of clutter, usually the sign of a keen collector. But Alan would appear to be ever so tidy and has his treasures carefully hidden away. They include royal items, with an autographed object from every king or queen back to Henry VII. He also has a collection of Daphne du Maurier material, being a bit of a fan of her writing.

Over an excellent lunch, I admired his great head of hair, just in case he might have taken any liberties, but no, it's all natural and genuine, lucky feller. He looks fit and tanned and appears much younger than his seventy-two years, which he has often been told.

'On TV, men over sixty have to have all their own hair. I can't think of any man of my age who appears regularly on TV who is bald. Just think about them – David Attenborough is ninety-five. What a grand head of hair he has. Melvyn Bragg, now in his eighties. Michael Palin, too.'

Alan never seems to stop working, yet appears so relaxed, never in a rush. He has regular columns in *BBC Gardeners' World* magazine and *Country Life*. He presents his Saturday morning programme on Classic FM. That day he was getting ready to go on location to film a new TV series and had recently finished his twelfth novel. Alison would rather he did slow down a bit, but he loves being busy. And active and in demand.

He didn't start writing his novels and memoirs until he was in his fifties, although by then he had loads of gardening books published. He happened to mention to Jilly Cooper, after he had interviewed her for a programme, that he was thinking of writing his first novel. She not only encouraged him but agreed to read the first five chapters and make suggestions, which was kind. But then kind people often attract kindness from others.

He and his wife have two daughters, Polly and Camilla. Rather posh names, considering his mum was Bessie. 'She hated being called Bessie – said that it was a name only given to cows and fire engines.' Both daughters are grown up and married and have two children each, giving Alan and Alison four grandchildren, two boys and two girls aged nine, eight, seven and six, all of whom were due to visit next week. Good job he has a large house with lots of rooms and a big garden and the sea to mess around in just a hundred yards away.

At the bottom of his front garden he has a boat house, also constructed from clapboard, in which Alan writes when he is on the Isle of Wight. The Royal Yacht Squadron and the other Cowes yacht clubs are just a few hundred yards away, but Alan is not a member. He still has a boat, but just a small 'day boat', in which he takes his grandchildren across the Solent for outings up the Beaulieu River.

He adores the Isle of Wight, can't keep away. When he has to go to London to present his Classic FM programme, he will often get up early and go just for the day, so desperate is he to get back to Cowes.

'If you look at England as a balloon, with all the counties painted on it, then you burst the balloon and immediately it will shrink and the print will become intense. But you might still make out all the different counties. That's like the Isle of Wight. We are all the counties of England – in miniature.'

Good simile, Alan, but I think you might have to work on it a bit, before you take it anywhere. He smiled. He can take being teased.

He and his wife are quiet, non-ostentatious Christians, who go to church occasionally. He helps various charities on the island and in Hampshire. Years ago he did some commercial work, which involved him lending his name to a range of gardening tools, but it's not something he does any more.

'Someone once told me many years ago that you are your own currency; spend it wisely. I try to live by that. I try to avoid diluting it.'

Alan's likes

- So much in the island is so lovely. And there is so much variety.
- My favourite place is Steephill Cove, down by the sea just along from Ventnor.

Alan's dislikes

- The chain ferry between East and West Cowes drives me nuts. We have to use it when we are coming over from the mainland in the car – if it's working. It is always breaking down for some reason, or else the tide is out and it has run aground. Grrr!
- Alison dislikes it when they won't deliver stuff from the mainland to our house in Cowes. And it has just happened to me. I ordered something last week from a London shop and they said, 'Sorry, we only deliver to the mainland.' I mean, we are part of the British Isles!

CHAPTER 23

Good times, bad times

Beach huts at Small Hope Beach, Shanklin

One of our simpler pleasures since we arrived in Ryde is taking a ride on a Vectis double-decker bus. Anywhere, really. I like standing at the little bus station at the end of the pier, looking at all the buses lined up, ready to shoot off to all parts of the island.

When our bus eventually arrives, usually a No. 8, heading down the coast, Claire and I always rush to get on first, then clamber upstairs to sit at the front, just like kids. We each have our freedom pass from London. Which amazingly works in the Isle of Wight. Oh, I do love anything free.

I always study the excellent local bus map, which covers the whole island. It is superior by far to the train timetable, which does not seem to exist (nor do the trains, for that matter, though for months we have been promised that the train service from Ryde down the coast to Shanklin is returning soon).

The Isle of Wight has just one railway line, the 8½-mile Island Line from Ryde Pier Head to Shanklin – a mere fraction of the 55-mile rail network it once boasted (though there is a heritage steam railway that connects with the Island Line at Smallbrook Junction). But Ryde still has as many as three railway stations: Ryde Pier Head, Ryde Esplanade and Ryde St John's Road. Ryde Esplanade railway station is right beside the bus station. The distance between Ryde Pier Head and Esplanade station must be the shortest distance between two stations anywhere in Britain. The line then goes into a tunnel and swoops under the Esplanade and, I like to think, under our house, though I have never heard it. That may have something to do with the Island Line being closed for an upgrade, which was then delayed owing to the Covid pandemic. I gather that before its temporary closure they used ancient 1930s London

Underground carriages on the line – I do hope there are some left when it opens again. The island certainly seems to be well served by buses, though a lot of them seem to head inland first to Newport, the capital, or end up there.

I clutch my bus map all the way, ticking off all the stages as they come over the intercom. Claire thinks this is potty. She just likes to stare out of the window, not knowing where she is.

On this particular bus journey, we were heading for Bembridge, at the easternmost point of the island. We got off before the village and walked along the waterfront, looking at all the houseboats, one of which is home to the Best Dressed Crab restaurant. We had been there twice and liked it. So romantic, sitting on a boat to eat.

We walked along the coast, heading for the other side of Bembridge. Since September 2020, we had been trying to walk the whole coast, but at the rate we walk it will probably take us ten years, if we live that long. Well, it'll certainly take us that long at the rate I go. When the tide is in and you have to clamber over the stones and rocks, it's hellish for my poorly knee. It's OK for Claire, of course. She is a fit young woman.

The tide was half out, so there was a bit of wet sand and seaweed, but it was OK for walking. This section was new to us and I could not really follow it on the map. While the bus map is excellent, the tourists' maps are too vague, too busy being pretty and colourful, promoting all the wonderful attractions.

I began to tire and was dying for a coffee but could only see an empty beach ahead, as if we had been shipwrecked. Even looking out to sea, it was all empty, no boats on the horizon. I realised we had walked round a bit of a peninsula so the familiar views we get from Ryde across to the Spinnaker at Portsmouth, and all the multitude of boats, were not there.

There seemed to be no habitation ahead, no sign of life, just some white cliffs in the far distance, which looked too far to reach before the incoming tide would cut us off. It's strange how, on a small island, you can sometimes feel totally alone in the world, as if you were on a desert island; but you know that up there, over the cliffs, there is life going on inland. We then spotted in the distance, right on the shore, what looked like a beach hut – or might it just be some bits of colourful driftwood piled up on the beach?

When we got nearer, we saw it was a wooden beach café, full of people, with wooden chairs and tables, and little areas with flowers and plants and overgrown grass, all very natural and artistic. From the accents we heard and the menu on display it could have been somewhere posh in Cornwall. It was simply called the Beach Hut. Its menu showed it specialised in lobster, crab and seafood platters. Such a shame it was too early in the day to have lunch, but we ordered coffee. I spoke to the couple who ran it. They said they opened in 2011. They now do deliveries, as the café is quite hard for people to find unless they know it is here. We made a note to come back and have a proper meal.

We had already found quite a few beach cafés, tucked away on apparently empty beaches, which looked at first like shipwrecks, but turned out to be lovely places to eat, offering excellent seafood. The best known beach café on the island is probably The Hut, near Yarmouth, which we will probably never visit, as it sounds as though it is full of thirty-something whizz-kids drinking flutes of champagne who have arrived in their speedboats from Southampton or come by helicopter from Chelsea. From Battersea heliport, it is only a twenty-five-minute flip.

We then cut inland and arrived at Foreland Road. I remembered that when Dylan played at the Isle of Wight festival in 1969, he stayed at Foreland Farm. I wondered if there was a blue plaque on it. I'd not seen any on the island so far. It started to rain so we sheltered in a handy bus stop and gave up trying to find the farm. Another time.

In my mind I still had at least twenty places and people on the island that I wanted to visit or meet, but I was beginning to realise I would never get round to them all in this first year. We walked through Bembridge, which has a pretty upmarket main street, and then down the hill to Pilot Boat Inn, where we had stayed on our first visit to the island. Opposite it, on the beach, is the Harbour View Café, which is not as arty or as boho-stylish as the Beach Hut, but we had enjoyed a meal there all those months ago. We had liked Michelle, the woman who runs it, and the sixth-former from Ryde School who had been working there as a waiter over his Christmas holidays.

It was now high summer and the café was full, but Michelle was there, smiling as ever. We managed to get a table outside, and immediately ordered a bottle of Pinot Grigio. Claire ordered half a lobster – she knows how to live, and also how to use the nutcracker thing to crack the shell and get the goodness out. I don't like lobster. No, it's not just the price. Lobster seems all texture and no taste to me. So I had a hamburger, which I had forgotten I don't like either, but the menu said the meat was locally sourced. We stayed quite late to finish the bottle and caught the bus home.

It had been a grand day out: we had had a good walk, discovered a new path and a new café, and eaten at another café we already knew and liked. So I don't quite know what happened next. We got home, feeling thoroughly pleased with ourselves, opened another bottle of wine and immediately started annoying each other. We had been bickering on and off about two subjects in particular over the last few weeks and now, before I could stop myself, I brought one of them up again, just as we were on the first drink.

Claire often repeats what her mother often repeated to her,

that there are two main reasons couples have rows – money and sex. I always say this is far too simplistic. And anyway, the two arguments we had that evening were nothing to do with either sex or money.

Going over the delights of the day, raving about the Beach Hut, I said we must take Flora and Richard and their daughters there. They will love it.

'No, you won't,' she said. 'We won't be here.'

Why could I not enjoy the pleasure of being at home here with the family? If Claire was adamant that she was going home before they arrived, why couldn't I stay for one night, to welcome them? Flora was collecting her two girls straight from school on the Friday, catching a train, and then the hovercraft. I would meet them off the hovercraft, take them briefly to our house, where they could have showers and a drink, then take them all for a slap-up meal at The Duck, just five minutes away. What's wrong with that?

'You always think of yourself,' she said.

'Oh yeah,' I said, 'what about you?' I then stupidly moved on to the new folding doors which she was desperate to have and had been researching for weeks. 'The folding doors are not for my pleasure,' I said. 'I don't want them. I know we decided you were in charge of the decor and furnishings of this house, but didn't we agree that if one person was violently against something, the other would give in and we wouldn't do it? Anyway, I don't want the folding doors.'

We had inherited double glass doors into the courtyard, but only one of them would open. This seemed fine to me, as the door that opened, the left-hand one, provided enough room for people to walk though or carry chairs out. But Claire had got it into her head that it was vital to have modern folding doors, so the whole doorway could be opened up. I said it was just a trendy fad, and that there was no need for them, what with the expense and the upheaval. Having the damp proofing done was expensive enough, but that was vital. Folding doors are just cosmetic.

'It will turn the courtyard into another room,' she explained, 'and, while I am in the kitchen cooking or getting drinks, I will be able hear all the chat outside, which I can't at the moment.' She confessed that she had been to see a firm who makes such doors to measure. It won't cost more than three thousand pounds. These days they are made of light aluminium. 'It will increase the value of the house,' she said.

'Bollocks,' I said. 'You know what happens with all houses. New owners rip out everything and start again, following whatever the latest fashions and follies. I remember, when we bought our London house in 1963, Margaret and I ripped out all the fireplaces because we were putting in central heating. Ten years later, we put all the fireplaces back. We had open fires *and* central heating. Folding windows, however trendy now, will not be the major selling point when this house gets sold. Anyway, I am not selling. Ever.'

So on we went, arguing away. Claire says I get argumentative after a few drinks, which I deny. Anyway, I had ruined a lovely day by raising two topics which had already been a source of discord between us. My fault, of course. It usually is the man's fault – not wanting anything changed, can't see the need, can't see what is worn, what is wrong and, of course, not wishing to spend more money, being a mean bastard. Which I am. I know that now.

This row was typical of most marital arguments. They are usually about trivial things but escalate into slanging matches. And these piddling, annoying little things can grow bigger, fester longer. I had rows like this with my wife, especially in the early days; and I am sure Claire had them with her past boyfriends.

I had lived on my own for two years after Margaret died.

Then, when I started to see Claire, it was only every weekend. Now for the first time we were close up and personal and, at times, rather intense, perhaps making up too much for the time we had had on our own – in Claire's case, many years living on her own. The six months we had spent together so far had seemed in many ways like six years – or even sixty – of marriage. Unless each of you is a complete robot, with no personality or views, then these petty irritations are inevitable. And, in a way, a good sign. Shows you care – about each other, the house, life together and all that.

Before bed, with us both still in a bit of a huff, I said, 'OK, then, I won't be here when Flora and Miles come.' As for the doors, let's wait another year. We have not had a full summer here yet. We don't know what the courtyard will be like at the height of summer or even if we will see any summer, with all the overhanging trees from next door.

So we went to bed, each of us still annoyed with the other, but I did manage to utter the mantra which Claire eventually echoed: WE ARE SO LUCKY...

CHAPTER 24

Dimbola

Dimbola Lodge, Julia Margaret Cameron's
home and workplace

Next day we had another splendid outing – and this time I did not ruin it. I find that apologising and taking the blame is always jolly helpful.

We went to visit the home of another eminent Victorian woman. Before coming to the Isle of Wight, I did not know that Julia Margaret Cameron, the pioneering photographer, had lived on the island. Nor did I know that Alfred Lord Tennyson had a house here – though more recently I had picked up that he had, which was why Bob Dylan had agreed to perform at the festival.

But I also did not know, until I read up on each of them before our visit, about the rumour that Tennyson had had an affair with Cameron. Just think of them getting it together, those two pillars of Victorian society and the Victorian arts world! What with Victoria and Albert in a permanent state of intimacy – judging from all the children they had together – and Alfred and Julia at it as well (allegedly), we had clearly alighted on the perfect island for a love nest.

Tennyson became poet laureate in 1850 and remained in that post until his death in 1892 – the longest reign of any poet laureate. He was born in Lincolnshire, the son of a vicar, but moved to London and became a national celebrity after the publication of 'In Memoriam A. H. H.' – a requiem for his friend Arthur Hallam, which was published the year he became laureate – taking over the duties from Wordsworth. Wordsworth himself had become a celebrity in later life and his gardener at Rydal Mount, who also cut his hair, sold locks of the great man's hair over the garden wall to gawping tourists. Tennyson, living in London, had even more fans and fame, enthralling the nation with such poems as 'The Lady of Shalott' and 'The Charge of the Light Brigade'.

In 1852, he and his wife Emily went househunting on the Isle of Wight. They were very taken by Farringford House, at Freshwater on the island's remote west coast. Tennyson's aim was 'to get away from the noise and smoke of town'. And, of course, the fans. They rented Farringford House in 1853, and bought it in 1856.

Julia Margaret Cameron, who had moved in the same social circles as the Tennysons in London, first visited the island in 1855. On one of her trips, she stayed with them for an extended period. In 1860, while her husband was in Sri Lanka tending to his coffee plantation, she bought two adjacent properties in Freshwater, just a short walk across the fields from Farringford, which she would convert into a single, spacious family home. Today, Tennyson's and Cameron's houses are – supposedly – open to the public. Our original plan had been to fit them both in on the same day but, alas, Farringford House seemed to be closed all the time, although the gardens were open.

Instead, we set off to look round Dimbola, Julia Margaret Cameron's home from 1860. I wondered where the name of the house came from and what there was to see. Would there be enough to make it worthwhile driving all that way? In under a year, we had already become little islanders, considering any trip to the other side of the island to be a journey to the far side of the known world. Yet it can be easily done in just under an hour from Ryde.

Dimbola, turned out to occupy a splendid position, just under half a mile from Freshwater Bay, with good views from all the front windows. In 1860, on buying the property, Julia knocked the two houses together and in 1870 built a new central tower, thereby creating quite a grand country house.

Julia was a dab hand at tarting up houses, a bit like Claire, really, forever seeing new things which she thought desperately needed doing. She once had an eminent artist friend staying who complained that, when having his afternoon rest in his bedroom – a bit like me by the sound of it – the sun was never quite on his bed. Within twenty-four hours, she had organised workmen to come and install a bay window through which the afternoon sun fell exactly on his bed. Imagine getting any workmen these days to arrive and do a job in twenty-four days, never mind twenty-four hours! If I had been Julia's husband, I would have said, 'Don't be potty, it doesn't need doing – it's just cosmetic. I am not spending good money on that sort of indulgence.' Fortunately for Julia, her husband was away a lot, tending to his estates. So he didn't know about all the changes she was making or how often she was popping across the fields to see her dear friend Alfred. Allegedly.

She was born Julia Margaret Pattle in Calcutta, India, in 1815 – one of seven daughters of a high official in the East India Company, all of whom were known for their vitality and style. 'To see one of the sisterhood flow into a room with sweeping robes and falling folds was an event in itself.' She was sent to England to school, then returned to India where she married Charles Hay Cameron. He was twenty years older, a widower, working for the Supreme Council of India. She established herself as a society hostess, holding lots of parties for the governor general.

When her husband retired in 1848, they moved back to London with their three children. Julia threw herself into London's literary and artistic circles, meeting Tennyson, the painter G. F. Watts and members of the Pre-Raphaelite Brotherhood.

In the 1850s and 1860s, acquiring a home on the Isle of Wight became very fashionable, thanks partly to Queen Victoria and other famous people like Tennyson. G. F. Watts and his very young bride, the actress Ellen Terry, also took a house at Freshwater. Ellen was just seven days short of her seventeenth birthday when she married Watts in 1864, who was thirty years older. Alas, she did a runner after one year of marriage. Goodness, what a good gossip all the Freshwater crowd must have had.

The presence on the island of this small colony of writers and artists drew a stream of distinguished visitors, including Charles Darwin, W. M. Thackeray, Lewis Carroll and Edward Lear. The situation sounds rather similar to the Lake District earlier in the century, when writers and artists of the day flocked to Grasmere and Ambleside and Keswick, hoping to pop in on Wordsworth, Robert Southey, Samuel Taylor Coleridge and Thomas De Quincey.

Julia did not pick up a camera till 1863, when she was aged forty-eight. Her husband was again abroad in Ceylon, looking after his coffee estates, when one of their daughters gave Julia a camera as a present. 'It may amuse you, Mother, to try to take photographs during your solitude at Freshwater.' It does not sound as if her life was really all that lonely while her husband was away. She was an inveterate social organiser, hosting the local quality as well as entertaining her artistic and literary friends from London.

Through the marriage of her favourite niece, she became great-aunt to Virginia Woolf, who was a frequent visitor to the island, usually staying with Anne Thackeray, the daughter of the novelist, at a house nearby. Thackeray's granddaughter later wrote that 'Freshwater in the time of Tennyson has been compared to Athens in the time of Pericles, as being the place to which all the famous men of the reign of Queen Victoria gravitated.'

And in the midst of these eminent Victorians was a society hostess, a daughter of the Raj, who turned herself into a celebrated photographer and went on to capture them all for posterity. She soon got to grips with her new present, converting an old greenhouse and chicken coop into her studio and workroom. She mastered the heavy plate camera, in its large wooden box, learned how to mix the necessary chemicals and created her own darkroom. Within just a year, she had been elected a member of the Photographic Society of London and had acquired a London dealer, Colnaghi. Two years later, she was awarded a gold medal in Berlin.

In the 1870s she would produce a series of images to illustrate Tennyson's *Idylls of the King*, a cycle of poems based on Arthurian legends, for which she got her family and friends to dress up as nymphs, angels and knights in armour. She also illustrated biblical stories and scenes from Shakespeare, which involved yet more people dressing up in costumes. Some critics derided her illustrative photographs as the work of an amateur, and they also mocked her use of soft focus. But it is Cameron's remarkable portraits of living people, which have been much admired, that reveal how talented she truly was.

It took her three years to persuade her good friend and best-known neighbour Tennyson to pose for her. It was an enormous drag, having to pose for a Victorian photographer. You had to sit still for up to an hour, without breathing or moving, and put up with lots of retakes, but most sitters were keen and willing. Photography was a technological wonder of the age and people were pleased to be immortalised. Across the nation, thousands of local photographers opened studios specialising in 'cartes de visite'; these were small photographic portraits mounted on a piece of card, which people gave out to their friends like visiting cards.

Tennyson, when he finally agreed, joked that he had become a victim, but he went on to recommend the experience to friends who visited him, such as Longfellow, the American poet. Tennyson described how he left Longfellow to Julia's mercies, 'You will have to do whatever she tells you. I will come back soon and see what is left of you.'

Julia often persuaded her sitters to adopt striking postures or wear bizarre costumes; she would then capture them at a strange angle – just like modern fashion photographers do – while she crouched in front of them, one eye watching through her wooden camera. Other distinguished Victorians who sat for her included Robert Browning, W. M. Rosetti, Thomas Carlyle, Alice Liddell, William Holman Hunt, Charles Darwin and Anthony Trollope.

The house today is a joy, much bigger and spacious than I was expecting, with a lovely tea-room and a restaurant covered in William Morris wallpaper. Upstairs there are about a dozen galleries, mostly devoted to Julia's works, from her literary illustrations to her studies of local children all dressed-up, plus her portraits of the great and the good.

In January 1864, having finally mastered the laborious photographic process, Julia Cameron took what she described as 'my very first success in Photography'. The rather serious-looking child in the portrait is eight-year-old Annie Wilhelmina Philpot, niece of George Granville Bradley – friend of Tennyson and future Dean of Westminster – in whose family the little girl was brought up following the early death of her mother.

The caption beneath the portrait quotes Julia's joyful reaction to the photograph: 'I was in transport of delight. I ran over all my house to search for gifts for the child...' I felt as if she had entirely made the picture I had printed, toned, framed and presented to her father the same day. Sweet sunny haired little Annie. No later prize has affected the memory of that joy.'

The caption to her portrait of Thomas Carlyle, a masterpiece of light and shade, in which every hair of his bushy beard seems to be illuminated, describes what happened when Julia went to Carlyle's house in Cheyne Walk, Chelsea, to photograph him, in the words of Carlyle's wife Jane. 'She was hardly to be restrained from forcing her way into Mr C's bedroom when he was changing his trousers. Thomas later growled in his Scottish brogue, "I'd have you know that I am in the hobbit of wurin clean lunen."' Julia sounds as though she was rather pushy, like all good snappers and reporters.

Claire and I spent two hours going through all the rooms, studying the prints, reading all the excellent captions. Two hours is a long time for me in a museum. I can usually do an art gallery in thirty minutes. The final rooms, upstairs, show the works of more contemporary photographers. That day there was a display of fashion photos from the sixties and seventies by Terry O'Neill. In them we saw poses and angles which Julia Cameron was already using 160 years ago.

Overall, I think the portrait of Julia's that I studied longest was her photograph of Ellen Terry: beautiful, sensitive and fragile – and just sixteen, the age she was when she married old Mr Watts.

Julia died while she was in Ceylon in 1879. She and her husband had returned to try to save his collapsing family coffee plantation. She had named her Freshwater house Dimbola, after the family estate in Ceylon.

The house later had several owners. It was bought in 1991 by a property company that obtained permission to demolish and redevelop the site. A local appeal was organised, the Julia Margaret Cameron Trust was created, funds were secured, grants obtained from the Department of Culture, Media and Sports. The house was saved and renovated. The hunt began for the originals of her photographs and the house and the collections were eventually opened to the public.

Osborne House is clearly the number one house on the Isle of Wight – the place where another, much more famous, woman once lived. Dimbola by comparison is small and of specialist interest. But I had known so little about Julia Cameron, and how talented and remarkable she had been. It was all so fascinating, that the visit stayed in my mind for many weeks.

I learned the origin of the name of the house during the visit but alas, I never found out if Julia and Alfred were ever more than just good friends. Local village gossip, I suspect.

CHAPTER 25

Mike and Bob

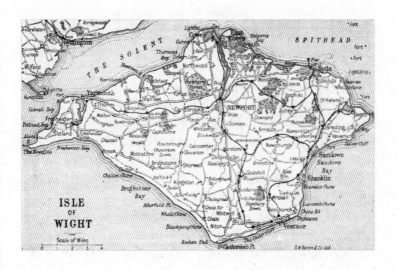

Roads, railways and landmarks of the
Isle of Wight, in a vintage postcard

There are six members of the House of Lords with homes on the Island at the last count – six Lords a-leaping, as they all sound pretty fit. There could even be a few more of them that I have not yet come across, lurking somewhere.

Six is a lot for a very small island, but I am sure the attractions for them are the same as for any other person of a certain age and class who either retires here or has a holiday home. The sea, the sea, all those views, all that sailing, the pleasure of being out of the limelight and the public eye, away from prying paparazzi and able to live quietly, among people who mostly don't know who the hell you are and don't really care.

Lord Fowler (formerly Norman Fowler), was a Tory health minister in the 1980s, as was Lady Bottomley – when she was plain Virginia Bottomley – during the following decade; her husband Peter remains an MP to this day. Lord Brabazon, the 3rd Baron Brabazon of Tara, has a home at Bembridge. Baron Oakeshott of Seagrove Bay is not far away, a couple of beaches along the coast.

Then there are two life peers who were friends of mine long before we came to the island. John Sharkey and his wife Astrid are neighbours in London. He used to be joint MD of Saatchi & Saatchi and became a Lib Dem peer in 2011, taking the title of Baron Sharkey of Niton Undercliff in the county of the Isle of Wight. I never knew they had an island home till I happened to tell Astrid of my plans to buy.

Their holiday home is hidden away at Niton. They bought it about thirty years ago when one of their daughters was on a school camp on the island. They came to visit her and saw a house they loved, which had a sign saying it had been sold. This did not deter them, so they put a note through the letterbox and – lo and behold – the sale had fallen through so they got it. Perseverance, eh? They live quiet and pretty invisible lives, on the island, unlike my other friend, Michael Grade.

It's not that Michael Grade is ultra-sociable but that he lives in the heart of Yarmouth and gets involved in various good works. When he walks around the local streets, going into local shops, everyone knows him and says, 'Hello.' Most of all he is a yachtie, a very keen racer, a member of two yacht clubs on the island, and is known and recognised by all those people who wear yellow corduroys in winter and pink shorts in summer. I have known Michael for thirty years – ever since he invited me to write a book about his family. At the time his uncles, Lew Grade and Bernie Delfont, were still alive, both of whom became life peers. More importantly, his grandma, Olga Winogradsky, was still alive, a redoubtable woman who escaped a pogrom in Russia back in 1912 and arrived in the East End of London, penniless, with her husband and two small boys under her arms. She went on to have a daughter and a third boy, Leslie, who was Michael's father.

Michael's parents separated when Michael was little, aged three, and he was brought up by his grandmother Olga. It was because he felt he owed her so much that he asked me to do the family history before she got too old. She died in 1981, by which time she was able to boast that she was the only Jewish momma in the world with two sons who were Lords.

Her three sons dominated British show business for decades, in the theatre and on TV and in films. Michael followed roughly in their footsteps, becoming a big cheese at both ITV and the BBC, of which he was chairman from 2004 to 2006, as well as running film companies and Channel 4. He became a life peer in 2011.

A life peer's title includes a location. There had already been a Lord Grade – Lew, who died in 1998, Lord Grade of Elstree.

'I said to my wife Francesca when I got the call, should I call myself Lord Grade of Charlton?' Michael has been a long-time supporter of Charlton Athletic, just as his dad was, and had been a director of the club for many years. 'Or should I call myself Lord Grade of Yarmouth?'

'Michael, there is no choice,' replied Francesca.

And Yarmouth is where they live today and have their main home, though they have a rented place in Chelsea for attending the House of Lords and other commitments. Michael invited me and Claire to have lunch with him at the Royal Solent Yacht Club, on the seafront next to Yarmouth pier, so very handy for his house – unlike his other yacht club, the Squadron, which is over in Cowes. It was a lovely sunny day and we sat outside in a peaceful, secluded position on the yacht club terrace, looking out at the boats, and at the ferries chugging in and out. In Yarmouth itself, the day-trippers were swarming into the little town, crowding its bijou streets and pretty little shops.

Doesn't it drive you mad in summer, being here, with all these people?, I asked Michael. We have other friends in Yarmouth who have told us they try to get away in summer, as it is just too popular.

'Oh, no, I love it,' was his response. I like walking round the streets, seeing all the visitors. I am pleased for the local shops and restaurants, the museums and souvenir places because the tourists are bringing them business.'

Michael never learned to sail as a boy; it was not part of the family's East End tradition. Lew and Bernie's exercise was more likely to be dancing. Lew Grade began his career as a professional dancer, and was especially proficient at the Charleston.

'But when I was a very little boy, about six or seven, my grandmother moved to Bournemouth. I remember looking out across the sea and being told that was the Needles in the distance. There was also a paddle steamer which went past; I think it was the *Waverley*. I remember telling myself I would sail to the Isle of Wight one day.'

It did not happen until he was thirty. He was by then married to Sarah Lawson. 'Her father was a keen yachtsman and got me interested. He had a boat at Lymington and took me sailing. We entered for a race during Cowes Week and it turned out to be a force-six gale, freezing cold and windy – absolutely appalling weather. "That'll teach you," said Sarah. And I said, "No – I loved it. Now I want to be able to do it properly."'

He bought himself a string of yachts, starting with the 45-foot *Grand Soleil*. He hired a skipper to sail it and to teach him the ropes.

Some years later, after his marriage to Sarah Lawson collapsed, he became friendly with Francesca Leahy. 'I first met her in Edinburgh where I was appearing at the TV festival. She was supposedly looking after me. I contacted her later and asked her out. One of the first things I asked her was if she was interested in sailing. If she had said no, that could have been it. But she said, yes, she loved it.'

Together, they went down to Lymington to sail his boat as often as possible. Their favourite trip was across the Solent to the Isle of Wight, either to Newtown Creek or Yarmouth.

'We were sitting in this exact spot, here in the Royal Solent Yacht Club, ten years ago, idly saying to each other wouldn't it be nice to have a place here. Francesca then happened to mention it to a local friend – and this friend introduced us to a woman who turned out to be a house-finder. She drove us round the island to some lovely houses for sale – then took us to this wreck of an old cottage. Stand up and you can see a bit of it. It's only a hundred yards away along the front. It needed so much work done, but the situation was incredible. We made an offer and got it – and spent a fortune doing it up. Francesca is an interior designer, so it was mostly her project and her creation. It was the only house we had seen which was right on the sea. Houses with actual sea frontage on the Isle of Wight tend to pass down the generations. They rarely come on the market, so we were very lucky.'

Did they not find getting workmen a hassle, with good ones being hard to book and then not turning up?

'Not really, we had no problems. We used to rent a cottage in Cornwall for several years and every time we had a problem we would ring a workman and he would say he was coming "drekly", meaning "directly". Which, of course, he never did. The average wait was four days. I asked one why they always said they would come directly when they never did. Oh, that's just what we say to all the visitors...'

The house is their main home and they were there full-time during all the lockdowns. They love it, as do their children and grandchildren. Their son Samuel, who went to Eton, is a very good yachtsman. He is also a musician, studying the double bass at the Royal College of Music. Michael also has children from his two previous marriages and has five grandchildren, all whom love coming to visit. Grandads do tend to be popular when they have their own boat and a stunning house on the sea.

After lunch, Michael took us to meet Francesca, who was busy working at home on some urgent design commissions and had therefore not been able to join us for lunch, and to see the cottage. It dates back to 1850 and was part of a little row of three cottages right on the water's edge.

Michael's house is right at the end, perched on the water, with its own little slipway, perfect for launching his own dinghy or rowing boat or going for a swim, straight out of the cottage. The sea views are uninterrupted and wonderful. To one side is not only the yacht club, but also the very handsome Yarmouth Pier, stretching out into the sea.

Today, Michael has a big yacht which he co-owns with a friend – a fifty-foot long craft made by the Shipman company. He has sailed the Atlantic in it three times and competed several times at Cowes Week. He was getting ready to do so in 2021 as well.

'The best I have done is second in my class. And I have a certificate on my wall to prove it.' It must be, er, rather costly, running such a smart yacht, I ventured. Apparently it takes ten to crew it, when they are racing in competitions. It sleeps six, which is handy when he is off sailing it round the island with friends and family. 'Sailing is not cheap,' said Michael. 'Everyone knows that. I once saw a yacht which was called *Never Again 2*. I know exactly what the owner meant by calling it that. But, oh, the pleasure I get out of sailing. All your problems and worries just fade away when you are at sea. You can't think about anything else except the winds and the tides. It is the most wonderful escape.

'I also enjoy golf and I apply the same principle to that as with my sailing. I am not all that brilliant at either golf or sailing, so I always chose to do them with nice people. [Multiple Olympic sailing medal-winner] Ben Ainslie is a friend of mine who also lives on the island. I was talking about sailing with him once and asking him whether I should get myself fitter and leaner to do it. As you can see, I am not quite as slim as I once was… Ben said to me, "I would never get off the start line if I lived on lettuce." So that's my principle. Eat and drink and sail – and enjoy life. And where better to do it than the Isle of Wight? I do love it here and have no plans ever to leave.'

Michael's likes

- The topography – whichever direction you go on the island or round the island, north, south, east or west, it is all stunning. I never tire of it.
- Yarmouth. I love the people and the community here.

- All the sea views of course, but especially at our cottage. We are so lucky to live in such a perfect spot.

Michael's dislikes

- None really – just the unreliability of the ferry service. Francesca the other day had her booking suddenly put back four hours and it totally ruined all her work and plans for that day.

After meeting a life peer, it seemed only fair to meet a common-or-garden MP. The MP for the Isle of Wight is Robert Seely, a Tory known locally as Bob. I hadn't heard of him before coming to the island, but since then I've read a fair bit about him in the local papers, the *County Press* and the *Observer*. Though I couldn't quite work out if they liked him. Local papers do tend to have their faves. Readers' letters also give away how popular their local MP is.

I didn't really want to get into local politics, as this is a personal, happy book, but Michael told me Bob was a good chap, worked hard for the island – and most of all, was an islander, who knew a lot about the place.

I mentioned his name to a few locals in our street and they said, 'Oh, he's island aristocracy; in with the nobs now, are you?'

He invited me and Claire to lunch, which was kind, to a part of the island we had not yet visited, around Brighstone, a village that sits between the downs that run across the island like a spine on one side and the remote southwest coast on the other, site of many a shipwreck in Victorian Britain. We had been along the coastal road that follows the south and southwestern coast several times on the way to Freshwater, but had not ventured inland. Gosh, it is lush, full of yummy thatched cottages, mellow brick mansions, sweet little lanes, charming churches and pretty shops. Rather like the Cotswolds, but with the sea thrown in for good measure.

Bob lives in a cottage at Mottistone, on an estate that used to be owned by the Seely family but was bequeathed to the National Trust by Lord John Seely, 2nd Lord Mottistone, on his death in 1963.

Bob is divorced. He has a girlfriend who works in local radio and is a standup comedian. She was on the radio reading the island news the day we popped by, so we didn't meet her. In fact, his cottage seemed very much a bachelor pad. He made us a lovely lunch which we had in the garden, all very efficient, with no fuss, almost like a military operation – but then the army has been one of his various careers.

Bob is aged fifty-five: 'attractive and handsome', so Claire said; 'fit and active-looking', so I said, jealously. He has swum the Solent several times and also plays the guitar. Quite a catch, I suppose.

He put me right on his place in the Seely family. Yes, they have been on the island for a couple of centuries and owned a chunk of it at one time. They even have a family dinosaur – the fossilised remains of a new type of Iguanodon were discovered on their land in the nineteenth century and was named after them – *Iguanodon seelyi*.

'The family has always had a passion for the island. A love for it and I inherited that when I was very young,' said Bob.

His part of the family made their money in land and coalmines in Nottinghamshire. The family's 'founder', Charles Seely, Bob's great-great-great-grandfather, was a Liberal MP who defended the Chartists and made his first fortune in the Agricultural Revolution and the second in the Industrial Revolution. He invited the Italian revolutionary Garibaldi to England in the mid-nineteenth century, infuriating Queen Victoria, his near neighbour on the island. She refused to speak to him for twenty-five years. The fact that he was also one of the very few republicans in Parliament probably didn't help his cause.

The Seelys have produced six MPs in the last seven generations, including Bob. Most have been Liberals. In fact, Bob was the first one knowingly elected as a Tory (a great-great-uncle was elected as a Conservative on the island while fighting in the Boer War, but it was assumed he had been put forward as a Liberal. He joined the Liberals a few years later, anyway).

Bob was born and brought up in Belsize Park, London. His father worked for the government and then became a barrister. His mother was German-born. His English grandfather, Bill Seely, was killed leading his artillery regiment, the South Notts Hussars, in 1942. Later in the war, Bob's German grandmother was killed by the Soviets.

Bob went to Harrow School and then set off into the world, looking for adventures. It began with a spell as a reporter on the *Sunday Mirror*, doing doorstep interviews. Then he moved abroad and, for five years, he was a stringer for *The Times* in Ukraine in the former Soviet Union, where he also wrote for the *Washington Post*.

In the early 2000s, he joined the army reserve and, a few years later, found himself mobilised to go to Iraq. He was put on full-time reserve service for the next decade and served in Afghanistan, Libya and in northern Iraq. He also found a cottage in the Isle of Wight. 'I discovered it out of the blue. It was down a winding, single-track lane which seemed to twist and turn for ever. At the end of it was my new home. It had always been my dream to re-make roots here. My earliest and best memories of childhood were the times spent on the island. At Brook or near Bonchurch, playing on the beach or climbing the rocks, looking for crabs and wondering what adventures I would have growing up.'

Several years later, midway during the 2017 election, the sitting MP for the Isle of Wight retired – or more accurately, 'was retired'. Bob applied for the nomination and won it on the first round. Today he has a large majority of 24,000. So, in theory a safe seat – although it's been Liberal twice before in living memory. The island is, by population, by far the largest constituency in the UK, roughly twice the size of the average and four times the size of the smallest Scottish constituency. 'I don't care whether the island is technically safe or not – it's my home and I want the best for it, so I am not going to be sitting on my backside taking it easy. It's my dream job. I don't take it for granted.'

He was at one point a junior ministerial aide, but voted against the government on various things – including the building of the HS2 rail route – and returned to the backbenches. 'Don't get me wrong, I'd love to be a minister, but getting a better deal for the island is the priority now – and, frankly, learning the art of being a good parliamentarian. You can't control much in politics, but you can decide what sort of MP you want to be. Too many people go into ministerial roles too quickly without learning how to be a decent MP first.'

He appears to be something of a free, independent thinker, with strong beliefs, not always prepared to follow all the party lines, but his passion is clearly for the Isle of Wight. 'It's fabulous to have the chance to be an MP, but I'd never be content unless I was representing the island. It's like being married to the right woman. If anyone else was MP here, I'd be forever plotting blue murder!'

He thinks the island gets overlooked by central government, especially when it comes to being granted funds. It sometimes seems to be ignored by the media – in the travel pages, for example. He gets fed up when they are writing about the delights of the Lake District or Cornwall and ignoring the Isle of Wight.

'I am a bit chippy about it. I do see these other places as our rivals, in a nice way – possibly we are getting better coverage then we used to; the island is being more appreciated as the special place it is. And let's face it, do we really want to be so overrun with tourists that we end up as crowded as Cornwall?'

He has worked hard to put the island on the map, managing to get the island special status from the Arts Council and – for the first time – the government to recognise that the island is an island. 'We are getting there, but it's only the beginning, there's a way to go yet. J. B. Priestley was right, the island should have been Britain's first national park; I wish we had gone down that route. However, with a possible change of law coming, the island can become Britain's first island park. We currently have a series of designated landscapes, but it's bizarre that they were not united in a single whole. I'm hoping we can make that happen.'

Bob is fascinated by the island's history – politically and culturally – and by the artists and poets who once lived here. 'After the Napoleonic Wars put an end to touring Europe, artists and writers instead turned to inspiration at home – and the island was one of the places they went to, as Turner's sketchbooks of the island showed. The Freshwater set around Tennyson included many of the intellectual giants of Victorian Britain, and they all came to stay on the island. If you look at Tennyson's work, and indeed that of his brother, you see at times the island reflected in it.'

Bob went on to recommend poetry collections by two twentieth-century writers who settled on the Isle of Wight: Henry de Vere Stacpoole's *In a Bonchurch Garden* and Alfred Noyes' *Orchard Bay*.

Turning back to the here and now, Seely worries about over-development. 'We need to protect the island and, frankly, invest more in our own people. We need housing for islanders, in the right places, well-built – like it used to be. What we don't need is low-density, car-dependent, greenfield development which is slowly suffocating our quality of life, our visitor economy and doing lasting damage to a landscape which has been celebrated by artists and poets. We don't want to end up looking like Poole,' he said, tongue-in-cheek. That backhander was rather wasted on me, as I have never been to Poole. Clearly, I won't go now.

Bob always tries to support and help local business, especially independent shops and producers. He said he rarely goes into a supermarket – though I did notice some of his lovely and generous lunch did come from Marks & Spencer's delicatessen and was delicious.

'We have fifty food producers on the island. I get my food from them – via Brighstone village store – most of the time. Supermarkets are depressing, anonymous places. We have lots of island milk, cheeses and yogurts, and seasonally available local vegetables. OK, we don't produce avocados (yet), but a lot of the UK's tomatoes come from the island's greenhouses. I still go to M&S for oatcakes, though.'

As an MP, his postbag and his surgeries are dominated by the same two main complaints I have heard all year from both islanders and visitors – the ferries and the roads.

'I feel the same pain as everyone else with the ferries. As for the roads, they are a lot better than they used to be. Most of them have been rebuilt in the past seven years. In general, I get frustrated when stuff isn't just right, but we need to remember, we live in a special place.'

Bob's Likes

- I love all of it, but if I had to name my favourite places they are: Brook Beach, Newtown Creek, Ventnor and Bonchurch, especially the path from Bonchurch down to the sea, Yarmouth and the estuary.

Bob's dislikes

- Low density, greenfield development.
- Idiots treating the Military Road as a racetrack.

CHAPTER 26

Museum of Ryde and Rude

The Royal Victoria Arcade, Ryde, 2014

After all the expeditions to places and people in far-flung parts of the island – well, some were at least twenty miles away – I at last managed to visit an attraction right on the my doorstep. It wasn't until the summer that I finally got into the Museum of Ryde – and also saw the Museum of Rude! Yes, they always give it an exclamation mark, which I never do. I always consider it the mark of an amateur.

All year I had seen notices and posters around the town about the world-famous Donald McGill 'saucy seaside' postcard museum.

The only two people I ever knew who actually had original artwork of the McGill postcards are Paul McCartney and the late Michael Winner. I was always so jealous when visiting them. The cost these days for the original artwork of one of his postcards is at least a thousand pounds.

The Donald McGill Museum is situated in the Royal Victoria Arcade in Union Street. It is part of the Museum of Ryde, in the basement, but it never seemed to be open when I was there. Obviously, it was closed during lockdown, as most things were, but even when the restrictions were eased, I never seemed to catch it open, despite visiting the arcade itself lots of times.

There are around fourteen shops and stalls in the arcade, mainly collectors' shops of the sort I can never resist, selling old books and magazines, records, postcards, ephemera and memorabilia. It also has a very attractive coffee bar in 1950s American style, with waitresses wearing bobby sox and flared frocks.

The Royal Victoria Arcade was opened in 1836 and named after Victoria when she was a princess – she did not become queen until the following year. It offered rather upmarket shopping for the local gentry and people of taste, with living accommodation above the shops. In the basement were workshops and kitchens.

The arcade fell derelict in the 1970s and – despite having been Grade II listed in 1952 – was once in danger of demolition, but it was saved by local worthies.

In 2011 the Historic Ryde Society was formed and they moved into the basement of the arcade and started showing their treasures, illustrating the history of Ryde, all donated by volunteers. The chairman today of the Historic Ryde Society today is Brian Harris. One of the reasons it took me so long to track him down – apart from the arcade always being closed – was that since we got here I had been confused by the fact that there is a separate body in the town called the Ryde Society, which looks after preservation.

Brian and his wife Sandy come from Coulsdon, Surrey. They have known each other all their lives because she lived next door to him when he was growing up. 'I was too lazy to go courting far afield. That's a joke – I would like to remain married...'

He worked for thirty-four years for BT as an engineer and was offered redundancy in 1998 on a good pension. He jumped at it and retired to Ryde. During the last twenty-three years, he has thrown himself full-time into voluntary work. He was on the Ryde council for many years and ended up mayor. But he has channelled most of his energy and enthusiasm into the Historic Ryde Society.

Brian kindly agreed to show me the museum the day before it was due to open publicly for the summer. Gosh, it was so exciting; I stepped carefully down the little wooden steps to the basement and Brian got out some large keys and unlocked the chains to the entrance. I had been ogling these steps for almost a year, wondering what lay behind the locked door – a dingy basement or some proper, vaulted cellars?

I was astounded by the size of it. There are sixteen rooms in all. Although they are basically cellar rooms, they are full size and full height, extending to the side under the adjoining shops. And every room is filled with the treasures and memorabilia and memories of Ryde. The work of gathering, cataloguing and organising the displays, as well as creating films featuring old clips of Ryde, has been carried out by the society's own volunteers. They have to pay £8,000 annual rent for the basement, so they charge visitors £4 for entry. And there is a membership fee to join the society. For two hours Brian never stopped talking. He explained in detail the contents of each of the rooms, all of which I found fascinating, although afterwards my head was reeling.

All aspects of the history of Ryde are here – the shops, breweries, buildings, the buses, the hovercraft, the aeroplanes and the Isle of Wight Rifles (a local regiment). It is amazing to think that the ten thousand or so items in the collection have only been gathered in the twelve years since the society was founded and the museum created.

One of the displays that is most popular with locals (and exiles returning to the island), is devoted to the local schools. They have school photographs from every island institution, plus scarves, blazers and examples of school reports. Another much-loved attraction is an old aluminium swing, shaped like a boat, hanging on chains, which was once in Puckpool Park. Brian says he often hears people of a certain age shouting in delight when they see the swing – immediately recalling the hours they spent swinging on it as children, sixty-odd years ago.

The display which Brian is clearly most proud of is the ice well. This was how the quality kept their food and drinks cool in the 1830s. Stately homes often had their own ice wells – or similar arrangements. Very often it was just a deep hole dug either outside or in a basement. In the winter, when there was real ice on local ponds or streams, they would wheelbarrow lumps of ice into the well. If they were lucky and the ice well was deep and cold enough, the ice would then stay frozen for months. Some of the ice was sold in buckets to local households in Ryde – the sort that needed ice to cool their champagne, such as those of the better class of naval officers.

Years ago Brian had heard that according to old plans and documents, there was an ice well in the basement. But when they moved into the building in 2011, they could not find it. It looked as though the entrance to it had been blocked up. Eventually they worked out where it might be and knocked through a wall which led into a little corridor – and there they found it. It was a massive hole in the ground, stone-lined, about twenty feet deep and ovoid in shape. This means it was circular but wider at the top than the bottom. According to Brian, it is the only integrally built ovoid ice well in the country, to take ice imported from Norway or the Great Lakes of North America. Beat that attraction, Lake District and Cornwall.

Alas, when it was located the ice well turned out to be filled with rubbish and decaying objects and very unpleasant-smelling water. It had not been used for at least a hundred years. It took Brian and several other volunteers six months just to empty the well. They disposed of four tons of rubbish. The things volunteers do, eh?

They then had to pump out all the remaining water. Luckily, Conrad Gauntlett of Rosemary Vineyard and Mermaid Gin fame (see Chapter 18) was on Ryde council with Brian at the time. He provided them with a pump and two men who worked for two days to take out all the water. Today the ice well is ever so clean and the stonework gleaming fresh. Looking down into it, it feels a bit scary, which amuses school children when they are touring the museum.

Also in the museum is a tribute to something once found in every seaside resort in the whole of the UK – the Great British saucy postcard, the best of them being created by the one and only Donald McGill. I had wondered how on earth a Donald McGill museum had come to be in Ryde, when as far as I knew he had no connection with the town.

Donald McGill was born in 1875 in London, near Regent's Park. His parents were Scots-Canadians. One of their ancestors gave his name to McGill University in Montreal. Donald's father was a retired captain, living on an inheritance, when he died of pleurisy in 1883. His mother and her seven children moved to Blackheath, southeast London. Donald was sent to Blackheath Proprietary School, which sounds rather posh, so there must have been a bit of money left. One of his best friends in school became the bishop of Wakefield. Aged sixteen, he sustained an injury while playing rugby which went untreated and resulted in his left foot being amputated.

He attended Blackheath School of Art for a year, then worked for several years as a draughtsman. One day he sent an amusing get-well card to a sick nephew. All his relations and friends found it so funny and artistic that they thought he should sell his cards. He went on to produce more than twelve thousand artworks from which were printed millions of saucy postcards. He didn't die rich because he only ever got three guineas for drawing each postcard. And, owing to the drama that unfolded towards the end of his life, even this income was drastically reduced.

From the 1880s onwards, British people on holiday at the seaside, having a good time and wanting a good laugh, loved the humorous cartoons of McGill. My collection features a lot of used postcards, on which the addresses and messages are still legible. And it is evident that a lot of the purchasers of McGill's cards were women, sending them home to other women for a bit of fun. They clearly enjoyed the double entendres and did not mind the fact that a lot of the jokes were at the expense of big, fat women or depicted men leering at attractive young women in bathing suits. Just to even up the sexes – and the targets of his bawdy humour – McGill's cards include plenty of weedy men being henpecked by their wives, or failing to get off with women. In Donald McGill's world, women's voluminous frocks are always being blown up by the wind and Scotsmen always wear kilts and are always mean.

His art was excellent: its colours bright and cheerful, the observations precise, and the depiction of details of the clothes and styles of the time perfectly up to date. His work reflects our social history, covering topics like the suffragettes and the First World War. While some po-faced clerics turned up their noses and the middle classes considered the cards vulgar, only fit for the industrial working classes, McGill acquired a following among the intellectuals of his day.

George Orwell, in an essay he wrote in *Horizon* magazine in 1941, remarked on the social significance of the postcards, which he saw as a continuation of the tradition of music-hall humour and a harmless form of rebelliousness. Orwell was unsure whether there was actually such a person as Donald McGill or if the name covered a group of cartoonists, but he was sure of the postcards' worth:

The genuine popular culture of England is something that goes on beneath the surface, unofficial and more or less frowned upon by the authorities. One of the things one notices if one looks directly at the common people, especially in the big towns, is that they are not puritanical. They are inveterate gamblers, drink as much beer as their wages will permit, are devoted to bawdy jokes and use probably the foulest language in the world. They have to satisfy these tastes in the face of astonishingly hypocritical laws – licensing laws, lottery acts, etc. – which are designed to interfere with everybody but in practice allow everything to happen.

Most people, both then and now, would hardly consider

McGill's jokes to be all that rude. In one of them, a lady is looking at a selection of seaside postcards in a window, being watched in the background by a vicar. 'The postcards down here are positively disgusting,' she says. 'I must send you one.'

His double entendres are pretty harmless. Often, McGill creates a play on words by using a word that does not normally have another meaning, but which, in the context of the cartoon, becomes suggestive. For instance, one of his cards depicts a woman who has fallen down with her legs in the air. 'I thought I would help,' says a passing man. 'I saw your predicament.' 'Did you?' the woman replies. 'Well, if you were a gentleman, you would not mention it.'

In another, two women in the street are looking up at a house. 'There's the vicar at the window, sponging his aspidistra,' says one. 'Horrid man,' observed the other. 'He ought to do it in his bathroom.'

It has to be said that a fair few of McGill's jokes are vulgar or trite or both, as when a smart lady is telling off a waiter. 'Take this jelly away, waiter. There are two things on this Earth that I like firm and one of them is jelly.'

Then there is the sales assistant in a department store who is helping a male customer – 'Gentleman's requisites? Yes, sir, go right though ladies underwear' – and the two chaps discussing a well-dressed young woman: 'She's a nice girl. Doesn't drink or smoke and only swears when it slips out.'

Up and down the country local watch committees went tut-tut over such blatant double entendres. They banned the rudest ones and passed the ones they deemed acceptable. Some of the cards in my collection have a stamp on the back bearing the stern judgement: 'Blackpool Postcard Censorship Board DISAPPROVED'.

In 1953, certain towns up and down the country that lacked censoring committees began an orchestrated attack on McGill's cards, with local vicars writing letters of complaint to the police, who were then forced to act. One of the towns that complained was Ryde, and cards were seized from five shops. In the ensuing case in the magistrates' court, many of the cards were declared obscene and were burnt – and the shopkeepers were fined. You can imagine how the Ryde shopkeepers felt when they journeyed to Shanklin, Cowes or Ventnor and saw the same cards still on display and being sold.

Worse was to follow. The next year, McGill's publishers were prosecuted in a court case at Lincoln. McGill and his publisher were found guilty of obscenity, fined and had to pay costs. McGill continued to work, but his sales were never the same again. He died in 1962 in Balham, aged eighty-seven, leaving two hundred sketches for new cartoons, meant for the following summer season.

So how did this amazing collection end up in the Ryde museum? In 1954, his cards were found to be obscene here, but he himself had no personal connections with the area. Brian gave me the name of the owner of the collection – but it took me a while to meet him, as he lives in Kew for part of the year.

He is called James Bissell-Thomas and he makes globes. What, I said. Globes? I didn't know anyone made globes today. His works, Globe Workshop, is just a few yards down from the arcade, on the other side of Union Street, a handsome if rather crumbling Grade II building with four fine Corinthian columns at the front entrance. But it was also closed when I tried to get in, so I did not realise it stretched all the way back to the street behind, Union Road, which was where I eventually met him.

Inside was an array of complicated-looking machines and piles of materials – and hundreds of globes in various stages of construction. James revived the craft in the UK in 1991, producing them by hand with three staff, supplying them to libraries, museums, collectors and the public.

James, now in his sixties, was born in Jersey. His parents moved to Barnes, south London. He went to art college and became apprenticed to a printer. He had no connection with the island until his eccentric brother Charles Gibaut Bissell-Thomas, an old Harrovian hippie who went to Sussex University, moved to Ryde and leased Appley Tower. One of a number of different names he adopted was 'Jungle Eyes'.

'He was a fruitarian, which meant he only ever ate nuts and mushrooms and fruit, which sadly probably contributed to his death in 2013.'

James had been making globes for some years and was looking for new premises, when he came to visit his brother in Ryde and found the derelict building for sale in Union Street. After endless complications, he managed to buy it for £90,000.

He had not heard of Donald McGill till he started researching postcards and learned that McGill's cards had been seized in Ryde. He ended up buying a massive hoard of McGill items, including original artworks, from a collector who had gone into administration, and then opened a Donald McGill museum on the Union Street side of his premises. Footfall was not great despite national coverage on TV and in the press. James found coach drivers were advising their passengers on the location of a Wetherspoons instead of suggesting places of cultural interest. As the museum was taking up too much of his time, he decided to loan the collection to the Ryde museum which means that more visitors get to see it.

James has now bequeathed the collection to the nation through the Arts Council bequeathment scheme. So the McGill collection will stay in Ryde, where it should help the museum to keep going. For ever and ever, we all hope, in that lovely arcade.

CHAPTER 27

How now brown Cowes

Sailing during Cowes Week, 1956

Claire was so looking forward to Cowes Week, being a yachtie. All year I have let her down, not being able to find someone with a yacht and too mean to hire one myself. I keep telling her, 'Don't worry, pet, if you meet a nice chap in pink corduroys who turns out to have a thirty-footer, you go off with him, have your fun. I don't mind in the least.'

Michael Grade has a whopper of a yacht – the one that takes ten to race it – but I think it might be a bit hairy for Claire at her age: all that being thrown around, lying backwards an inch above the water and being shouted at. I am told the language at sea is appalling.

We have been reduced to rubber-necking all year, oohing and ahhing at lovely yachts in the distance when we walk along Ryde Sands. At least at Cowes Week we should have a more intimate experience – we'll be able to watch thousands of racing yachts up close and personal from the promenade at Cowes.

We decided not to go the first weekend. As it had not been held the previous year, we were convinced it would be chocka: the crowds, my dears, the yelling, the hooray-Henrying. So, we plumped for the Monday, which we assumed would be a quieter day.

Cowes Week has been going since 1832 and has only ever been cancelled for the two world wars and the dreaded Covid. This year, 2021, it was set to bounce back, just like the old glory days, and Cowes would doubtless come to a standstill.

Where to park? We wondered about using our new best friend Alan Titchmarsh's drive, but decided that would be a bit cheeky. We set off really early and, amazingly, found excellent free parking on the coast road, near Gurnard. Then we walked along the sea front towards Cowes.

Claire got very excited when we spotted our first race, just a hundred yards or so out at sea – a host of golden yachts, nodding and dancing in the breeze. In fact, most of the first lot we saw racing seemed to have brown sails, which I thought rather attractive. The colour might have had something to do with the class they were in. But what do I know? All day long, and all week long, there were endless races for so many different classes and sizes and conditions of yachts. Claire, despite going on endlessly about her years of sailing round the island with that earlier boyfriend, was pretty useless. She had no more idea than I had about which sort of race we were watching.

But, oh, the fun, watching them tacking and turning, swerving to catch the wind, suddenly veering away as if going in the wrong direction, looking lost, but waiting for the right moment and the right wind to sneak back on the right route and dash to the front of the race.

As we walked, we came across waves of other boats, different races which had set off at different times, with a variety of colours and sizes. The sails were billowing, fluttering and flapping like butterflies in a sea-green field.

We still couldn't work out what was going on, but when we got past Egypt Point, after the beach café and on a little stretch of green grass with some seats, I had a coffee and a sit down. I began to hear voices in my ears. How strange. Am I hearing things in my old age?

I looked around. Claire was on the shore, watching. Then I realised the seat I was sitting on was in front of a lamp-post and attached to the lamp-post was a loudspeaker, carrying live radio commentary. How marvellous. How jolly useful for all those idiots who didn't know what was going on. I assumed the commentators were on the viewing balcony at the Royal Yacht Squadron, where we had been when I had interviewed the secretary. It was totally empty then. It must now be crammed with experts and techies, all shouting and waving and ever so excited. And, of course, knowledgeable.

I wanted to walk right along the front, to the Squadron and beyond, to take in the whole experience, but Claire was already complaining about the noise of cannons going off, affecting her ears. So, I walked on my own. The crowds were not as large as I thought they would be. There was quite a lot of space, easy to push through.

I remarked on this to a few boatmen waiting for customers and official-looking types with binoculars and they agreed it was not as crowded this year. They suggested it was partly the continuing impact of Covid but they thought it was mainly due to the absence of the Royal Yacht *Britannia*. When she was in her pomp, she always turned up for Cowes Week and was a big attraction in herself. She has now been decommissioned. Today, *Britannia* is permanently berthed at a dock in Leith where she has become a popular visitor attraction.

I managed to get up close to the little row of bright, gleaming cannons outside the RYS. I had seen them on our earlier visit, but thought they were just for show. I hadn't appreciated that they really did work. These small-scale cannons came from a miniature sailing frigate, the *Royal Adelaide*, which the 'Sailor King', William IV, commissioned for himself and sailed on Virginia Water Lake, near Windsor. They look rather dinky from afar but, close up, I could see they were about five feet long and made of well-polished brass. A youngish woman in uniform was poking a stick down each one, presumably loading them with gunpowder. When a whistle blew, she set them off. Then what a noise, what a bang, for a little cannon. No wonder Claire did not want to hear them. I was brought up during the war and got used to loud bangs.

There were so many races still going on, one after the other, that I reckon there must have been about a thousand yachts out racing that day. The starting line, when I eventually worked it out, was a stretch of the sea in front of the Squadron marked out by two large buoys. You could see the yachts manoeuvring with the wind, hoping to be poised correctly when the shot sounded – then, whoosh, they were all off. It was amazing how much speed they could get up from a standing start, if they had positioned themselves to their best advantage.

I met up with Claire again and we watched for another hour or so, then walked to the end of the promenade to admire the marquees, stalls and shops selling yachtie tackle, binoculars, clothes, food and drinks. We watched until midday and then walked slowly into Cowes, up the High Street, heading for the Medina bookshop where we had an appointment. And also an invitation to lunch...

I had recently met Medina's owner, Peter Harrigan, at the Monkton Arts music festival, run by Jenna and Dawn. And I saw him again at an event where Ray Foulk was talking about his book on Dylan at the Isle of Wight Festival – *Stealing Dylan from Woodstock*. (Peter was there as Ray's publisher as he also runs a publishing company, Medina Books.)

At the bookshop, ahead of lunch, we were introduced to Peter's staff. Any author knows that it is vital to make yourself known to all local bookshops and their staff, try your best to charm and ingratiate yourself, hoping they will shift loads of your work.

Peter's cottage was up an unmarked road beside a forest. Joining us for lunch was Mohammed from Saudi Arabia who looks after Medina's books in the Arab world. I was amazed and impressed that a little publishing firm in Cowes manages to sell its books in the Middle East. I used to be a publisher myself in the Lake District, so I know selling any of your own books anywhere is a struggle. A local publisher traditionally publishes books about his own patch and expects to concentrate on selling them there. So how does a little firm in Cowes find a market in Saudi Arabia?

Peter is seventy-one, born in Cowes, but way back is of Irish extraction. His mother was a Sivell. Like Seely, Sivell is a long-established island surname although unlike like the Seelys – with their well-known politicians – Peter's best-known ancestor was a brandy smuggler. Peter went to school on the island, Carisbrooke grammar school, and then to Birmingham University. He drifted into PR after university and did promotion for those amazing 1969 and 1970 Isle of Wight pop festivals, helping his fellow local grammar-school boy, Ray Foulk, get the festival going. Until then, neither of them had any previous experience of such events. Next thing, he was working with Dylan and Jimi Hendrix.

'But I didn't exactly like the music scene or the people in it,' said Peter. 'Especially those behind the scenes.' So, following the third Isle of Wight festival, he signed up for Voluntary Service Overseas (VSO). 'Lots of graduates did it in the sixties, as their gap year, before deciding what to do in life. I was hoping to be sent to somewhere exotic and lovely such as the Caribbean. Instead, I found myself being sent to Nigeria as a teacher.'

He spent four years in Nigeria, working for the British Council, and also doing a little bit of freelance work for BBC West Africa and writing pieces for the state newspaper in Nigeria. Back in London he returned to the pop world for a couple of years, working on shows at Wembley; then by chance he met someone from Saudi Arabia who said there was a job vacancy for someone to teach trainees for Saudi Arabian Airlines. Peter knew nothing about planes but he had some teaching experience.

He spent the next twenty-five years in Saudi Arabia, working for their airline, developing their training programme. They had a staff of 60,000, so there was a lot of training to be done. At the time, Saudi Airlines was the biggest Arabian airline, but it is now overshadowed by Emirates.

It was while in Saudi, meeting government people, making contacts and doing a bit of journalism, that he started writing articles for a glossy magazine in Riyadh, run and funded by the Riyadh Development Corporation. From working on magazines sponsored by a government agency, he moved on to publishing high-quality illustrated books, also sponsored by Saudi government bodies. Like the magazines, they were given out free to customers and contacts. He was given the budget to commission, research and photograph stories from experts about Saudi history, architecture, the desert and camels. Nothing political or controversial about human rights, of course.

In my journalistic career I have often been on foreign jaunts to Arabian and other countries and been given very impressive free books. They look amazing and impressive, so you take them, as hacks love free gifts. You plan to read them, but at the airport, you think, nah, I am not going to lug this all the way back to Blighty. So you dump them. What a waste.

Peter came back home to the Isle of Wight in 2007 and carried on publishing his Saudi-sponsored books with his company Medina Publishing, named after the river and estuary on the island. You see the word 'Medina' in the names of many island firms and businesses. The River Medina flows through the middle of the Isle of Wight from its source near Chale in the far south, practically bisecting the island. But, ha ha, Medina is also the name of one of the sacred cities of Saudi Arabia, one of the major pilgrimage shrines of the Middle East. Excellent name for a publishing firm that wants to sell books in Arabia.

'When I got back to Cowes, I decided I had to have some sort of premises. I had several books commissioned and two or three people working with me on my Saudi books. By chance, a local estate agent told me that a barber's shop had come on the market the day before – right in the middle of Cowes High Street. I went to look at it. It was still a barber's shop, hairdressers clipping away. I thought its situation would be excellent for my publishing firm. It had always been a shop of some sort, with good frontage. I decided to open a book shop downstairs and call it the Medina Bookshop, and have my publishing company upstairs.'

Today, he has a total of twelve staff based in the shop, plus Mohammed, who is based mainly in Saudi, where he has a wife and children. He spends around two months each year in the Cowes office.

Peter has enough Arabian books under contract to keep him occupied for the next few years. He currently has five books on the go – commissioned by the Dubai government, which wants suitably lavish books about the glories of the emirate to give to VIP visitors to the Dubai Expo 2022. Peter gets paid a set fee to produce the books, which he uses to commission words and photographs and to pay for their editing, production and printing. The finished books are then shipped over to the Middle East. He has all the contacts, knows how things work and is very knowledgeable about Saudi life after a quarter of a century living there.

It sounds like a lucrative deal, but such arrangements with kingdoms or political dynasties can suddenly change. Your contacts lose their influence. Your face does not fit any more. Contracts can be cancelled. So, in the last few years, he has branched out and now also publishes books on local Isle of Wight subjects; these include a rather handsome volume about food and chefs on the island, with recipes and beautiful photographs. They are produced to the same high standards as his Arabian books, but in this case he has to sell them himself. That's where having a bookshop helps.

He has already published two books by Ray Foulk about the Isle of Wight festival and intends to continue to work with subjects and writers connected to the island, getting sponsorship if he can. It isn't really vanity publishing, because Peter has to like the books' content in the first place. However, he does not pay his authors an advance, and sometimes they have to contribute to the costs, but they do get a share of the profits. This arrangement is quite common in local book publishing, where publishers often can't afford to pay the author an advance on royalties, as traditional commercial publishers do. It has to be said of Peter's books that the results look much more professional than would be the case if the books had been self-published (in other words, if the authors had done everything for themselves). Medina has properly trained and experienced staff who know how to create handsome-looking books.

Good luck to him. And good luck to anyone else trying to establish a new business in Cowes on the little old Isle of Wight – and hoping to shift the product. Particularly when that's not just to mainland England, but also to far-flung Arabian kingdoms.

CHAPTER 28

Festival and finale

The Isle of Wight Festival, 1970; probably
the largest musical event of its time

ohn Giddings (remember him? See Chapter 14) had said he would try to get us VIP tickets for the Isle of Wight Festival and, lo and behold, his offer came to pass and the festival went ahead – huzzah! – despite some lingering Covid restrictions. What an exciting event with which to finish our exciting first year.

I got carried away and enquired about helicopter flights, as that is how the star bands have traditionally arrived at the festival. I know how to treat a gel... And I hate having to put up with those traffic jams round Newport.

A helicopter flight would really get me in Claire's good books. Not that she's been hard done by up to now – not only did she get VIP seats to the hottest event on the island, but over the year have I not taken her to lunch with Lord Grade at his yacht club, to Alan Titchmarsh's lovely clapboard mansion, on a conducted tour of Osborne House by the curator, umpteen suppers at the Dell, and several Chinese takeaways? Oh, so many excitements and treats. I know, I do spoil her.

I rang the helicopter people and asked how much it would be to fly from Ryde to the festival site. I know Princess Anne recently flew from the recreation ground behind our house, so it must be possible. It would depend on air traffic control, they said, but from London to the festival field they charge £4,500 – one-way, one person only. Gulp. I said, 'Thanks. Will let you know.' Gawd, no wonder putting on pop festivals is so expensive.

In the end we got the special festival shuttle bus from Ryde Pier on the Sunday evening. But I still moaned about the cost: fourteen pounds return. Bloody hell. Normally with our freedom passes all buses on the island cost us nothing. The bus was quite empty, apart from a few gaggles and giggles of girls aged about thirty, with sparkly hairbands, lights flashing, lots of makeup, the odd tattoo in strange places, all laughing and screaming, clearly already tanked up for the night ahead. They had probably been like this all weekend. Some were carrying groundsheets and blankets, ready for an all-nighter.

I felt even more ancient than ever. This was going to be my first open-air pop concert, as it was for Claire. Yes, I have been to the O2 and Wembley and the Forum in Kentish Town over the years to see the latest pop sensation, but never anything out in the open air. Dear God, do you know how old I am?

The bus dropped us off at gate A2 – which appeared to be a massive bus terminal, with buses coming from all corners of the island. We queued at the entrance, clutching our Covid cards to prove we had been vaccinated twice – but, alas, the rules had changed. We now had to have a swab and get tested for Covid. Oh, God, what a drag. We were handed a little packet each with capsules and a little plastic phial. I could not even open it. My fingers are so stiff these days. A girl at the entrance did it for me, then showed me how to push a swab up my nose, mix it with a solution and squeeze a bit onto a plastic tray till it revealed the result. My test showed just one line rather than two, meaning I was OK. Phew. No wonder the queues were so enormous, if all visitors had to do this. And no wonder Covid has cost the nation billions – though the manufacturers of these kits must have made a fortune.

Having got our Covid all-clear, we were still not allowed inside the festival site proper. I flashed the printout of our invite to the VIP lounge, as sent by John Giddings' office – but was told we now needed to pick up another pass. Where from? From gate A6. And where is that? At a least a mile away, she said. I hoped she was joking.

We went back on the road, which was now half for cars going one way only while the other was reserved for pedestrians. I reckoned it would take me half an hour, as I am a slow walker these days, unlike Claire. I started moaning like hell. Oh, no, we are going to spend all evening on this stupid road instead of being at the festival, oh God, what a mistake. I spotted a taxi on the other side, but going the right way, and flagged him down. He said he was not allowed to stop but, having stopped him, I then talked him into giving us a lift to gate A6.

Then the same thing happened. We couldn't find the box office or any official who had any idea about where we should be. We explained we had VIP invites and were sent to an area which turned out to be for disabled VIPs. We said our VIP area is the Black Star bar – where is that?

Next we were directed across the main arena, where fifty thousand people were singing and roaring, watching Supergrass. It was hell getting through the crowd, especially the ones lying down on blankets and rugs, drinking and eating. It was like fighting our way through a human mountain. But we found the right bar at last. I could see all the VIP ticket-holders on a balcony enjoying themselves. But the security guard would not let us in. We did not have the right wristband. We would have to go to the box office, back at A5. Oh, God, all that way, fighting our way through the mass of teeming humanity again. I said, 'That's it. I'm going home. I am too old for all this nonsense.' Claire agreed. She had had enough as well.

We spotted the box office huts on our way out, though most of them appeared closed and locked. But one of them was still open. The young girl at the counter turned out to be ever so helpful and checked on her computer. She gave us the right wristbands and John Giddings' assistant, Flo, appeared in minutes – on a buggy. She then drove us all the way to the proper entrance to the VIP lounge at the rear of the site. Oh, bliss. We had done it.

I went straight for the free food and drink while Claire found a seat. There were about five hundred people in the VIP lounge.

I discovered that almost all of our fellow VIPs had paid for their tickets, and that it had cost each of them about £1000 to be in this exclusive zone with a very good view of the main stage. I went out on the balcony to see a group called The Script performing. I had not heard of them. Earlier in the week Tom Jones had appeared, and Liam Gallagher, Snow Patrol and Kaiser Chiefs, all of whom I had heard of. I am not totally out of touch.

Liam Gallagher, I read later, had arrived by helicopter. On returning to the mainland, he fell out of the helicopter and badly bruised his face and nose. No, he was not tired and emotional. It appears to have been an accident. Good job I didn't hire a helicopter, after all.

The leader of The Script came down off the stage and mingled with the crowd, still singing, and I could detect his Irish accent. The audience was going wild. The next group was officially top of the bill, the main attraction, Duran Duran. Very polished and smooth, but it seemed to me the crowd had been more excited by The Script. Perhaps they were all too young to remember Duran Duran in their heyday.

I got talking to a builder from Tunbridge Wells who was there with his wife, two teenage daughters and two friends. They had been staying in white luxury tents which you could hire. I think it might be called 'glamping'. The tents came complete with tickets for all the events and all meals, including breakfast. I asked him how much he had paid for the three nights. And was astounded – £22,000. 'My God,' I said. 'That is four times what I paid for my London house.'

'Oh, it's been well worth it. I could easily have spent that in Spain for the six of us – and the girls would have got bored. Here they had live groups all day long to listen to. They thought they were in heaven.'

During the festival there were 150 groups performing. Looking round the site, which we had been forced to do, alas, I had seen how enormous it was, covering 250 acres and stretching well over a mile, all filled with stages and caravans, facilities and lights. It must have needed hundreds of electricians and riggers to put it all up and take it all down, plus the techies to operate it all, and security and staff. I asked John afterwards how many staff they had taken on for that festival. He said five thousand people. Wow.

I could now understand what he had told me earlier in the year – that, by his reckoning, the festival brings in £10 million each year for the island economy.

On the bus home, exhausted, we were more than glad we had persevered and not gone home. It had been a wonderful experience, exciting and rather uplifting, seeing so many thousands of youngish people, couples, families and groups, clearly enjoying themselves. I would like to have danced, but Claire would not let me. My wife and children were the same. They got embarrassed whenever I got up to dance at family gatherings. Spoilsports. At eighty-five, I still consider I am a good little mover.

One big surprise was how well-behaved the crowd were. I saw no drunks, no drugs and no fighting. Everyone was so happy and cheerful, so pleased to be there. As we were.

It made a perfect ending for what had been, for us, a momentous year. At our age, starting a new life in a new place was probably a bit foolhardy, especially deciding to do so in a year still so badly affected by Covid. But we did it, all the same.

Neither of us has any regrets about the house – it proved every bit as lovely as we first imagined it would be. I still love it dearly and so does Claire. It lifts up my heart and my spirits just to open the front gate, walk down the little red tiled path past the cactus, see the stained-glass door and read the name 'Victoria Lodge'.

There have, of course, been far more jobs to be done than I expected, and endless expenditure replacing items. I kept a list in my little cottage notebook. The two biggest costs were the £2,600 for damp proofing and £1,500 for the drains, but we couldn't avoid them. Buying new furniture, table, chairs, shelves, beds, bedding, wardrobe, mirror, TV, lights, vacuum cleaner, washing machine, dishwasher, oven, desk, rug, oh God, the list goes on for pages – that came to another £3,000. Then we paid three different handymen to put the stuff together and for odd jobs.

On top of the total cost of buying the house – £315k, including stamp duty and legal fees – I suppose we spent another £8,000 once we were in. But perhaps that's not so much, really, when you are buying a house that's at least 150 years old.

Our new neighbours a few doors along, Neil and Denise from Aberdeen, who are finally moving in after a year of work, have spent £100,000 doing up their house, which is very similar to ours, though it has a lovely, good-sized garden. But it was a total wreck, and they did get it for a bargain price.

We don't really miss having a proper garden, as we didn't want the hassle of having to maintain it, but the lack of much sun in the courtyard is something of a disappointment. The tropical trees and plants that have grown over the wall from the next-door garden are lovely, but they do reduce our midday sun. Still, we mustn't forget that only three minutes away, virtually on our doorstep, is that glorious long sandy beach.

One routine we got into in the early autumn was going out at around six o'clock, when most holidaymakers have gone home or to their digs, and finding a seat on the seawall of Ryde Marina. We sit with our backs to the sea, looking at the boats in front of us bobbing in the harbour. Or not bobbing, as the case may be. Because the tide goes out so far on that stretch of the Solent, the marina is more often than not just a sea of mud, with the boats marooned and motionless. Yet there is usually a lone yachtsman on one of the decks, tinkering with their lanyards, mizzen sails, or whatever it is they tinker with. Or, like us, they are quietly sitting, drinking and watching the sun set.

Beyond the harbour, we can see all of the town of Ryde, the church spires and the handsome Victorian mansions. Then we turn right to admire that enormous pier and watch the sun going down behind it. Ah, so romantic. A bottle of Pinot Grigio also helps the tender moments.

The beach itself is perhaps the best and most wonderful natural feature of Ryde. I never tire of it, no matter how many times a day I walk along it. The enormous tides, going out at least half a mile, mean that no two days ever feel the same. Another joy is to sit at the Dell café, on the bend of the beach on the way to Seaview, looking back towards Ryde.

I derive great pleasure from poking around the town of Ryde itself. It is not a tourist trap, like Cowes, or middle-class, like Seaview. It has real, ordinary locals, going about their ordinary local business, as they have done for centuries. I love all the independent shops, the little cafés, the Victorian arcade, the old-fashioned hardware store, the handsome buildings with strange pillars and statues on the top, which you don't notice at first, until you stop and look up high. Then you smile, for it is just so potty having statues so high up, on top of a building where they can't be seen.

And Ryde has proved much nicer than we expected. Some of the pink corduroy brigade over in Cowes and Yarmouth were a bit snotty about Ryde when they heard we were moving there, suggesting it was rough and run down. I now know they have got it totally wrong. There are some remarkable buildings in Ryde, period houses and beautiful streets and squares, such as Vernon Square, filled with architectural gems. Yes, many of them could do with some tender loving care, but it means the prices are a bargain compared with similar gems in West Wight.

As for the island, we couldn't stop exploring it, which is

why the book has turned out to be longer than I had planned. All the new places and all the new people were so fascinating. And yet we never got round to visiting one of the best-known treasures on the island, Carisbrooke Castle. And I never met any of the star yachties on the island, such as Sir Ben Ainslie or Dame Ellen MacArthur. Another time, another book.

So, what were the highlights? Looking back, some of the unexpected, lesser-known places – such as Dimbola – jump out. And the simpler pleasures, like travelling on the hovercraft. Osborne House was fabulous, but then we expected it to be. And I must not forget the world's one and only Donald McGill museum. Since my first visit I have bought another ten sets of the repro saucy cards. Some lucky recipients are going to be very blessed.

As for the people, I had never met Alan Titchmarsh before, so that was fun, and Bob Seely, for an MP, he was entertaining as well. Wayne Whittle, I hope to stay friends with him, and Father Stephen in his camper van. Peter Harrigan at the Medina bookshop in Cowes, with his speciality of publishing books about Saudi Arabia: I could not have predicted meeting someone like him a year ago. And Jenna and her mother Dawn at Monkton Arts, what a remarkable job they have done.

The island seems richer, more varied and bigger than we ever thought when we first arrived here. It is ten out of ten for the house. And top marks for the island, as well. But what about the third new project we blithely embarked upon just a year ago?

Us. Me and Claire.

We have been properly living together at last. How did that go?

It was a bit late in life for two mature people – one of them very set in his ways – to attempt to live together full time. And, well, there were some bumps and hiccups along the way. Some rather upsetting at the time. Looking back, I should have expected some, I suppose. Love at any age, old or young, is never without tensions, misunderstandings, annoyances, huffs and puffs. You can behave like a teenager, however ancient you are. And it was hard on Claire for me to expect her suddenly to accommodate my desires and demands, whims and wishes.

We have gone back to London more often than we had planned, just for quick visits, to check on our respective houses, both of which have a tenant in them. Mostly we wanted to see our families and our grandchildren, catch up on family and local affairs, and in my case, return for work-related reasons, to meet publishers and editors.

But we were here during every time of the year, including Christmas and New Year, when the island was empty of all tourists and second-homers. Going back for the odd few days every month or so gave us a break from each other, especially when I was clearly beginning to irritate Claire. And coming back again to each other and to our 'love nest' – a phrase Claire does not like but which amuses me – confirmed just how much we had missed each other. We hope our relationship will last.

I think this might well be my last book. It will be my 103rd published book since my first, a novel called *Here We Go, Round the Mulberry Bush*, came out in 1965. I am counting here *every* book I have ever had published – non-fiction, fiction, children's books, guidebooks, collections. It's my list. And now I am going to draw a line under it.

I do have one other manuscript, the life of a famous Hollywood star, which never got published as the person changed his mind, after I had written 100,000 words. He is now dead, so I hope to find a publisher one day. Meanwhile, I will busy and amuse myself with various magazine and newspaper columns. They are easy. I only have one subject: me.

The trouble with my doing this sort of book, interviewing so many real people, using their real names and recording real facts about them, is that I always let them read what I have written so they can confirm they are happy with it.

I know that many well-known travel writers, the sort who describe their year in Tuscany or go across Europe on the Orient Express, or ride a camel across Arabia, actually do the journey and meet the people. But then, when they come to write the book, while they may not make things up, people and incidents get blended together, get given different names and locations, so they can't be identified. I wish I had done that this time.

I have spent the last two months letting all the people in this book read what I have written about them. Over 95 per cent were thrilled, loved it, had no objections, found my description of meeting them a delight and amusing, even when I was teasing them. But two people were not happy and changed their minds about certain things they had told me when I interviewed them. Instead of trying to persuade them, I dropped them entirely. I didn't want them to be unhappy.

I must have done thirty books in this format, about real people, either biographies or social history or travel, starting with my second book in 1966 which was called *The Other Half*, about the new poor and the new rich. I don't remember getting in a state with the process of writing a book of this sort in the past. I think it is partly age – but also bloody modern technology. I have constantly been losing chapters, deleting them or being unable to find them or find the right version. Also, my fingers have got stiffer. I make so many mistakes when I have to copy and paste, and then have to correct them.

So, having turned eighty-six in January 2022, I don't think I will have the physical energy and dexterity to do this sort of book again. Mentally and emotionally I can still do it, as I love meeting and interviewing new people, finding out about their lives, asking them cheeky questions. But I feel now I want an easier life, in the lovely cottage, pottering around the island, on the beach, walking round Ryde. Ah... bliss.

It was a bit mad in a way, starting this adventure at our ages, a new house in a new place, but at least neither of us fell ill during the year, which could well have happened. Though as I write, with the first year now over, each of us has suddenly got annoying ailments which will need treatment of some sort.

But I am starting a new project, of a different sort, which I would like to share with you: the Isle of Wight Book Awards.

For thirty-eight years since I founded the award in 1984, I have been the one of the judges of the Lakeland Book of the Year, the only regional book awards in the whole country. It now has a life and vitality of its own, with six different categories of prizes and up to eighty new books entered each year. The results and awards are given out at a grand literary lunch and it has become one of the social highlights of the Lake District year.

It was meeting Peter Harrigan, at the Medina Bookshop, and the local MP Bob Seely – who turned out to have a rather fine collection of Isle of Wight books – which sparked the idea of book awards for the island. There will be three judges – the other two being Joanna Trollope and Alan Titchmarsh. We have three sponsors lined up – Hovertravel, the Isle of Wight Festival and the leading local estate agent, Hose Rhodes Dickson. The first grand awards lunch will be held at the Island Yacht Club in Cowes in September 2022. It is hoped that the Isle of Wight Book Awards will run every year, forever. Hurry, hurry and look: www.iowbookawards.co.uk.

The object is to promote the Isle of Wight – and books. Words are about the only thing on this Earth which last. I mean words of the sort contained in books, printed on paper. Unlike those stupid texts and emails, using computers which get upgraded all the time and then become obsolete. Books are here forever. So do keep this one safe.